D1527545

SOUL AND FORM

SOUL AND FORM

by Georg Lukacs

Translated by
Anna Bostock

THE MIT PRESS
Cambridge, Massachusetts

First MIT Press edition, 1974

Library of Congress catalog card number: 74-12828

ISBN: 0 262 12066 6

Printed in the United States of America.

PN
45
L713
1974

Contents

On the Nature and Form of the Essay

A Letter to Leo Popper

My friend,

THE ESSAYS intended for inclusion in this book lie before me and I ask myself whether one is entitled to publish such works—whether such works can give rise to a new unity, a book. For the point at issue for us now is not what these essays can offer as "studies in literary history", but whether there is something in them that makes them a new literary form of its own, and whether the principle that makes them such is the same in each one. What is this unity—if unity there is? I make no attempt to formulate it because it is not I nor my book that should be the subject under discussion here. The question before us is a more important, more general one. It is the question whether such a unity is possible. To what extent have the really great writings which belong to this category been given literary form, and to what extent is this form of theirs an independent one? To what extent do the standpoint of such a work and the form given to this standpoint lift it out of the sphere of science and place it at the side of the arts, yet without blurring the frontiers of either? To what extent do they endow the work with the force necessary for a conceptual re-ordering of life, and yet distinguish it from the icy, final perfection of philosophy? That is the only profound apology to be made for such writings, as well as the only profound criticism to be addressed to them; for they are measured first and foremost by the yardstick of these questions, and the determining of such an objective will be the first step towards showing how far they fall short of attaining it.

The critique, the essay—call it provisionally what you will—as a work of art, a genre? I know you think the question tedious; you feel that all the arguments for and against have been exhausted long ago. Wilde and Kerr merely made familiar to everyone a truth that was already known to the German Romantics, a truth whose ultimate meaning the Greeks and Romans felt, quite unconsciously, to be self-evident: that criticism is an art and not a science. Yet I believe—and it is for this reason alone that I venture to importune you with these observations—that all the discussions have barely touched upon the essence of the real question: what *is* an essay? What is

1

its intended form of expression, and what are the ways and means whereby this expression is accomplished? I believe that the aspect of "being well written" has been too one-sidedly emphasized in this context. It has been argued that the essay can be stylistically of equal value to a work of the imagination, and that, for this reason, it is unjust to speak of value differences at all. Yet what does that mean? Even if we consider criticism to be a work of art in this sense, we have not yet said anything at all about its essential nature. "Whatever is well written is a work of art." Is a well-written advertisement or news item a work of art? Here I can see what so disturbs you about such a view of criticism: it is anarchy, the denial of form in order that an intellect which believes itself to be sovereign may have free play with possibilities of every kind. But if I speak here of criticism as a form of art, I do so in the name of order (i.e. almost purely symbolically and non-essentially), and solely on the strength of my feeling that the essay has a form which separates it, with the rigour of a law, from all other art forms. I want to try and define the essay as strictly as is possible, precisely by describing it as an art form.

Let us not, therefore, speak of the essay's similarities with works of literary imagination, but of what divides it from them. Let any resemblance serve here merely as a background against which the differences stand out all the more sharply; the purpose of mentioning these resemblances at all will be to limit our attention to genuine essays, leaving aside those writings which, useful though they are, do not deserve to be described as essays because they can never give us anything more than information, facts and "relationships". Why, after all, do we read essays? Many are read as a source of instruction, but there are others whose attraction is to be found in something quite different. It is not difficult to identify these. Our view, our appreciation of classical tragedy is quite different today, is it not, from Lessing's in the *Dramaturgy*; Winckelmann's Greeks seem strange, almost incomprehensible to us, and soon we may feel the same about Burckhardt's Renaissance. And yet we read them: why? On the other hand there are critical writings which, like a hypothesis in natural science, like a design for a machine part, lose all their value at the precise moment when a new and better one becomes available. But if—as I hope and expect—someone were to write a new *Dramaturgy*, a *Dramaturgy* in favour of Corneille and against Shakespeare—how could it damage Lessing's? And what did Burckhardt and Pater, Rhode and Nietzsche do to change the effect upon us of Winckelmann's dreams of Greece?

"Of course, if criticism were a science . . ." writes Kerr. "But the imponderables are too strong. Criticism is, at the very best, an art."

And if it were a science—it is not so impossible that it will become one—how would that change our problem? We are not concerned here with replacing something by something else, but with something essentially new, something that remains untouched by the complete or approximate attainment of scientific goals. Science affects us by its contents, art by its forms; science offers us facts and the relationships between facts, but art offers us souls and destinies. Here the ways part; here there is no replacement and no transition. In primitive, as yet undifferentiated epochs, science and art (and religion and ethics and politics) are integrated, they form a single whole; but as soon as science has become separate and independent, everything that has led up to it loses its value. Only when something has dissolved all its content in form, and thus become pure art, can it no longer become superfluous; but then its previous scientific nature altogether forgotten and emptied of meaning.

There is, then, a science of the arts; but there is also an entirely different kind of expression of the human temperament, which usually takes the form of writing about the arts. Usually, I say, for there are many writings which are engendered by such feelings without ever touching upon literature or art—writings in which the same life-problems are raised as in the writings which call themselves criticism, but with the difference that here the questions are addressed directly to life itself: they do not need the mediation of literature or art. And it is precisely the writings of the greatest essayists which belong to this category: Plato's *Dialogues*, the texts of the mystics, Montaigne's *Essays*, Kierkegaard's imaginary diaries and short stories.

An endless series of almost imperceptible, subtle transitions leads from here to imaginative writing. Think of the last scene in the *Heracles* of Euripides: the tragedy is already over when Theseus appears and discovers everything that has happened—Hera's terrible vengeance on Heracles. Then begins the dialogue about life between the mourning Heracles and his friend; questions akin to those of the Socratic dialogues are asked, but the questioners are stiffer and less human, and their questions more conceptual, less related to direct experience than in Plato. Think of the last act of *Michael Kramer*, of the *Confessions of a Beautiful Soul*, of Dante, of *Everyman*, of Bunyan—must I quote further examples?

Doubtless you will say that the end of *Heracles* is undramatic and Bunyan is. . . . Certainly, certainly, but why? The *Heracles* is undramatic because every dramatic style has this natural corollary, that whatever happens within human souls is projected into human actions, movements and gestures and is thus made visible and palpable to the senses. Here you see Hera's vengeance overtaking Heracles, you see Heracles in the blissful enjoyment of victory before vengeance is upon him, you see his frenzied gestures in the madness which Hera has dealt to him and his wild despair after the storm, when he sees what has happened to him. But of what comes after you see nothing at all. Theseus comes—and you try in vain to determine by other than conceptual means what happens next: what you see and hear is no longer a true means of expression of the real event, and that the event occurs at all is deep down a matter of indifference to you. You see no more than that Theseus and Heracles leave the stage together. Prior to that some questions are asked: what is the true nature of the gods? Which gods may we believe in, and which not? What is life and what is the best way of bearing one's sufferings manfully? The concrete experience which has led up to these questions is lost in an infinite distance. And when the answers return once more into the world of facts, they are no longer answers to questions posed by real life—questions of what these men must do or refrain from doing in this particular situation. These answers cast a stranger's eye upon all facts, for they have come from life and from the gods and know scarcely anything of Heracles' pain or of its cause in Hera's vengeance. Drama, I know, also addresses questions to life, and in drama, too, the answer comes from destiny— and in the last analysis the questions and answers, even in drama, are tied to certain definite facts. But the true dramatist (so long as he is a true poet, a genuine representative of the poetic principle) will see *a life* as being so rich and so intense that almost imperceptibly it becomes *life*. Here, however, everything become undramatic because here the other principle comes into effect: for the life that here poses the question loses all its corporeality at the moment when the first word of the question is uttered.

There are, then, two types of reality of the soul: one is *life* and the other *living*; both are equally effective, but they can never be effective at the same time. Elements of both are contained in the lived experience of every human being, even if in always varying degrees of intensity and depth; in memory too, there is now one, now the other, but at any one moment we can only feel one of these two forms. Ever since there has been life and men have sought to understand and order life, there has been this duality in their lived experience. But the struggle for priority and pre-eminence between the two has mostly been fought out in philosophy, so that the battle-cries have always had a different sound, and for this reason have gone unrecognized by most men and have been unrecognizable to them. It would seem that the question was posed most clearly in the Middle Ages, when thinkers divided into two camps, the ones maintaining that the *universalia*—concepts, or Plato's Ideas if you will— were the sole true realities, while the others acknowledged them only as words, as names summarizing the sole true and distinct things.

The same duality also separates means of expression: the opposition here is between image and "significance". One principle is an image-creating one, the other a significance-supposing one. For one there exist only things, for the other only the relationships between them, only concepts and values. Poetry in itself knows of nothing beyond things; for it, every thing is serious and unique and incomparable. That is also why poetry knows no questions: you do not address questions to pure *things*, only to their relationships, for—as in fairy-tales—every question here turns again into a thing resembling the one that called it into being. The hero stands at the crossroads or in the midst of the struggle, but the crossroads and the struggle are not destinies about which questions may be asked and answers given; they are simply and literally struggles and crossroads. And the hero blows his miraculous horn and the expected miracle occurs: a thing which once more orders life. But in really profound criticism there is no life of things, no image, only transparency, only something that no image would be capable of expressing completely. An "imagelessness of all images" is the aim of all mystics, and Socrates speaks mockingly and contemptuously to Phaedrus of poets, who never have nor ever could worthily celebrate the true life of the soul. "For the great existence which the immortal part of the soul once lived is colourless and without form and impalpable, and only the soul's guide, the mind, can behold it."

You may perhaps reply that my poet is an empty abstraction and so, too, is my critic. You are right—both are abstractions, but not, perhaps, quite empty ones. They are abstractions because even Socrates must speak in images of his "world without form", his world on the far side of form, and even the German mystic's "imagelessness" is a metaphor. Nor is there any poetry without some ordering of things. Matthew Arnold once called it *criticism of life*. It represents the ultimate relationships between man and destiny and world, and without doubt it has its origin in those profound regions, even if, often, it is unaware of it. If poetry often refuses all questioning, all taking up of positions, is not the denial of all questions in itself an asking of questions, and is not the conscious rejection of any position in itself a position? I shall go further: the separation of image and significance is itself an abstraction, for the significance is always wrapped in images and the reflection of a glow from beyond the image shines through every image. Every image belongs to our world and the joy of being in the world shines in its countenance; yet it also reminds us of something that was once there, at some time or another, a somewhere, its home, the only thing that, in the last analysis, has meaning and significance for the soul. Yes, in their naked purity they are merely abstractions, those two limits of human feeling, but only with the help of such abstractions can I define the two poles of possible literary expression. And the writings which most resolutely reject the image, which reach out most passionately for what lies behind the image, are the writings of the critics, the Platonists and the mystics.

But in saying this I have already explained why this kind of feeling calls for an art form of its own—why every expression of this kind of feeling must always disturb us when we find it in other forms, in poetry. It was you who once formulated the great demand which everything that has been given form must satisfy, the only absolutely universal demand, perhaps, but one that is inexorable and allows of no exception: the demand that everything in a work must be fashioned from the same material, that each of its parts must be visibly ordered from one single point. And because all writing aspires to both unity and multiplicity, this is the universal problem of style: to achieve equilibrium in a welter of disparate things, richness and articulation in a mass of uniform matter. Something that is viable in one art form is dead in another: here is practical, palpable proof of the inner divorce of forms. Do you remember how you explained to me the living quality of human figures in certain heavily stylized mural paintings? You said: these frescoes are painted between pillars, and even if the gestures of the men depicted in them are stiff like those of puppets and every facial expression is only a mask, still all this is more alive than the columns which frame the pictures and form a decorative unity with them. Only a little more alive, for the unity must be preserved; but more alive all the same, so that there may be an illusion of life. Here, however, the problem of equilibrium is posed in this way: the world and the beyond, image and transparency, idea and emanation lie in the two cups of a scale which is to remain balanced. The deeper down the question reaches—you need only compare the tragedy with the fairy-tale—the more linear the images become, the smaller the number of planes into which everything is compressed, the paler and more matt the radiance of the colours, the simpler the richness and multiplicity of the world, the more mask-like the expressions of the characters. But there are other experiences, for the expression of which even the simplest and most measured gesture would be too much—and too little; there are questions which are asked so softly that beside them the sound of the most toneless of events would be crude noise, not musical accompaniment; there are destiny-relationships which are so exclusively relationships between destinies as such that anything human would merely disturb their abstract purity and grandeur. I am not speaking here of subtlety or depth: those are value categories and are therefore valid only within a particular form. We are speaking of the fundamental principles which separate forms from one another—of the material from which the whole is constructed, of the standpoint, the world-view which gives unity to the entire work. Let me put it briefly: were one to compare the forms of literature with sunlight refracted in a prism, the writings of the essayists would be the ultra-violet rays.

There are experiences, then, which cannot be expressed by any gesture and which yet long for expression. From all that has been said you will know what experiences I mean and of what kind they are. I mean intellectuality, conceptuality as sensed experience, as immediate reality, as spontaneous principle of existence; the world-view in its undisguised purity as an event of the soul, as the motive force of life. The question is posed immediately: what is life, what is man, what is destiny? But posed as a question only: for the answer, here, does not supply a "solution" like one of the answers of science or, at purer heights, those of philosophy. Rather, as in poetry of every kind, it is symbol, destiny and tragedy. When a man experiences such things, then everything that is outward about him awaits in rigid immobility the outcome of the struggle between invisible forces to which the senses have no access. Any gesture with which such a man might wish to express something of his experience would falsify that experience, unless it ironically emphasized its own inadequacy and thus cancelled itself out. A man who experiences such things cannot be characterized by any outward feature—how then can he be given form in a work of literature? All writings represent the world in the symbolic terms of a destiny-relationship; everywhere, the problem of destiny determines the problem of form. This unity, this coexistence is so strong that neither element ever occurs without the other; here again a separation is possible only by way of abstraction. Therefore the separation which I am trying to accomplish here appears, in practice, merely as a shift of emphasis: poetry receives its profile and its form from destiny, and form in poetry appears always only as destiny; but in the works of the essayists form *becomes* destiny, it is the destiny-creating principle. This difference means the following: destiny lifts things up outside the world of things, accentuating the essential ones and eliminating the inessential; but form sets limits round a substance which otherwise would dissolve like air in the All. In other words, destiny comes from the same source as everything else, it is a thing among things, whereas form—seen as something finished, i.e. seen from outside—defines the limits of the immaterial. Because the destiny which orders things is flesh of their flesh and blood of their blood, destiny is not to be found in the writings of the essayists. For destiny, once stripped of its uniqueness and accidentality, is just as airy and immaterial as all the rest of the incorporeal matter of these writings, and is no more capable of giving them form than they themselves possess any natural inclination or possibility of condensing themselves into form.

That is why such writings speak of forms. The critic is one who glimpses destiny in forms: whose most profound experience is the soul-content which forms indirectly and unconsciously conceal within themselves. Form is his great experience, form—as immediate reality—is the image-element, the really living content of his writings. This form, which springs from a symbolic contemplation of life-symbols, acquires a life of its own through the power of that experience. It becomes a world-view, a standpoint, an attitude vis-à-vis the life from which it sprang: a possibility of reshaping it, of creating it anew. The critic's moment of destiny, therefore, is that moment at which things become forms—the moment when all feelings and experiences on the near or the far side of form receive form, are melted down and condensed into form. It is the mystical moment of union between the outer and the inner, between soul and form. It is as mystical as the moment of destiny in tragedy when the hero meets his destiny, in the short story when accident and cosmic necessity converge, in poetry when the soul and its world meet and coalesce into a new unity that can no more be divided, either in the past or in the future. Form *is* reality in the writings of critics; it is the voice with which they address their questions to life. That is the true and most profound reason why literature and art are the typical, natural subject-matter of criticism. For here the end-point of poetry can become a starting-point and a beginning; here form appears, even in its abstract conceptuality, as something surely and concretely real. But this is only the typical subject-matter of the essay, not the sole one. For the essayist needs form only as lived experience and he needs only its life, only the living soul-reality it contains. But this reality is to be found in every immediate sensual expression of life, it can be read out of and read into every such experience; life itself can be lived and given form through such a scheme of lived experience. Because literature, art and philosophy pursue forms openly and directly, whereas in life they are no more than the ideal demand of a certain kind of men and experiences, a lesser intensity of critical capacity is needed to experience something formed than to experience something lived; and that is why the reality of form-vision appears, at the first and most superficial glance, less problematic in the sphere of art than in life. But this only seems to be so at the first and most superficial glance, for the form of life is no more abstract than the form of a poem. Here as there, form becomes perceptible only through abstraction, and there as here the reality of form is no stronger than the force with which it is experienced. It would be superficial to distinguish between poems according to whether they take their subject-matter from life or elsewhere; for in any case the form-creating power of poetry breaks and scatters whatever is old, whatever has already been formed, and everything becomes unformed raw material in its hands. To draw such a distinction here seems to me just as superficial, for both ways of contemplating the world are merely standpoints taken up in relation to things, and each is applicable everywhere, although it is true that for both there exist certain things which, with a naturalness decreed by nature, submit themselves to one particular standpoint and others which can only be forced to do so by violent struggles and profound experiences.

As in every really essential relationship, natural effect and immediate usefulness coincide here: the experiences which the writings of the essayists were written to express become conscious in the minds of most people only when they look at the pictures or read the poem discussed and even then they rarely have a force that could move life itself. That is why most people have to believe that the writings of the essayists are produced only in order to explain books and pictures, to facilitate their understanding. Yet this relationship is profound and necessary, and it is precisely the indivisible and organic quality of this mixture of being-accidental and being-necessary which is at the root of that humour and that irony which we find in the writings of every truly great essayist—that peculiar humour which is so strong that to speak of it is almost indecent, for there is no use in pointing it out to someone who does not spontaneously feel it. And the irony I mean consists in the critic always speaking about the ultimate problems of life, but in a tone which implies that he is only discussing pictures and books, only the inessential and pretty ornaments of real life—and even then not their innermost substance but only their beautiful and useless surface. Thus each essay appears to be removed as far as possible from life, and the distance between them seems the greater, the more burningly and painfully we sense the actual closeness of the true essence of both. Perhaps the great Sieur de Montaigne felt something like this when he gave his writings the wonderfully elegant and apt title of "Essays". The simple modesty of this word is an arrogant courtesy. The essayist dismisses his own proud hopes which sometimes lead him to believe that he has come close to the ultimate: he has, after all, no more to offer than explanations of the poems of others, or at best of his own ideas. But he ironically adapts himself to this smallness—the eternal smallness of the most profound work of the intellect in face of life—and even emphasizes it with ironic modesty. In Plato, conceptuality is underlined by the irony of the small realities of life. Eryximachos cures Aristophanes of hiccups by making him sneeze before he can begin his deeply meaningful hymn to Eros. And Hippothales watches with anxious attention while Socrates questions his beloved Lysis—and little Lysis, with childish malice, asks Socrates to torment his friend Menexenos with questions just as he has tormented him. Rough guardians come and break up the gently scintillating dialogue, and drag the boys off home. Socrates, however, is more amused than anything else: "Socrates and the two boys wanted to be friends, yet were not even able to say what a friend really is." I see a similar irony in the vast scientific apparatus of certain modern essayists (think only of Weininger), and only a different expression of it in the discreetly reserved manner of a Dilthey. We can always find the same irony in every text by every great essayist, though admittedly always in a different form. The mystics of the Middle Ages are the only ones without inner irony—I surely need not tell you why.

We see, then, that criticism and the essay generally speak of pictures, books and ideas. What is their attitude towards the matter which is represented? People say that the critic must always speak the truth, whereas the poet is not obliged to tell the truth about his subject-matter. It is not our intention here to ask Pilate's question nor to enquire whether the poet, too, is not impelled towards an inner truthfulness and whether the truth of any criticism can be stronger or greater than this. I do not propose to ask these questions because I really do see a difference here, but once again a difference which is altogether pure, sharp and without transitions only at its abstract poles. When I wrote about Kassner I pointed out that the essay always speaks of something that has already been given form, or at least something that has already been there at some time in the past; hence it is part of the nature of the essay that it does not create new things from an empty nothingness but only orders those which were once alive. And because it orders them anew and does not form something new out of formlessness, it is bound to them and must always speak "the truth" about them, must find expression for their essential nature. Perhaps the difference can be most briefly formulated thus: poetry takes its motifs from life (and art); the essay has its models in art (and life). Perhaps this is enough to define the difference: the paradoxy of the essay is almost the same as that of the portrait. You see why, do you not? In front of a landscape we never ask ourselves whether this mountain or that river really is as it is painted there; but in front of every portrait the question of likeness always forces itself willy-nilly upon us. Give a little more thought, therefore, to this problem of likeness—this problem which, foolish and superficial as it is, drives true artists to despair. You stand in front of a Velasquez portrait and you say: "What a marvellous likeness," and you feel that you have really said something about the painting. Likeness? Of whom? Of no one, of course. You have no idea whom it represents, perhaps you can never find out; and if you could, you would care very little. Yet you feel that it is a likeness. Other portraits produce their effect only by colour and line, and so you do not have this feeling. In other words, the really significant portraits give us, besides all other artistic sensations, also this: the life of a human being who once was really alive, forcing us to feel that his life was exactly as shown by the lines and colours of the painting. Only because we see painters in front of their models fight such a hard battle for this ideal expression—because the look and the battle-cry of this battle are such that it cannot be anything else than a battle for likeness—only for this reason do we give this name to the portrait's suggestion of real life, even though there is no one in the world whom the portrait could be like. For even if we know the person represented, whose portrait we may call "like" or "unlike"—is it not an abstraction to say of an arbitrarily chosen moment or expression that this is that person's likeness? And even if we know thousands of such moments or expressions, what do we know of the immeasurably large part of his life when we do not see him, what do we know of the inner light which burns within this "known" person, what of the way this inner light is reflected in others? And that, you see, is more or less how I imagine the truth of the essay to be. Here too there is a struggle for truth, for the incarnation of a life which someone has seen in a man, an epoch or a form; but it depends only on the intensity of the work and its vision whether the written text conveys to us this suggestion of that particular life.

The great difference, then, is this: poetry gives us the illusion of life of the person it represents; nowhere is there a conceivable some-one or something against which the created work can be measured. The hero of the essay was once alive, and so his life must be given form; but this life, too, is as much inside the work as everything is in poetry. The essay has to create from within itself all the pre-conditions for the effectiveness and validity of its vision. Therefore two essays can never contradict one another: each creates a different world, and even when, in order to achieve a higher universality, it goes beyond that created world, it still remains inside it by its tone, colour and accent; that is to say, it leaves that world only in the inessential sense. It is simply not true that there exists an objective, external criterion of life and truth, e.g. that the truth of Grimm's, Dilthey's or Schlegel's Goethe can be tested against the "real" Goethe. It is not true because many Goethes, different from one another and each profoundly different from *our* Goethe, may convince us of their life : and, conversely, we are disappointed if our own visions are presented by others, yet without that vital breath which would give them autonomous life. It is true that the essay strives for truth : but just as Saul went out to look for his father's she-asses and found a kingdom, so the essayist who is really capable of looking for the truth will find at the end of his road the goal he was looking for : life.

The illusion of truth ! Do not forget how slowly and with how much difficulty poetry abandoned that ideal. It happened not so very long ago, and it is highly questionable whether the disappearance of the illusion was entirely advantageous. It is highly questionable whether man should want the precise thing he sets out to attain, whether he has the right to walk towards his goal along straight and simple paths. Think of the chivalresque epics of the Middle Ages, think of the Greek tragedies, think of Giotto and you will see what I am trying to say. We are not speaking here of ordinary truth, the truth of naturalism which it would be more accurate to call the triviality of everyday life, but of the truth of the myth by whose power ancient tales and legends are kept alive for thousands of years. The true poets of myths looked only for the true meaning of their themes; they neither could nor wished to check their pragmatic reality. They saw these myths as sacred, mysterious hieroglyphics which it was their mission to read. But do you not see that both worlds can have a mythology of their own? It was Friedrich Schlegel who said long ago that the national gods of the Germans were not Hermann or Wotan but science and the arts. Admittedly, that is not true of the *whole* life of Germany, but it is all the more apt as a description of *part* of the life of every nation in every epoch—that part, precisely, of which we are speaking. That life, too, has its golden ages and its lost paradises; we find in it rich lives full of strange adventures and enigmatic punishments of dark sins; heroes of the sun appear and fight out their harsh feuds with the forces of darkness; here, too, the magic words of wise magicians and the tempting songs of beautiful sirens lead weaklings into perdition; here too there is original sin and redemption. All the struggles of life are present here, but the stuff of which everything is made is different from the stuff of the "other" life.

We want poets and critics to give us life-symbols and to mould the still-living myths and legends in the form of our questions. It is a subtle and poignant irony, is it not, when a great critic dreams our longing into early Florentine paintings or Greek torsos and, in that way, gets something out of them for us that we would have sought in vain everywhere else—and then speaks of the latest achievements of scientific research, of new methods and new facts? Facts are always there and everything is always contained in facts, but every epoch needs its own Greece, its own Middle Ages and its own Renaissance. Every age creates the age it needs, and only the next generation believes that its fathers' dreams were lies which must be fought with its own new "truths". The history of the effect of poetry follows the same course, and in criticism, too, the continuing life of the grandfather's dreams—not to mention those of earlier generations—is barely touched by the dreams of men alive today. Consequently the most varied "conceptions" of the Renaissance can live peacefully side by side with one another, just as a new poet's new Phèdre, Siegfried or Tristan must always leave intact the Phèdre, Siegfried or Tristan of his predecessors.

Of course there is a science of the arts; there has to be one. The greatest essayists are precisely those who can least well do without it: what they create must be science, even when their vision of life has transcended the sphere of science. Sometimes its free flight is constrained by the unassailable facts of dry matter; sometimes it loses all scientific value because it is, after all, a vision, because it precedes facts and therefore handles them freely and arbitrarily. The essay form has not yet, today, travelled the road to independence which its sister, poetry, covered long ago—the road of development from a primitive, undifferentiated unity with science, ethics and art. Yet the beginning of that road was so tremendous that subsequent developments have rarely equalled it. I speak, of course, of Plato, the greatest essayist who ever lived or wrote, the one who wrested everything from life as it unfolded before his eyes and who therefore needed no mediating medium; the one who was able to connect his questions, the most profound questions ever asked, with life as lived. This greatest master of the form was also the happiest of all creators: man lived in his immediate proximity, man whose essence and destiny constituted the paradigmatic essence and destiny of his form. Perhaps they would have become paradigmatic in this way even if Plato's writing had consisted of the driest notations—not just because of his glorious form-giving—so strong was the concordance of life and form in this particular case. But Plato met Socrates and was able to give form to the myth of Socrates, to use Socrates' destiny as the vehicle for the questions he, Plato, wanted to address to life about destiny. The life of Socrates is the typical life for the essay form, as typical as hardly any other life is for any literary form—with the sole exception of Oedipus' life for tragedy. Socrates always lived in the ultimate questions; every other living reality was as little alive for him as his questions are alive for ordinary people. The concepts into which he poured the whole of his life were lived by him with the most direct and immediate life-energy; everything else was but a parable of that sole true reality, useful only as a means of expressing those experiences. His life rings with the sound of the deepest, the most hidden longing and is full of the most violent struggles; but that longing is—simply—longing, and the form in which it appears is the attempt to comprehend the nature of longing and to capture it in concepts, while the struggles are simply verbal battles fought solely in order to give more definite limits to a few concepts. Yet the longing fills that life completely and the struggles are always, quite literally, a matter of life and death. But despite everything the longing which seems to fill that life is not the essential thing about life, and neither Socrates' life nor his death was able to express those life-and-death struggles. If this had been possible, the death of Socrates would have been a martyrdom or a tragedy—which means that it could be represented in epic or dramatic form. But Plato knew exactly why he burned the tragedy he wrote in his youth. For a tragic life is crowned only by its end, only the end gives meaning, sense and form to the whole, and it is precisely the end which is always arbitrary and ironic here, in every dialogue and in Socrates' whole life. A question is thrown up and extended so far in depth that it becomes the question of all questions, but after that everything remains open; something comes from outside—from a reality which has no connection with the question nor with that which, as the possibility of an answer, brings forth a new question to meet it— and interrupts everything. This interruption is not an end, because it does not come from within, and yet it is the most profound ending because a conclusion from within would have been impossible. For Socrates every event was only an occasion for seeing concepts more clearly, his defence in front of the judges only a way of leading weak logicians *ad absurdum*—and his death? Death does not count here, it cannot be grasped by concepts, it interrupts the great dialogue— the only true reality—just as brutally, and merely from the outside, as those rough tutors who interrupted the conversation with Lysis. Such an interruption, however, can only be viewed humoristically, it has so little connection with that which it interrupts. But it is also a profound life-symbol—and, for that reason, still more profoundly humorous—that the essential is always interrupted by such things in such a way.

The Greeks felt each of the forms available to them as a reality, as a living thing and not as an abstraction. Alcibiades already saw clearly what Nietzsche was to emphasize centuries later—that Socrates was a new kind of man, profoundly different in his elusive essence from all other Greeks who lived before him. But Socrates, in the same dialogue, expressed the eternal ideal of men of his kind, an ideal which neither those whose way of feeling remains tied to the purely human nor those who are poets in their innermost being will ever understand: that tragedies and comedies should be written by the same man; that "tragic" and "comic" is entirely a matter of the chosen standpoint. In saying this, the critic expressed his deepest life-sense: the primacy of the standpoint, the concept, over feeling; and in saying it he formulated the profoundest anti-Greek thought.

Plato himself, as you see, was a "critic", although criticism, like everything else, was for him only an occasion, an ironic means of expressing himself. Later on, criticism became its own content; critics spoke only of poetry and art, and they never had the fortune to meet a Socrates whose life might have served them as a springboard to the ultimate. But Socrates was the first to condemn such critics. "It seems to me," he said to Protagoras, "that to make a poem the subject of a conversation is too reminiscent of those banquets which uneducated and vulgar people give in their houses. . . . Conversations like the one we are now enjoying—conversations among men such as most of us would claim to be—do not need outside voices or the presence of a poet. . . ."

Fortunately for us, the modern essay does not always have to speak of books or poets; but this freedom makes the essay even more problematic. It stands too high, it sees and connects too many things to be the simple exposition or explanation of a work; the title of every essay is preceded in invisible letters, by the words "Thoughts occasioned by. . . ." The essay has become too rich and independent for dedicated service, yet it is too intellectual and too multiform to acquire form out of its own self. Has it perhaps become even more problematic, even further removed from life-values than if it had continued to report faithfully on books?

When something has once become problematic—and the way of thinking that we speak of, and its way of expression, have not become problematic but have always been so—then salvation can only come from accentuating the problems to the maximum degree, from going radically to its root. The modern essay has lost that backdrop of life which gave Plato and the mystics their strength; nor does it any longer possess a naïve faith in the value of books and what can be said about them. The problematic of the situation has become accentuated almost to the point of demanding a certain frivolity of thought and expression, and this, for most critics, has become their life-mood. This has shown, however, that salvation is necessary and is therefore becoming possible and real. The essayist must now become conscious of his own self, must find himself and build something of his own out of himself. The essayist speaks of a picture or a book, but leaves it again at once—why? Because, I think, the idea of the picture or book has become predominant in his mind, because he has forgotten all that is concretely incidental about it, because he has used it only as a starting-point, a springboard. Poetry is older and greater—a larger, more important thing—than all the works of poetry: that was once the mood with which critics approached literature, but in our time it has had to become a conscious attitude. The critic has been sent into the world in order to bring to light this *a priori* primacy over great and small, to proclaim it, to judge every phenomenon by the scale of values glimpsed and grasped through this recognition. The idea is there before any of its expressions, it is a soul-value, a world-moving and life-forming force in itself: and that is why such criticism will always speak of life where it is most alive. The idea is the measure of everything that exists, and that is why the critic whose thinking is "occasioned by" something already created, and who reveals its idea, is the one who will write the truest and most profound criticism. Only something that is great and true can live in the proximity of the idea. When this magic word has been spoken, then everything that is brittle, small and unfinished falls apart, loses its usurped wisdom, its badly fitting essence. It does not have to be "criticism": the atmosphere of the idea is enough to judge and condemn it.

Yet it is now that the essayist's possibility of existence becomes profoundly problematic. He is delivered from the relative, the inessential, by the force of judgement of the idea he has glimpsed; but who gives him the right to judge? It would be almost true to say that he seizes that right, that he creates his judgement-values from within himself. But nothing is separated from true judgement by a deeper abyss than its approximation, the squint-eyed category of complacent and self-satisfied knowledge. The criteria of the essayist's judgement are indeed created within him, but it is not he who awakens them to life and action: the one who whispers them into his ear is the great value-definer of aesthetics, the one who is always about to arrive, the one who is never quite yet there, the only one who has been called to judge. The essayist is a Schopenhauer who writes his *Parerga* while waiting for the arrival of his own (or another's) *The World as Will and Idea*, he is a John the Baptist who goes out to preach in the wilderness about another who is still to come, whose shoelace he is not worthy to untie. And if that other does not come—is not the essayist then without justification? And if the other does come, is he not made superfluous thereby? Has he not become entirely problematic by thus trying to justify himself? He is the pure type of the precursor, and it seems highly questionable whether, left entirely to himself—i.e., independent from the fate of that other of whom he is the herald—he could lay claim to any value or validity. To stand fast against those who deny his fulfilment within the great, redeeming system is easy enough: a true longing always triumphs over those who lack the energy to rise above the vulgar level of given facts and experiences; the existence of the longing is enough to decide the outcome. For it tears the mask off everything that is only apparently positive and immediate, reveals it as petty longing and cheap fulfilment, points to the measure and order to which even they who vainly and contemptibly deny its existence —because measure and order seem inaccessible to them—unconsciously aspire. The essay can calmly and proudly set its fragmentariness against the petty completeness of scientific exactitude or impressionistic freshness; but its purest fulfilment, its most vigorous accomplishment becomes powerless once the great aesthetic comes. Then all its creations are only an application of the measure which at last has become undeniable, it is then something merely provisional and occasional, its results can no longer be justified purely from within themselves. Here the essay seems truly and completely a mere precursor, and no independent value can be attached to it. But this longing for value and form, for measure and order and purpose, does not simply lead to an end that must be reached so that it may be cancelled out and become a presumptuous tautology. Every true end is a real end, the end of a road, and although road and end do not make a unity and do not stand side by side as equals, they nevertheless coexist: the end is unthinkable and unrealizable without the road being travelled again and again; the end is not standing still but arriving there, not resting but conquering a summit. Thus the essay seems justified as a necessary means to the ultimate end, the penultimate step in this hierarchy. This, however, is only the value of what it *does*; the fact of what it *is* has yet another, more independent value. For in the system of values yet to be found, the longing we spoke of would be satisfied and therefore abolished; but this longing is more than just something waiting for fulfilment, it is a fact of the soul with a value and existence of its own: an original and deeprooted attitude towards the whole of life, a final, irreducible category of possibilities of experience. Therefore it needs not only to be satisfied (and thus abolished) but also to be given form which will redeem and release its most essential and now indivisible substance into eternal value. That is what the essay does. Think again of the example of the *Parerga*: whether they occurred before or after the system is not a matter simply of a time-sequence; the time-historical difference is only a symbol of the difference between their two natures. The *Parerga* written before the system create their preconditions from within themselves, create the whole world out of their longing for the system, so that—it seems— they can give an example, a hint; immanently and inexpressibly, they contain the system and its connection with lived life. Therefore they must always occur before the system; even if the system had already been created, they would not be a mere application but always a new creation, a coming-alive in real experience. This "application" creates both that which judges and that which is judged, it encompasses a whole world in order to raise to eternity, in all its uniqueness, something that was once there. The essay is a judgement, but the essential, the value-determining thing about it is not the verdict (as is the case with the system) but the process of judging.

Only now may we write down the opening words: the essay is an art form, an autonomous and integral giving-of-form to an autonomous and complete life. Only now would it not be contradictory, ambiguous and false to call it a work of art and yet insist on emphasizing the thing that differentiates it from art: it faces life with the same gesture as the work of art, but only the gesture, the sovereignty of its attitude is the same; otherwise there is no correspondence between them.

It was of this possibility of the essay that I wanted to speak to you here, of the nature and form of these "intellectual poems", as the older Schlegel called those of Hemsterhuys. This is not the place to discuss or decide whether the essayists' becoming conscious of their own nature, as they have been doing for some time past, has brought perfection or can bring it. The point at issue was only the possibility, only the question of whether the road upon which this book attempts to travel is really a road; it was not a question of who has already travelled it or how—nor, least of all, the distance this particular book has travelled along it. The critique of this book is contained, in all possible sharpness and entirety, in the very approach from which it sprang.

Florence, October 1910.

Platonism, Poetry and Form

RUDOLPH KASSNER

"TIME AND again I have met people who played an instrument exceedingly well and even composed after a fashion, yet afterwards, in ordinary life, were perfect strangers to their music. Is that not odd?" This is the question we find, either openly or indirectly stated, in every text by Rudolf Kassner. The smallest of his reviews seeks to supply an answer to it, and in every person he analyses (mostly they are poets, critics, painters) the only thing that interests him, the only thing he concentrates upon, is what leads up to this problem: how people behave "in ordinary life", how art and life confront each other, how each shapes and transforms the other and how a higher organism grows out of the two—or why it does not. Is style a matter of a person's whole life? If so, how and wherein does style manifest itself? Is there, in an artist's life, a strong, continuously ringing melody, persistent to the very end, that makes everything necessary, that resolves everything in itself, a melody in which everything divergent finds unity at last? Does a great life's work make a great man of its author, and where, in art, does it become apparent if the artist is a great man, made all of a piece?

Who are the men who thus appear in Kassner's critical works? The very fact that such a question can be asked determines (if only negatively) Kassner's place among present-day critics. In the company of those alive today he is the only *active* critic—the only one who visits his shrines himself, who chooses for himself what sacrifices he will make to conjure up the spirits of only those men who can answer the questions he wants to ask. Kassner is no photosensitive plate for chance impressions, but a quite sovereignly positive critic: positive in the choice of those he writes about. He has never engaged in polemics nor ever written criticism in a polemical mood. The bad, the inartistic simply does not exist for him, he does not even see it, let alone want to attack it. Positive, too, in his presentation of his chosen subjects: their failures do not interest him, and the borderline between failure and success only to the extent that it may be inseparably connected with the nature of the man in question, only in so far as it forms

19

the negative pole of his highest achievement, a background to the great, symbolic act of his life. Everything else falls away as soon as Kassner looks at an artist. The suggestive power of his *not seeing* is so great that his glance strips off the husk, and we feel at once that the husk is mere chaff and only what Kassner sees as the kernel is important. One of his main strengths is that there is so much he does not see. When he speaks of Diderot, for instance, he sees nothing of the encyclopaedist whom the literary historians would have us see, nothing of the founder of bourgeois drama, nothing of the herald of new ideas; he does not distinguish between Diderot's theism, deism and atheism; even the Germanic cloudiness so often pointed out by psychologists disappears from his field of vision. Then, after he has swept away everything banal, he constructs in front of our eyes a new Diderot—forever restless, forever searching, the first impressionist and individualist, the man for whom every new opinion, every new method is only a means of finding himself or understanding others—or even, simply, of coming into contact with others; a Diderot who overestimates the whole world because for him that is the only way of enhancing himself; a Diderot full of contradictions, often a mere windbag, a phrasemonger, who yet, at a few great, exceptional moments—and only at those moments—finds a style which still lives on in the rhythm of our longings.

Let us then speak about the men Kassner writes about. Two types of men occur in his writings, the two principal types of all those who live in art: the creative artist and the critic, or—to employ Kassner's terminology—the poet and the Platonist. He distinguishes between them sharply, with a conservative, almost dogmatic decisiveness. He is an enemy of modern sensibility, of blurred outlines, of jumbled styles which permit "men of imagination who have trouble with verse to write poems in prose". A different means of expression befits each type of soul: the poet writes in verse, the Platonist in prose, and —most important distinction of all—"poetry has laws, prose has none".

The poet writes in verse, the Platonist in prose. The one lives within the strict security of a structure of laws, the other in the thousand hazards and vagaries of freedom—the one in a radiant and enchanting perfection-within-itself, the other in the infinite waves of relativity. The one sometimes holds things in his hand and contemplates them, but mostly he soars above them on mighty wings; the other is always close to things and yet distant from them in eternity; it seems as though he could possess them, yet he is doomed to long for them forever. Perhaps both are equally homeless, both stand equally outside life, but the poet's world (although he never reaches the world of real life) is an absolute one in which it is possible to live, whereas the Platonist's world has no substantiality. The poet says either 'Yes' or 'No', the Platonist believes and doubts all at once, at the same moment. The poet's lot may be tragic, but the Platonist may not even become a hero of tragedy; "he is," says Kassner, "a Hamlet bereft even of a murdered father".

They are opposite poles. They almost complement one another. But whilst the poet's problem consists in not noticing the Platonist, for the Platonist the decisive problem is to discover the truth about the poet, to find the right words to define the poet. The true type of poet has no thoughts—that is to say, when he has thoughts they are merely raw materials, a mere occasion for rhythm; like everything else, they are only voices in a chorus, they comprehend nothing and oblige to nothing. The poet can learn nothing because his vision is always rounded and complete. The poet's form is verse, is song; for him everything resolves itself in music. "Within the Platonist lives something for which he seeks but cannot find a rhyme anywhere": he will always long for something he can never reach. For him, too, a thought is only raw material, only a road which he travels in order to arrive somewhere, but the road in itself is the ultimate, irreducible fact of his life; he develops incessantly, yet never reaches any goal. What he wanted to say is always more—or less—than what he succeeds in saying, and only the silent accompaniment of things unsaid makes music of his writings. He can never say all there is to say about himself, can never wholly surrender himself to anything; his forms are never completely filled, or else they cannot encompass everything he wants them to encompass. Analysis, prose, is his form. The poet always speaks about himself, no matter of what he sings; the Platonist never dares to think aloud about himself, he can only experience his own life through the works of others, and by understanding others he comes closer to his own self.

The really typical poet (according to Kassner, only Pindar, Shelley and Whitman may, perhaps, be counted as such without reservation) is never problematic, the true Platonist always—which, when both are men determined to live their lives to the uttermost limits of their logic, comes down, in a very profound sense, to the same thing. Expression and the way to a goal, verse and prose become a life-problem only when the two contrasting types combine within a single man—which must inevitably happen in the course of history. Thus—to quote a few of Kassner's examples—Greek tragedy as written by Euripides, the disciple of Socrates, became Platonic if compared with Greek tragedy in the hands of Aeschylus; thus the French chivalresque epic develops, in the hands of a Wolfram von Eschenbach, from Platonism to Christianity—i.e., in the opposite direction.

Wherein lies the problem? And where is the solution? In the purest types the work and the life coincide—or, rather, only that part of their life which can be related to the work is valid and has to be taken into consideration. The life is nothing, the work is all; the life is mere accident, the work is necessity itself. "When Shelley wrote," says Kassner, "he took leave of the real world"; and the work of a Pater, a Ruskin, a Taine absorbed all those possible aspects of their lives which might perhaps have been in contradiction with it. A problem arises when the Platonist's eternal uncertainty threatens to cast a shadow over the white brilliance of the verse, when the heaviness of his sense of distance weighs down the poet's soaring lightness, or when there is a danger that the poet's divine frivolity may falsify the Platonist's profound hesitations and rob them of their honesty. With such men the problem consists in finding a form spacious enough to contain the conflicting trends, rich enough to force a unity upon them, a form whose very fullness, the very fact of its refusal to be burst asunder, may give it strength. For such men one of the directions is the goal and the other the danger; one is the compass, the other the desert; one is the work and the other life. Between the two, a life-and-death struggle is fought out for a victory which could unite the two opposing camps, which could turn to advantage the weakness, the very frailty of the defeated force; a struggle full of dangers precisely because the one extreme might counterbalance the other and the result might be an empty mediocrity.

A real solution can only come from form. In form alone ("the only possible thing" is the shortest definition of form known to me) does every antithesis, every trend, become music and necessity. The road of every problematic human being leads to form because it is that unity which can combine within itself the largest number of divergent forces, and therefore at the end of that road there stands the man who can create form: the artist, in whose created form poet and Platonist become equal.

Away with everything accidental! Such is the goal. And towards it struggled Werther and Friedrich Schlegel and Benjamin Constant's Adolphe (whom Kassner holds to be Kierkegaard's predecessor); and all of them were beautiful and interesting and authentic during the first act of their lives, when to be interesting, original and witty was still enough. Yet as soon as they started on the weary road towards universal, model-creating life (these are only different words for the concept of form), they disintegrated, flattened out, committed suicide or decayed inwardly. Kierkegaard did achieve a noble and rigorous life-system constructed on a Platonist basis; but in order to get there he had to conquer the aesthete, the poet within himself; he had to live all the poet's qualities to the very end so as to be able to fuse them into the whole. Life for him became what writing is for the poet, and the poet hidden within him was like the tempting siren-song of life. Robert Browning went exactly the opposite way. By nature he was never at rest, he could not find a fixed point any-where in life; there was no expression that he would have dared to consider final, no writing large enough to contain what he lived and felt—until, at last, he found the music for his Platonism in a curious form of abstract-lyrical, impressionist-abstract drama (or, shall we say, in fragments of drama, in monologues and situations), through which the purely accidental part of his life became symbolic and necessary.

Likewise Baudelaire's artistry unites the man—who amounts to little, almost to nothing, and belongs nowhere—with the poet, who is everything, is eternal, and who also belongs nowhere. Thus Rossetti's art grows into his life, and what were originally purely artistic, stylistic demands are transformed into life-feelings. Thus Keats' life outgrows his poetry because he thinks his being-as-a-poet through to the end, embraces a saintly asceticism, renounces life; and the two—life, in the particular case of Keats, as the backdrop to verse—combine to a new and higher unity.

From the accidental to the necessary: that is the road of every problematic human being. To arrive where everything becomes necessary because everything expresses the essence of man, nothing but that, completely and without residue—where everything becomes symbolic, where everything, as in music, is only what it means and means only what it is!

The poet's form has always soared above his life, the Platonist's always failed to capture life; the artist's form absorbed all shadows into itself and the intensity of its radiance is all the greater for such drinking-up of darkness. Only in the artist's form can a balance be achieved between the Platonist's heavy-footed hesitations and the poet's weightless arrow-flight; in the artist's form, the always hidden object of the Platonist's longing—the longing for certainty, for dogma—grows out of poetry: and Platonism introduces the many-coloured richness of lived life into the divine unison of the poet's songs.

Perhaps life exists as a reality only for the man in whose feelings there is such dissonance. Perhaps 'life' is just a word which means, for the Platonist, the possibility of being a poet, and for the poet the possibility of being the Platonist hidden in his soul—and only he can live in whose soul these two elements are fused in such a way that their fusion can give birth to form.

Kassner is one of the most Platonist writers in world literature today. The longing for certainty, for measure and dogma, is unbelievably alive in him and unbelievably hidden, wrapped in fierce ironies, veiled by rigid theories. His doubts and hesitations, which make him renounce all measure and force him to see man in the stark light of isolation rather than within the harmony of any great synthesis, are sublime. Kassner sees syntheses, as it were, with his eyes shut; when he looks at anything, he sees so many minute details that every summing-up must appear as a lie, a conscious falsification. Nevertheless he follows his longing, he closes his eyes in order to see things as a whole—as values—but then his honesty immediately forces him to look at them again, and they become once more separate, isolated, floating in a vacuum. The fluctuation between these two poles determines Kassner's style. It is beautiful at the moments when he is looking at something, when the apprehended syntheses are filled with real content and the facts are still encapsuled in values, when they are not yet strong enough to break the bonds of dreamed connections between them. And it is beautiful when he shuts his eyes, when things seen in wonderfully close detail join the endless dancing throng of a frieze round the walls of a fairy-tale castle hall: they are still alive, but only as symbols, as decorations. Kassner is the passionate dreamer of the great unifying line, but his conscientiousness also makes him an impressionist. The consequent quality makes for the glowing intensity and, at the same time, the impenetrable fogginess of his style.

We have said that the Platonist's world has no substantiality. The world created by a poet is always real, even when it is woven out of dreams, because its substance is more unified and more alive. The critic's way of creation is like the way of a Homeric hero when, for a brief moment, he brings to life the shade of another hero, languishing in Hades, with the blood of a sacrificial lamb. The inhabitants of two worlds confront one another, a man and a shade, the man wants to learn only one thing from the shade, the shade has come back to life in order to give only one answer—and only for the duration of the question and the answer, spoken together, does each exist for the other. The Platonist never creates a man; that man lives already or has lived somewhere else, no matter where, independently from his will and power; he can only conjure up shades and demand an answer to a question (only in this is the critic wholly sovereign), a question of whose significance the one who is questioned may never have been aware.

The Platonist is a dissector of souls, not a creator of men. Hofmannsthal in one of his dialogues makes Balzac differentiate between two types of men: the life-capacity of one is crystallized in drama, that of the other in the epic, so that one can imagine men who could live in a play but not in an epic. Perhaps these distinctions could be carried through all literary forms and a scale of life-capacities established according to each. One thing is certain—that if the drama stood at one end of the scale, the essay (to use just one word to describe all the Platonists' writings) would have to stand at the other. And this is not a scholastic classification; it has deep reasons within the soul. In the same dialogue Balzac defines one of these reasons. He says that he does not believe in the existence of characters, whereas Shakespeare does; he, Balzac, is not interested in men, but only in destinies.

In one of Kassner's latest dialogues one of the speakers denies that the other has character, saying that his memory is too good: he cannot bear anything to be repeated, every repetition is for him wrong, foolish, superfluous and useless; yet it is impossible to assign value—more than that, it is impossible to live—without any repetition. There is also a technical factor: Kerr, writing of Hauptmann's *The Red Cockerel*, points out that when the villainous old shoemaker Fielitz risks his life for the sake of the fleet, this touch—although brilliantly observed—fails to produce the desired effect. It does not convince because Hauptmann makes the point only once and never repeats it; and while it may seem natural for such a thing to be mentioned only once in the course of a play, it is nevertheless bound to seem artificial. A dramatic character is unthinkable without permanent characteristics; in the perspective of drama we simply do not see people without such characteristics; their momentary ones are forgotten in an instant. This repetition of a trait is nothing other than the technical equivalent of a profound faith in the constancy of characteristics, of character. The Platonist, as we have already said in different words, does not believe in repetitions, which for both spiritual and technical reasons are the fundamental precondition for creating characters.

That is why the subjects of his essays, but not the heroes of his experiments in the short story, appear to be alive. I can see Kassner's Robert and Elizabeth Browning, his Hebbel, Kierkegaard, Shelley and Diderot, but I totally fail to see his Adalbert von Gleichen or Joachim Fortunatus. I can remember things they have thought or seen, but these are not connected with anything sensual, visible or audible in my mind. I do not see them. I see the Brownings alive before me— but perhaps they are only the shades of the Brownings, perhaps Kassner's words only suggest that these shades, conjured up from books, have put on the armour they wore in life, that they retain the gestures, the tempo and rhythm of their life; perhaps what, for a moment, looked like the creation of living persons is only an invocation of ghosts.

Certainly Browning has to have lived if Kassner is to attempt to
awaken him to a new life. For Goethe it was not necessary that
Egmont or Tasso should have lived, nor for Swinburne (although he
was not a powerful creator of character) that Mary Stuart should
have lived; but the Platonist Pater can bring Watteau alive through
the diary of a young girl, whilst the girl herself dissolves in mists. It
is not true to say, therefore, that both types of artist possess the same
kind of talent for creation, and are merely led by external circumstances to choose, say, the essay or the drama form. Each, if he is a
true artist, will find that art form which is appropriate to him according to his own capacity to live (or, more accurately, to create men).
That is why the Platonist, if he wants to speak of himself, must work
through the destinies of others (and in these others the life which is
already given, already formed by reality and therefore unchangeable,
must be especially rich) so as to penetrate to the most deeply hidden
intimacies of his own soul. His all-dissecting eye can only see men of
flesh and blood by concentrating on such powerful realities. It sometimes seems to me that the honesty of the true critic—that honesty
which forces him to try to treat his models so scrupulously, to draw
them always as they really were—arises from a profound recognition
of his own limits. The critic, whose strength lies in making connections, comes closest to creativity when he is firmly anchored in
undeniable reality.

Once more: the poet and the Platonist are opposite poles. Every
Platonist speaks his most significant words when he speaks about
the poet. Perhaps there is a mystic law which decides which poet
shall be allotted to which critic, so that he may then speak about
him in this special way. Perhaps the degree to which poetry and
Platonism are mixed in each artist determines who, in this sense,
shall be for ever more the other's psychological antipode; perhaps, in
a mystical-mathematical sense, the sum of Platonism and poetry in
both together is always constant, so that it takes the purest Platonist
to appreciate and love the purest poet, the visionary who has nothing
of the Platonist about him. It is for this reason, perhaps, that of all
Kassner's writings I regard the essay on Shelley as the most lyrical
and subtle—Shelley who meant little even to so pure-blooded a
Platonist as Emerson. Kassner finds his most resonant, most elevated
and telling language when writing about Shelley, perhaps just
because he is in every respect so immeasurably far from him; perhaps,
when describing Shelley's style, he is speaking about himself. "They
are," he says of Shelley's images, "as though woven out of light, air
and water, their colours are those of the rainbow, their tone that of
the echo, their duration, if I may call it thus, that of a rising and
falling wave." There could be no better or truer way of describing

Shelley's style—or Kassner's. For Shelley's style is also his: but in Shelley there were no shadows, whilst in Kassner the dark glow of shadows is everywhere.

1908

The Foundering of Form Against Life

SÖREN KIERKEGAARD AND REGINE OLSEN

> Fair youth beneath the trees, thou canst not leave
> Thy song, nor ever can those trees be bare;
> Bold lover, never, never canst thou kiss,
> Though winning near the goal—yet do not grieve;
> She cannot fade, though thou hast not thy bliss,
> For ever wilt thou love, and she be fair!
>
> Keats: *Ode on a Grecian Urn*

1

WHAT is the life-value of a gesture? Or, to put it another way, what is the value of form in life, the life-creating, life-enhancing value of form? A gesture is nothing more than a movement which clearly expresses something unambiguous. Form is the only way of expressing the absolute in life; a gesture is the only thing which is perfect within itself, the only reality which is more than mere possibility. The gesture alone expresses life: but is it possible to express life? Is not this the tragedy of any living art, that it seeks to build a crystal palace out of air, to forge realities from the insubstantial possibilities of the soul, to construct, through the meetings and partings of souls, a bridge of forms between men? Can the gesture exist at all, and has the concept of form any meaning seen from the perspective of life?

Kierkegaard once said that reality has nothing to do with possibilities; yet he built his whole life upon a gesture. Everything he wrote, every one of his struggles and adventures, is in some way the backdrop to that gesture; perhaps he only wrote and did these things to make his gesture stand out more clearly against the chaotic multiplicity of life. Why did he do it? How could he do it—he of all men, who saw more clearly than any other the thousand aspects, the thousand-fold variability of every motive—he who so clearly saw how everything passes gradually into its opposite, and how, if we look really close, we see an unbridgeable abyss gaping between two

28

barely perceptible nuances? Why did he do this? Perhaps because the gesture is one of the most powerful life-necessities; perhaps because a man who wants to be "honest" (one of Kierkegaard's most frequently used words) must force life to yield up its single meaning, must grasp that ever-changing Proteus, so firmly that, once he has revealed the magic words, he can no longer move. Perhaps the gesture—to use Kierkegaard's dialectic—is the paradox, the point at which reality and possibility intersect, matter and air, the finite and the infinite, life and form. Or, more accurately still and even closer to Kierkegaard's terminology: the gesture is the leap by which the soul passes from one into the other, the leap by which it leaves the always relative facts of reality to reach the eternal certainty of forms. In a word, the gesture is that unique leap by which the absolute is transformed, in life, into the possible. The gesture is the great paradox of life, for only in its rigid permanence is there room for every evanescent moment of life, and only within it does every such moment become true reality.

Whoever does more than merely play with life needs the gesture so that his life may become more real for him than a game that can be played by an infinite choice of moves.

But can there really be a gesture vis-à-vis life? Is it not self-delusion—however splendidly heroic—to believe that the essence of the gesture lies in an action, a turning towards something or a turning away: rigid as stone and yet containing everything immutably within itself?

2

In September 1840 it happened that Sören Aaby Kierkegaard, Master of Arts, became engaged to Regine Olsen, State Councillor Olsen's eighteen-year-old daughter. Barely a year afterwards he broke off the engagement. He left for Berlin, and when he returned to Copenhagen he lived there as a noted eccentric; his peculiar ways made him a constant target for the humorous papers, and although his writings, published under a variety of pen-names, found some admirers because they were so full of wit, they were hated by the majority because of their "immoral" and "frivolous" contents. His later works made still more open enemies for him—namely, all the leaders of the ruling Protestant Church: and during the hard fight he fought against them—contending that the society of our time is not a Christian one and indeed makes it practically impossible for anyone to remain a Christian—he died.

A few years previously Regine Olsen had married one of her earlier admirers.

3

What had happened? The number of explanations is infinite, and every newly published text, every letter, every diary entry of Kierkegaard's has made it easier to explain the event and at the same time harder to understand or appreciate what it meant in Sören Kierkegaard's and Regine Olsen's life.

Kassner, writing about Kierkegaard in unforgettable and unsurpassable terms, rejects every explanation. "Kierkegaard," he writes, "made a poem of his relationship with Regine Olsen, and when a Kierkegaard makes a poem of his life he does so not in order to conceal the truth but in order to be able to reveal it."

There is no explanation, for what is there is more than an explanation, it is a gesture. Kierkegaard said: I am a melancholic; he said: I was a whole eternity too old for her; he said: my sin was that I tried to sweep her along with myself into the great stream; he said: if my life were not a great penitence, if it were not the *vita ante acta*, then. . . .

And he left Regine Olsen and said he did not love her, had never really loved her, he was a man whose fickle spirit demanded new people and new relationships at every moment. A large part of his writings proclaims this loudly, and the way he spoke and the way he lived emphasized this one thing in order to confirm Regine Olsen's belief in it.

. . . And Regine married one of her old admirers and Sören Kierkegaard wrote in his diary: "Today I saw a beautiful girl; she does not interest me. No married man can be more faithful to his wife than I am to Regine."

4

The gesture: to make unambiguous the inexplicable, which happened for many reasons and whose consequences spread wide. To withdraw in such a way that nothing but sorrow may come of it, nothing but tragedy—once it was clear that their encounter had to be tragic—nothing but total collapse, perhaps, just so long as there was no uncertainty about it, no dissolving of reality into possibilities. If what seemed to mean life itself to Regine Olsen had to be lost to her, then it had to lose *all* meaning in her life; if he who loved Regine Olsen had to leave her, then he who left her had to be a scoundrel and a seducer, so that every path back to life might remain open to her. And since Sören Kierkegaard's penitence was to leave life, that penitence had to be made the greater by the sinner's mask, chivalrously assumed, which disguised his real sin.

Regine's marriage to another man was necessary for Kierkegaard. "She has grasped the point very well," he wrote, "she understands that she must get married." He needed her marriage so that nothing uncertain, nothing vague should remain about the relationship, no further possibility, only this one thing: the seducer and the jilted girl. But the girl consoles herself and finds the way back to life. Under the seducer's mask stands the ascetic who, out of asceticism, voluntarily froze in his gesture.

The transformation of the girl follows in a straight line from her beginning. Behind the fixedly smiling mask of the seducer frowns, as fixedly, the real face of the ascetic. The gesture is pure and expresses everything. "Kierkegaard made a poem of his life."

5

The only essential difference between one life and another is the question whether a life is absolute or merely relative; whether the mutually exclusive opposites within the life are separated from one another sharply and definitively or not. The difference is whether the life-problems of a particular life arise in the form of an either/or, or whether "as well as" is the proper formula when the split appears. Kierkegaard was always saying: I want to be honest, and this honesty could not mean anything less than the duty—in the purest sense of the word—to live out his life in accordance with poetic principles; the duty to decide, the duty to go to the very end of every chosen road at every crossroads.

But when a man looks about him, he does not see roads and cross-roads, nor any sharply distinct choices anywhere; everything flows, everything is transmuted into something else. Only when we turn away our gaze and look again much later do we find that one thing has become another—and perhaps not even then. But the deep meaning of Kierkegaard's philosophy is that he places fixed points beneath the incessantly changing nuances of life, and draws absolute quality distinctions within the melting chaos of nuances. And, having found certain things to be different, he presents them as being so unambiguously and profoundly different that what separates them can never again be blurred by any possible nuance or transition. Thus Kierkegaard's honesty entails the paradox that whatever has not already grown into a new unity which cancels out all former differences, must remain divided forever. Among the things you have found to be different you must choose one, you must not seek "middle ways" or "higher unities" which might resolve the "merely apparent" contradictions. And so there is no system anywhere, for it is not possible to *live* a system; the system is always a vast palace, while its creator can only withdraw into a modest corner. There is never any room for life in a logical system of thought; seen in this way, the starting point for such a system is always arbitrary and, from the perspective of life, only relative—a mere possibility. There is no system in life. In life there is only the separate and individual, the concrete. To exist is to be different. And only the concrete, the individual phenomenon is the unambiguous, the absolute which is without nuance. Truth is only subjective—perhaps; but subjectivity is quite certainly truth; the individual thing is the only thing that *is*; the individual is the real man.

And so there are some major, typical cycles of possibilities in life, or stages to use Kierkegaard's language: the aesthetic, the ethical, the religious stage. Each is distinct from the other with a sharpness that allows of no nuances, and the connection between each is the miracle, the leap, the sudden metamorphosis of the entire being of a man.

6

This, then, was Kierkegaard's honesty: to see everything as being sharply distinct from everything else, system from life, human being from human being, stage from stage: to see the absolute in life, without any petty compromises.

But is it not a compromise to see life as being without compromises? Is not such nailing down of absoluteness, rather, an evasion of the duty to look at *everything*? Is not a stage a "higher unity", too? Is not the denial of a life-system itself a system—and very much so? Is not the leap merely a sudden transition? Is there not, after all, a rigorous distinction hidden behind every compromise, hidden behind its most vehement denial? Can one be honest in face of life, and yet stylize life's events in literary form?

7

The inner honesty of Kierkegaard's gesture of separation could only be assured if everything he did was done for Regine Olsen's sake. The letters and diary entries are full of it: had they remained together, not even Regine's bubbling laughter would have broken the sombre silence of his terrible melancholy; the laughter would have been silenced, the lightness would have fallen wearily to the stony ground below. No one would have benefited from such a sacrifice. And so it was his duty (whatever it may have cost him from the point of view of human happiness, of human existence) to save Regine Olsen's life.

But the question is whether Regine's life was the only thing he saved. Was not the very thing which, as he believed, made it necessary for them to part, essential to his own life? Did he not give up the struggle against his melancholy (a struggle which might have been successful) because he loved it more dearly, perhaps, than anything else, and could not conceive of life without it? "My sorrow is my castle," he once wrote, and elsewhere he said (I quote only a few examples to stand for many more): "In my great melancholy I still loved life, for I loved my melancholy." And writing about Regine and himself: ". . . she would have been ruined and presumably she would have wrecked me, too, for I should constantly have had to strain myself trying to raise her up. I was too heavy for her, she too light for me, but either way there is most certainly a risk of overstrain."

There are beings to whom—in order that they may become great—anything even faintly resembling happiness and sunshine must always be forbidden. Karoline[1] once wrote of Friedrich Schlegel: "Some thrive under oppression, and Friedrich is one of them—if he were to enjoy the full glory of success even once, it would destroy what is finest in him." Robert Browning rewrote Friedrich Schlegel's tragedy in the sad history of Chiappino, who was strong and noble, delicate and capable of deep feeling so long as he remained in the shadows and his life meant only wretchedness and fruitless longing; when misfortune raised him higher than he had ever hoped in his wildest dreams or most foolish rantings, he became empty, and his cynical words could barely disguise the pain he felt at becoming conscious of that emptiness—the emptiness which came with "good fortune". (Browning called this disaster "a soul's tragedy".)

Perhaps Kierkegaard knew this, or perhaps he sensed it. Perhaps his violently active creative instinct, released by the pain he felt immediately after the break with Regine, had already claimed in advance this only possible release. Perhaps something inside him knew that happiness—if it was attainable—would have made him lame and sterile for the rest of his life. Perhaps he was afraid that happiness might not be unattainable, that Regine's lightness might after all have redeemed his great melancholy and that both might have been happy. But what would have become of him without his melancholy? Kierkegaard is the sentimental Socrates. "Loving is the only thing I'm an expert in," he said. But Socrates wanted only to recognize, to understand human beings who loved, and therefore the central problem in Kierkegaard's life was no problem for Socrates. "Loving is the only thing I'm an expert in," said Kierkegaard, "just

[1] Karoline Schelling (1763–1809), an active participant in the German Romantic movement, was married for some years to Wilhelm Schlegel, Friedrich's elder brother. (*Trans.*)

give me an object for my love, only an object. But here I stand like
an archer whose bow is stretched to the uttermost limit and who is
asked to shoot at a target five paces ahead of him. This I cannot do,
says the archer, but put the target two or three hundred paces further
away and you will see!"

Remember Keats' prayer to nature:

> A theme! a theme! great nature! give a theme;
> Let me begin my dream.

To love! Whom can I love in such a way that the object of my
love will not stand in the way of my love? Who is strong enough,
who can contain everything within himself so that his love will
become absolute and stronger than anything else? Who stands so
high above all others that whoever loves him will never address a
demand to him, never be proved right against him—so that the love
with which he is loved will be an absolute one?

To love: to try never to be proved right. That is how Kierkegaard
described love. For the cause of the eternal relativity of all human
relationships, of their fluctuations and, therefore, of their pettiness,
is that it is now the one who is right, and now the other; now the
one who is better, nobler, more beautiful, and now the other. There
can be constancy and clarity only if the lovers are qualitatively different from one another, if one is so much higher than the other that
the question of right and wrong (in the broadest sense) can never be
posed, even as a question.

Such was the ideal of love of the ascetic mediaeval knights, but it
was never to be as romantic again. Kierkegaard's psychological
insight robbed him of the naïve belief (naïve for a Kierkegaard) that
the beloved woman whom the troubadours renounced in order to be
able to love her in their own fashion—or even the dream image of
such a woman, who can never and nowhere be real—might be different enough from reality for their love to become absolute. This,
I believe, was the root of Kierkegaard's religiosity. God can be loved
thus, and no one else but God. He once wrote that God is a demand
of man, and man clings to this demand to escape from the wretchedness of his condition, to be able to bear his life. Yes, but Kierkegaard's
God is enthroned so high above everything human, is separated from
everything human by such absolute depths—how could he help a
man to bear his human life? I think he could, and for that very
reason. Kierkegaard needed life to be absolute, to be so firm that it
tolerated no challenge; his love needed the possibility of embracing
the whole, without any reservation whatsoever. He needed a love
without problems, a love in which it was not now the one, now the
other that was better, not now the one, now the other that was right.

My love is sure and unquestionable only if I am never in the right: and God alone can give me this assurance. "You love a man," he wrote, "and you want always to be proved wrong against him, but, alas, he has been unfaithful to you, and however much this may pain you, you are still in the right against him and wrong to love him so deeply." The soul turns to God because it cannot subsist without love, and God gives the lover everything his heart desires. "Never shall tormenting doubts pull me away from him, never shall the thought appal me that I might prove right against him: before God I am always in the wrong."

9

Kierkegaard was a troubadour and a Platonist, and he was both these things romantically and sentimentally. In the deepest recesses of his soul burned sacrificial flames for the ideal of a woman, but the self-same flames fed the stake upon which the self-same woman was burned. When man stood face to face with the world for the first time, everything that surrounded him belonged to him, and yet each separate thing always vanished before his eyes and every step led him past each separate thing. He would have starved to death, tragically, absurdly, in the midst of all the world's riches, had woman not been there from the start—woman who knew from the start how to grasp things, who knew the uses and the immediate significance of things. Thus it was that woman—within the meaning of Kierkegaard's parable—saved man for life, but only in order to hold him down, to chain him to the finiteness of life. The real woman, the mother, is the most absolute opposite of any yearning for infinity. Socrates married Xanthippe and was happy with her only because he regarded marriage as an obstacle on the way to the Ideal and was glad to be able to overcome the difficulties of marriage: much in the way that Suso's[1] God says: "You have always found recalcitrance in all things; and that is the sign of my chosen ones, whom I want to have for myself."

Kierkegaard did not take up this struggle; perhaps he evaded it, perhaps he no longer needed it. Who knows? The world of human communion, the ethical world whose typical form is marriage, stands between the two worlds of Kierkegaard's soul: the world of pure poetry and the world of pure faith. And if the foundation of the ethical life, "duty", appears firm and secure compared with the "possibilities" of the poet's life, its eternal evaluations are yet, at the same time, eternal fluctuations compared with the absolute certainties of the religious. But the substance of those certainties is air,

[1] Heinrich Suso or Seuse (1300–1366), German mystic. (Trans.)

and the substance of the poet's possibilities is likewise air. Where is the dividing line between the two?

But perhaps this is not the question to ask here. Regine Olsen was for Kierkegaard no more than a step on the way that leads to the icy temple of nothing-but-the-love-of-God. Committing a sin against her merely deepened his relationship to God; loving her with suffering, causing her to suffer, helped to intensify his ecstasies and to fix the single goal of his path. Everything that would have stood between them if they had really belonged to each other only gave wing to his flight. "I thank you for never having understood me," he wrote in a letter to her which he never sent, "for it taught me everything. I thank you for being so passionately unjust towards me, for that determined my life."

Even abandoned by him, Regine could only be a step towards his goal. In his dreams he transformed her into an unattainable ideal: but the step that she represented was his surest way to the heights. In the woman-glorifying poetry of the Provençal troubadours, great faithlessness was the basis for great faithfulness; a woman had to belong to another in order to become the ideal, in order to be loved with real love. But Kierkegaard's faithfulness was even greater than the troubadours', and for that very reason even more faithless: even the deeply beloved woman was only a means, only a way towards the great, the only absolute love, the love of God.

10

Whatever Kierkegaard did, and for whatever reason, it was done only to save Regine Olsen for life. However many inner meanings the gesture of rejection may have had, outwardly—in Regine Olsen's eyes—it had to be univocal. Kierkegaard sensed that for Regine there was only one danger, that of uncertainty. And because, for her, no life could grow out of her love of him, he wanted with all his strength—sacrificing his good name—that she should feel nothing but hate for him. He wanted Regine to consider him a scoundrel, he wanted her whole family to hate him as a common seducer; for if Regine hated him, she was saved.

Yet the break came too suddenly, even though long and violent scenes had helped to prepare the way. Regine suddenly had to see Kierkegaard as different from the man she had previously known; she had to re-evaluate every word and every silence of every minute they had spent together if she was to feel that the new was indeed connected with the old—if she was to see Kierkegaard as a whole man; and from that moment onwards she had to see whatever he might do in that new light. Kierkegaard did everything to make this easier for her, to channel the current of her newly formed images in a single direction—the direction he wanted, the only one he saw as leading to the right goal for Regine: the direction of hate against himself.

This is the background to Kierkegaard's erotic writings—especially the *Diary of a Seducer*—and it is this that gives them their radiance, received from life itself. An incorporeal sensuality and a plodding, programmatic ruthlessness are the predominant features of these writings. The erotic life, the beautiful life, life culminating in pleasure, occurs in them as a world-view—and as no more than that; a way of living which Kierkegaard sensed as a possibility within himself, but which not even his subtle reasoning and analysis could render corporeal. He is, as it were, the seducer *in abstracto*, needing only the possibility of seduction, only a situation which he creates and then enjoys to the full; the seducer who does not really need women even as objects of pleasure. He is the platonic idea of the seducer, who is so deeply a seducer and nothing else that really he is not even that; a man so remote, so far above all other humans that his appeal can scarcely reach them any longer, or if it does, then only as an incomprehensible, elemental irruption into their lives: the absolute seducer who appears to every woman as the eternal stranger, yet who (Kierkegaard was incapable of noticing this aspect), just because he is so infinitely remote, barely avoids appearing comic to any woman who, for whatever reason, is not destroyed when he looms up on the horizon of her life.

We have already said that the role of the seducer was Kierkegaard's gesture for Regine Olsen's sake. But the possibility of being a seducer was already latent in him, and a gesture always reacts back upon the soul that makes it. In life there is no purely empty comedy: that is perhaps the saddest ambiguity of human relationships. One can play only at what is there: one cannot play at anything without it somehow becoming part and parcel of one's life; and although it may be kept carefully separate from the game, life trembles at such play.

Regine, of course, could only see the gesture, and the effect of the gesture forced her to re-evaluate everything in her life so that it became the exact opposite of what it had been before. At least, that was what Kierkegaard wanted, and on this he staked everything. But something that has been lived in corporeal reality can, at most, only be poisoned by the realization that it was a mere game; a reality can never be completely and unchallengeably re-evaluated; only one's view of that reality and the values one attaches to that view can change. What had passed between Regine and Kierkegaard was life, was living reality, and it could only be shaken and irretrievably confounded in retrospect, as the result of a forced re-evaluation of

motives. For if the present forced Regine to see Kierkegaard differently, then this way of seeing him was sensual reality only for
the present; the reality of the past spoke in a different voice, and
could not be silenced by the feebler voice of her new knowledge.

Soon after the actual break Kierkegaard wrote to Bösen, his only
dependable friend, that if Regine knew with what anxious care he
had arranged everything and carried it through once he had decided
that the break had to come, she would by that very fact recognize
his love for her. When, after Kierkegaard's death, Regine read his
posthumous writings, she wrote to Dr. Lund, his relative: "These
pages put our relationship in a new light, a light in which I too saw
it sometimes, but my modesty forbade me to think that it was the
true light; and yet my unshakable faith in him made me see it like
that again and again."

Kierkegaard himself felt something of this uncertainty. He felt
that his gesture remained a mere possibility in Regine's eyes, just as
Regine's gesture had in his own eyes. The gesture was in no way
sufficient to create solid reality between them. If there was a way in
which he could find true reality, it was the way to Regine: but to
travel that way, however cautiously, would have been to destroy
everything that he had accomplished so far. He had to remain frozen
in his outwardly rigid, inwardly uncertain posture because, for all
he knew, everything in her life might really be settled and certain,
after all. Perhaps, if he had made a move towards her, he would have
encountered living reality? But only perhaps. Ten years after the
breaking off of the engagement he still did not dare to meet her.
Perhaps her marriage was only a mask. Perhaps she loved him as
before, and a meeting would have cancelled out all that had
happened.

11

But it is impossible even to maintain the rigid certainty of one's
gesture—if indeed it ever is a real certainty at all. One cannot, however much one may want to, continually disguise so deep a
melancholy as a game, nor can one ever definitively conceal such
passionate love under an appearance of faithlessness. Yes, the gesture
reacts back upon the soul, but the soul in turn reacts upon the
gesture which seeks to hide it, it shines forth from that gesture and
neither of the two, neither gesture nor soul, is capable of remaining
hard and pure and separate from the other throughout a lifetime.
The only way of somehow achieving the outwardly preserved purity
of the gesture is to make sure that, whenever the other person

momentarily abandons his stance, this is always misunderstood. In this way accidental movements, meaningless words carelessly spoken, acquire life-determining significance; and the reflex produced by the gesture is in turn strong enough to force the impulse back into the same self-chosen stance. When they parted, Regine asked Kierkegaard almost childishly, in the midst of tearful pleas and questions, whether he would still think of her from time to time, and this question became the *leitmotif* of Kierkegaard's whole life. And when she became engaged, she sent him greetings expecting a sign of approval, but by doing so she set off quite another train of thought in his uncomprehending mind. When he could no longer bear the weight of the mask and thought that the time had come for mutual explanations, Regine, by agreement with her husband, returned his letter unopened, making a gesture of certainty to make sure that everything should remain uncertain for ever more—since in any case, for her it had always been so—and to make sure that, once Kierkegaard was dead, she herself should grieve over the uncertainty she had created by refusing to hear his explanation. Whether they met or did not meet, the pattern was always the same: a hasty impulse leading out of the gesture, then a hasty return to the gesture —and the other's failure to understand both.

12

Where psychology begins, monumentality ends: perfect clarity is only a modest expression of a striving for monumentality. Where psychology begins, there are no more deeds but only motives for deeds; and whatever requires explanation, whatever can bear explanation, has already ceased to be solid and clear. Even if something still remains under the pile of debris, the flood of explanations will inexorably wash it away. For there is nothing less solid in the world than explanations and all that rests upon them. Whatever exists for a reason may have been its opposite for another reason— or, under slightly changed circumstances, for the same reason. Even when the reasons remain the same—but they never do—they cannot be constant; something that seemed to sweep the whole world away at a moment of great passion becomes minutely small when the storm is over, and something that was once negligible becomes gigantic in the light of later knowledge.

Life dominated by motives is a continual alternation of the kingdoms of Lilliput and Brobdingnag; and the most insubstantial, the most abysmal of all kingdoms is that of the soul's reason, the kingdom of psychology. Once psychology has entered into a life, then it is all up with unambiguous honesty and monumentality. When psychology rules, then there are no gestures any more that can comprise life and all its situations within them. The gesture is unambiguous only for as long as the psychology remains conventional.

Here poetry and life part company and become tragically, definitively distinct. The psychology of poetry is always unambiguous, for it is always an *ad hoc* psychology; even if it appears to ramify in several directions, its multiplicity is always unambiguous; it merely gives more intricate form to the balance of the final unity. In life, nothing is unambiguous; in life, there is no *ad hoc* psychology. In life, not only those motives play a role which have been accepted for the sake of the final unity, and not every note that has once been struck must necessarily be silenced in the end. In life, psychology cannot be conventional, in poetry it always is—however subtle and complex the convention. In life, only a hopelessly limited mind can believe in the unambiguous; in poetry, only a completely failed work can be ambiguous in this sense.

That is why, of all possible lives, the poet's life is the most profoundly unpoetic, the most profoundly lacking in profile and gesture. (Keats was the first to recognize this.) That which gives life to life becomes conscious in the poet; a real poet cannot have a limited mind about life, nor can he entertain any illusions about his own life. For a poet, therefore, all life is merely raw material; only his hands, doing spontaneous violence to living matter, can knead the unambiguous from the chaos of reality, create symbols from incorporeal phenomena, give form (i.e. limitation and significance) to the thousandfold ramifications, the deliquescent mass of reality. That is why a poet's own life can never serve as the raw material to which he will give form.

Kierkegaard's heroism was that he wanted to create forms from life. His honesty was that he saw a crossroads and walked to the end of the road he had chosen. His tragedy was that he wanted to live what cannot be lived. "I am struggling in vain," he wrote, "I am losing the ground under my feet. My life will, after all, have been a poet's life and no more." A poet's life is null and worthless because it is never absolute, never a thing in itself and for itself, because it is always there only *in relation to something*, and this relation is meaningless and yet it completely absorbs the life—for a moment at least; but then life is made up of nothing but such moments.

Against this necessity, the life of Kierkegaard—whose mind was never limited—waged its royally limited struggle. It might be said that life cunningly gave him all that it could give and all that he could ask for. Yet life's every gift was mere deception; it could never, after all, give him reality, but only lure him deeper and deeper, with every appearance of victory and success—like Napoleon in Russia—into the all-devouring desert.

This much his heroism did achieve, in life as in death. He lived in such a way that every moment of his life became rounded into the grand gesture, appearing statuesquely sure, carried through to the end; and he died in such a way that death came at the right time, just when he wanted it and as he wanted it. Yet we have seen how unsure his surest gesture was when seen from close by; and even if death overtook him at the climax of his most real, most profound struggle, even if it came as he wanted it to come, so that, dying, he could be the blood-witness of his own struggle, yet he could not be its real blood-witness. For, despite everything, his death pointed at several possibilities. In life, everything points at more than one possibility, and only *post facto* realities can exclude a few possibilities (never all of them, so that only one central reality is left). But even those open the way to a million new ones.

He was fighting the Christianity of his time when death overtook him. He stood in the midst of violent struggle; he had nothing more to seek in life outside that struggle, and he could scarcely have been fighting any harder. (Some incidental factors, too, made his death fateful. Kierkegaard had lived off his capital all his life, regarding interest as usury in the way religious men did in the Middle Ages; when he died, his fortune was just running out.) When he collapsed in the street and they took him to hospital, he said he wanted to die because the cause he stood for needed his death.

And so he died. But his death left every question open: Where would the path which broke off suddenly at his grave have led to if he had gone on living? Where was he going when he met his death? The inner necessity of death is only in an infinite series of possible explanations; and if his death did not come in answer to an inner call, like an actor taking his cue, then we cannot regard the end of his path as an end and we must try to imagine the further meanderings of that path. Then even Kierkegaard's death acquires a thousand meanings, becomes accidental and not really the work of destiny. And then his purest and most unambiguous gesture of his life—vain effort!—was not a gesture after all.

1909

On the Romantic Philosophy of Life

NOVALIS

> Das Leben eines wahrhaft kanonischen Menschen
> muss durchgehends symbolisch sein.[1]
> Novalis: Blütenstaub

THE background is the dying eighteenth century: the century of rationalism, of the fighting, victorious bourgeoisie conscious of its triumph. In Paris, dreamy doctrinaires were thinking through every possibility of rationalism with their cruel and bloodthirsty logic, while at German universities one book after another undermined and destroyed the proud hope of rationalism—the hope that nothing was ultimately out of reason's reach. Napoleon and the intellectual reaction were already frighteningly near; after a new anarchy that was already on the point of collapse, the old order was looming up once more.

Jena at the end of the eighteenth century. An episode in the lives of a few human beings, of no more than episodic significance for the world at large. Everywhere the earth resounds with battles, whole worlds are collapsing, but here, in a small German town, a few young people come together for the purpose of creating a new, harmonious, all-embracing culture out of the chaos. They rush at it with that inconceivable, reckless naïvety that is given only to people whose degree of consciousness is morbidly high, and to these only for a single cause in their lives and then again only for a few moments. It was a dance on a glowing volcano, it was a radiantly improbable dream; after many years the memory of it still lives on in the observer's soul as something bewilderingly paradoxical. For despite all the wealth of what they dreamed and scattered, "still there was something unhealthy about the whole thing". A spiritual tower of Babel was to be erected, with nothing but air for its infrastructure; it had to collapse, but when it did, its builders broke down too.

[1] "The life of a truly canonical person must be symbolic throughout." (*Trans.*)

1

Friedrich Schlegel once wrote that the French Revolution, Fichte's doctrine of science and Goethe's *Wilhelm Meister* represented the greatest events of the age. This juxtaposition is characteristic of the tragedy and greatness of the German cultural movement. For Germany, there was only one way to culture: the inner way, the way of revolution of the spirit; no one could seriously envisage a real revolution. Men destined for action had to fall silent and wither away, or else they became mere utopians and played games with bold possibilities in the mind; men who, on the other side of the Rhine, would have become tragic heroes could, in Germany, live out their destinies only in poetic works. Thus Schlegel's observation, if we properly evaluate the time and the circumstances, is surprisingly just and objective; it is astonishing that he places the French Revolution as high as he does, for in the minds of German intellectuals Fichte and Goethe represented real events in real life, whereas the Revolution could have little concrete meaning. Since outward progress could not be thought of, every energy turned inwards and soon "the land of poets and thinkers" surpassed all others by the depth, subtlety and power of its interiority. But this made the gap between the peaks and the plains ever greater; if those who arrived at the top became dizzy at the depth of the abysses, if the thinness of the Alpine air took their breath away, it was all in vain, for the descent had already become impossible: all those below lived in centuries long past. To take them higher, so that life on the mountain-tops might become less isolated and more secure for those who dwelt there, was just as impossible. The only path led still higher, towards a deadly solitude.

Everything seemed out of joint. Every summit projected into empty space. The effects of rationalism had been dangerous and destructive enough: rationalism had dethroned all existing values, at least theoretically, and those who had the courage to oppose it had nothing to guide them but an atomistic, anarchic emotional reaction. But when Kant appeared on the scene to destroy the proud armouries of both warring parties, there seemed to be nothing any longer capable of creating order in the ever-increasing mass of new knowledge or in the opaque depths below.

Goethe alone achieved it. In that sea of moody, untamed individualisms, his tyrannically conscious cult of the self is an island resplendent with flowers. All around him individualism was going to rack and ruin, was becoming an anarchy of instincts, a triviality that lost itself in a welter of moods and details, a pathetic renunciation; he alone was able to find order for himself. He had the strength to wait quietly until good fortune brought him fulfilment—and also the strength to reject, with cold equanimity, everything that spelt danger for him. He had the art of fighting in such a way that he never staked his innermost essence nor ever sacrificed any of it on compromises and arrangements. His conquests were of such a kind that newly discovered deserts turned into gardens at his mere glance, and when he renounced something, the power and harmony of possession was only heightened by the loss.

Yet all the forces unleashed in that century stormed within him too, and his flashes of lightning had to tame titans who raged within him more fiercely, perhaps, than those who, through their own unrestraint, were hurled into the depths of Tartarus. He faced all dangers, but he crushed every one of them underfoot; he suffered all the torments of loneliness, but he prepared himself always to stand alone. Every echo was for him a surprise, a happy, happiness-creating accident; but the whole of his life was a great, cruel and glorious necessity where every loss had to bring as much enrichment as every gain.

The truest way of speaking of the early Romantics would surely be to describe in the utmost detail what Goethe meant to each of them at each moment of their lives. Then one would see jubilant victory and speechless tragedy, great hopes, daring adventures, long voyages, and would hear two war-cries merging into a single shout of battle: to reach him! to surpass him!

2

Jena at the end of the eighteenth century. A few steeply rising trajectories cross here for a moment; men who have always lived in loneliness discover with intoxicating joy that others are thinking in accordance with the same rhythm as their own and feeling in a way which seems to fit into the same system. They were as different from one another as can be conceived, and it sounds like a romantic fairy-tale that they were able to love one another—that, even if for a short time, they could believe in the possibility of continuing their ascent together.

Of course the whole thing was really no more than a big literary salon, even if scattered over the whole of Germany. It was the founding of a new literary group on a social basis. Germany's most independent and headstrong personalities came together in it. Each of them climbed his own long, hard path to reach the point from where he could at last see sunlight and a wide view opening up before him; each suffered all the torments of a man driven out into the wilderness, thirsting for culture and intellectual communion, and the tragic, ecstatic pain of an idealism stretched to breaking-point. They felt that the way they had gone, the way that each young generation of the newly-awakened Germany had gone before them, led into nothingness; and almost simultaneously they saw the possibility of coming from the nothing into a something, of freeing themselves from the anarchy of living as mere litterati—a necessity forced upon them by outward circumstances—and hastening towards fruitful, culture-creating new goals.

Not so long before, Goethe had finally arrived at such a goal. Perhaps it was this that rescued the new generation from the constant, aimless, energy-devouring, energy-destroying agitation which for half a century had been the undoing of Germany's greatest men. Today we should probably call the thing they were striving for "culture"; but they, when for the first time it stood before their eyes as a redeeming, a possible goal, had a thousand poetic formulae to describe it and saw a thousand ways of coming nearer to it. They knew that each of their paths must lead to it, they felt that every conceivable experience had to be accepted and lived through in order that the "invisible church" which it was their mission to build should be all-embracing and full of riches. It looked as though a new religion were about to be created, a pantheistic, monistic religion which worshipped progress, a religion born of the new truths and discoveries of the new science. Friedrich Schlegel believed that in the all-penetrating force of idealism which revealed itself in the natural sciences before it became conscious as a philosophy, before it united the consciousness of the age, there lay concealed a myth-engendering force which only needed to be awakened into life in order to provide a ground which would be as strong and as collective as that of the Greeks for poetry, art and every life-expression. This mythology was not simply an ideal demand of those whose highest aspiration was to create a new style; it also became the infrastructure of a new religion. For they often called this goal of theirs a religion, and indeed it was with a purely religious exclusivity and single-mindedness that their questing spirit subordinated every other aim to it. Hardly anyone at the time could put in clear language what that goal was, and even today it is not easy to compress its meaning into any formula. The question, of course, was put to them quite clearly and unambiguously by life itself. A new world seemed to be in process of creation, bringing forth human beings with new life-possibilities; but the old, still persisting life was so constituted, and the new life, too, developed in such a way that no place could be found in it for its best sons. It was becoming more and more difficult and problematic for the great men of the age simply to exist, to belong to life, to occupy a place, to take up a stand. Everywhere and in every work of art, the question asked was: how can one, how ought one to live

today? They looked for an ethic of genius ("genius is the natural
condition of man," said Novalis) and, beyond it, for a religion of
genius—since even ethics could only be a means of attaining that
distant goal, that final harmony. The old religions, the Middle Ages,
Goethe's Greece, Catholicism, all were no more than makeshift
symbols for this new longing which, in their passionate will for unity,
elevated every feeling into a religion : everything small and everything great, friendship and philosophy, poetry and life.

And the apostles of this new religion gathered in their salons in
Berlin and Jena and discussed in passionate paradoxes the programme
of the new conquest of the world. Then they started a review, a very
clever, very bizarre one, very profound and completely esoteric,
whose every line betrayed the impossibility of its having any practical effect whatsoever. And if it had had one nevertheless. . .? "Still
there was something unhealthy about the whole thing. . . ."

3

Goethe and Romanticism. I think that what has been said already
makes it clear where the connection between them lies—and perhaps
still more clear where their ways part. Of course the Romantics, too,
were aware of both; every point at which they came near to Goethe
was a source of proud joy to them, and most of them dared only to
hint, timidly and stealthily, at what it was that divided them from
him. *Wilhelm Meister* was the decisive experience for them all, yet
only Karoline[1] remained faithful to the Goethean way of life and
only Novalis had the courage to say openly that it had to be
abandoned. He was the one who most clearly saw Goethe's
superiority to himself and his friends : he saw that everything which
remained mere method and idea with them, was turned into action
by Goethe; that in trying to cope with their own problems, they
could only produce reflections which were in turn problematic,
whereas Goethe actually transcended his; that they sought to create
a new world where the genius, the poet of that world, might find a
home, whereas Goethe found his home in the life of his own time.

Yet he saw just as clearly what Goethe had had to sacrifice in
order to find that home, and his whole being rebelled against the idea
that this solution was the only possible one. He too dreamed of the
ultimate harmony of *Wilheim Meister* as his life's goal, and with the
same clarity as Goethe he saw how fraught with danger were the
beginnings and the paths of that journey. Yet he believed that
Goethe had reached his goal a poorer man than the reaching of it
demanded.

[1] See footnote on p. 33. (*Trans.*)

Here the way of Romanticism and Goethe's way part. Both seek a balance of the same opposing forces, but Romanticism wants a balance in which its intensity can remain unimpaired. Its individualism is tougher, more self-willed, more conscious, more uncompromising than Goethe's, but by stretching this individualism to its uttermost limits, Romanticism wants to achieve the ultimate harmony.

Poetry is its ethic, morality its poetry. Novalis once said that morality was, at root, poetry; Friedrich Schlegel thought that all genuine and spontaneous originality was morally valuable in itself. Yet the Romantics' individualism was not meant to isolate them. "Our thinking is a dialogue, our feeling sympathy," said Novalis. The aphorisms and fragments of the *Athenaeum*—the most characteristic and lyrically truest expression of their programme—were not one work of any single individual; in many cases it is not even possible to identify their originator. In writing these aphorisms and fragments, the Romantics were concerned with emphasizing the directions and lines of thought common to them all; sometimes they synthesized the most widely differing ideas in the form of an aphorism simply in order to produce the effect of homogeneity and to avoid a single personality coming too strongly to the fore.

They wanted to create a culture, to make art learnable, to organize genius. They wanted—as in the great epochs of the past—every newly created value to become an inalienable possession, they wanted progress no longer to be subject to accident. They clearly saw that the only possible basis for such a culture was an art born of technology and the spirit of matter. They wanted to dedicate themselves to the art of putting words together just as goldsmiths had once given their lives to studying gold ore. But to produce a work of art, even a perfect one, could not be an ultimate goal for them; if anything possessed real value, it had that value only as a formative means. "To become a god, to be a man, to educate oneself—all these are different ways of expressing the same meaning," says Friedrich Schlegel, and Novalis adds: "Poetry is the specific mode of action of the human mind." This is not art for art's sake, it is pan-poetism.

It is the ancient dream of a golden age. But their golden age is not a refuge in a past that has been lost forever, only to be glimpsed from time to time in beautiful old legends—it is a goal whose attainment is the central duty of everyone. It is the "blue flower" which dreaming knights have to seek everywhere and always; it is the Middle Ages which they romantically worship, it is the Christianity they embrace; nothing is unattainable; a time must come when the impossible will be unknown. "People accuse poets of exaggeration," writes Novalis. "But it seems to me that poets do not exaggerate nearly enough. . . . They do not know what forces they have under their control, what worlds belong to them." This is why *Wilhelm Meister* disappointed him, this is why he said that it was essentially an anti-poetic work, "a *Candide* levelled at poetry".

By saying this he pronounced his death-sentence upon the book, for to the Romantics poetry was the centre of the entire world. The world-view of Romanticism is the most authentic pan-poetism: everything is poetry and poetry is "the one and the all". Never and for no one was the word "poet" so full of meaning, so holy, so all-embracing as for the German Romantics. It is true that in later times, too, many men and many poets have been ready to offer sacrifices at the altar of poetry; but what made Romanticism unique was that it extended to the whole of life: it was not a renunciation of life, nor a refusal of its riches; Romanticism seemed to offer the only possibility of achieving the goal without renouncing anything along the way. The goal of the Romantics was a world in which men could lead real lives. They spoke, with Fichte, of the "I". In this sense they were egoists: servants and fanatics of their own development, to whom everything mattered and had value only in so far as it contributed to their growth. "We are not yet 'I'," wrote Novalis. "But we can and must become 'I', we are the buds of becoming-'I'." The poet is the only human being who corresponds to the norms, he alone has the full possibility of "becoming-'I'". Why is this so?

An epoch which longs for culture will find its centre only in the arts; the less culture there is and the more intensely it is missed, the stronger the desire for it. But here what mattered was a passive capacity for experiencing life. The Romantics' philosophy of life was based—even if never quite consciously so—on their passive life-experiencing capacity. For them the art of living was one of self-adaptation, carried through with genius, to all the events of life. They exploited to the full and raised to the status of necessity everything that fate put in their path; they poeticized fate, but did not mould or conquer it. The path they took could only lead to an organic fusion of all given facts, only to a beautiful harmony of images of life, but not to controlling life.

Yet this path was the only possibility open to their longing for the great synthesis of unity and universality. They looked for order, but for an order that comprised everything, an order for the sake of which no renunciation was needed; they tried to embrace the whole world in such a way that out of the unison of all dissonances might come a symphony. To combine this unity and this universality is possible only in poetry, and that is why poetry for the Romantics became the centre of the world. In poetry alone they found a natural possibility of resolving all contradictions and bringing them together into higher harmony; in poetry alone was it possible to allocate to every separate thing its appointed place, simply by giving it a little more or a little less emphasis. Everything becomes a symbol in poetry, but then everything, in poetry, is *only* a symbol; everything has a meaning but nothing can claim value for itself and in itself. The Romantics' art of living was poetry as action; they transformed the deepest and most inward laws of poetic art into imperatives for life.

Where everything is properly understood and deeply lived, there can be no real contradictions. Whatever other roads they appeared to travel, the Romantics looked for their own "I", and the rhythm of their seeking created friendships and kinships, but not an identity of direction. At the root of their agreements and their differences lay only words; even their opinions were, at best, only ways towards the real values—generally imperfect and provisional expressions of feelings not yet mature enough to be given form. A sense of rhythm and social tact (the two concepts mean the same) were what made all the unresolved dissonances disappear. If Goethe had not intervened, the Schlegels would have printed Schelling's *Heinz Widerporst* and Novalis' *Christendom* side by side in the same issue of the *Athenaeum*. Convictions could not separate anyone from anyone else —their life-value was considered to be far too small. Every endeavour, whatever its goal, was received with irony, but, viewed symbolically, it was—if it so deserved—acknowledged as a religion.

The egoism of the Romantics is strongly coloured with social feeling. They hoped that the intense unfolding of the personality would in the end bring human beings really close to one another; in that unfolding they themselves sought their salvation from loneliness and chaos. They were deeply convinced that their uncompromising, self-willed manner of writing would produce the right and necessary communion between writers and readers and would ensure that popularity which was one of the highest aims of all Romantics. They clearly saw that the absence of such communion was the sole reason why the glorious development of individual forces characteristic of their time never ripened into cultural deeds. They hoped to develop such communion out of their small, closed circle, and they succeeded—within that circle and for a few years. So long as they, who came from the most different directions and followed the most different paths, appeared to be travelling along the same great road, they wanted to regard every divergence as something merely external, to consider only what they had in common as important; and this harmony was meant to be no more than the modest prelude to a greater, truer harmony to come. Yet it was enough for a few values to become slightly displaced in the minds of a few of them, and the "Hansa" disintegrated, the harmony became a deafening sequence of cacophonous sounds.

A seemingly deliberate withdrawal from life was the price of the Romantic art of living, but this was conscious only at the surface, only within the realm of psychology. The deep nature of this withdrawal and its complex relations were never understood by the Romantics themselves and therefore remained unresolved and devoid of any life-redeeming force. The actual reality of life vanished before their eyes and was replaced by another reality, the reality of poetry, of pure psyche. They created a homogeneous, organic world unified within itself and identified it with the real world. This gave their world the quality of something angelic, suspended between heaven and earth, incorporeally luminous; but the tremendous tension that exists between poetry and life and gives both their real, value-creating powers was lost as a result. And they did not even look for it, they simply left it behind on their heroically frivolous flight towards heaven; they were scarcely aware any longer that it existed. Only in this way could they achieve their universality, but because of this they could not recognize its limitations. These limitations were for them neither a tragedy—as they are for men who live life through to its end—nor ways towards a real, authentic œuvre whose greatness and strength would reside, precisely, in that it kept heterogeneous things apart and created a new, unified stratification of the world finally cut loose from reality. These limitations meant for them a collapse, an awakening from a beautiful, feverish dream, a melancholy end without enrichment, without the promise of a new beginning. Because they identified the cosmos they had created in their dreams with the real world, they could not arrive at a clear division anywhere; because of this they could believe that action is possible without renunciation and that poetry-making is possible within reality. Yet all action, every deed, every act of creation is limiting. No action can be performed without renouncing something, and he who performs an action can never possess universality. This is why, almost imperceptibly, the ground slipped away under their feet and their monumental, powerful constructions were gradually transformed into sandcastles and finally dissolved into thin air. The dream of advancing side by side dissolved like a fine mist, too, and a few years later scarcely a single one of them could understand the other's language; and the deepest dream of all, the hope of the culture to come, went the same way. But by now they had enjoyed the intoxication of belonging to a community and could no longer continue their ascent by solitary, separate paths. Many became mere imitators of their own youth; some, worn out by the comfortless

search for a new religion and the dismal sight of increasing anarchy
—a sight which merely helped to intensify their desire for order—
returned with resignation into the quiet waters of the old religions.
And so it happened that men who had once set out to remould and
re-create an entire world became pious converts. "Still there was
something unhealthy about the whole thing."

4

So far we have not said very much about Novalis, and yet he has
been our central subject throughout. No one emphasized the
exclusive importance of the ultimate goals more stubbornly than this
delicate youth doomed to an early death; no one was more at the
mercy of all the hazards of the Romantic way of life—and yet he
was the only one among all these great theoreticians of the art of
living who succeeded in leading a harmonious life. Each of the others
became dizzy at the sight of the abyss which spread before their feet
even on the brightest days, and each fell from the heights into that
abyss; only Novalis succeeded in wresting a life-enhancing strength
from the ever-present danger. The danger which threatened him was
more brutal, more physical than that of the others, and yet (or perhaps just because of this) he was able to draw the greatest life-energy
from it.

The danger which threatened him was death—his own and that
of the people who were closest to his soul. The programme of his life
could take only one form : to find the proper rhymes for these deaths
in the poem into which he made his life—and to fit his life
harmoniously, as an unassailable fact, in between these deaths. To
live in such a way that death would come in answer to a cue, not as
an interruption; but for this to be possible, the inner laws and beauty
of everything he did had to demand that it remain a fragment forever. To survive the death of his beloved, but in such a way that the
melody of his pain was never wholly hushed, and that a new time-
reckoning began with that death; in such a way that his own certain
death should stand in a deep inner relation to the beloved's death,
and that the short life fitted in between the two deaths should
nevertheless be rich and full of lived experience.

In Novalis the tendencies of Romanticism find their most intense
expression. Romanticism always consciously refused to recognize
tragedy as a form of life (though not, of course, as a form of literary
creation). The highest aspiration of Romanticism was to make tragedy
disappear completely from the world, to resolve tragic situations in
an untragic way. Here, too, Novalis' life was the most Romantic:
his destiny always placed him in situations from which another man

would have drawn nothing but suffering or tragic ecstasy, yet whatever his hand touched turned into gold and nothing could come his way that did not enrich him. He was always face to face with pain, he was forced again and again to sink to the very depths of despair, yet he smiled and was happy.

The young Friedrich Schlegel noted down the first conversation that ever took place between them. Both were twenty years old. Novalis asserted with fiery vehemence that "there is nothing evil in the world, and everything is bringing us closer to another golden age". Many years later, at the end of his life, the hero of Novalis' only novel expressed the same feeling when he said that "fate and soul are but two different names for a single concept".

Fate struck him more than once, brutally and ruthlessly. But he surrendered everything to fate and became richer than before. After a troubled youth it seemed as though a young girl were to become the fulfilment of all his dreams; she died, and nothing was left to him but his belief that he too would soon follow her into the grave. He did not think of suicide nor of being consumed by his sorrow; he was unshakeably convinced that he could devote himself serenely and calmly to what was left of his life, and that it would not be for long. He wanted to die, did he not? Surely his will was strong enough to call for death, to make death come?

But life came instead and stood in his way. It showed him unwritten poems, radiant and soaring; luminous paths that led further than the whole of Goethe. It spread before him all the innumerable wonders of the new sciences, their perspectives pointing into infinity, their possibilities destined to create new worlds. It led him into the world of action and he had to recognize that nothing could be dry or sterile for him, that everything turned into harmony at his approach; even a government official's existence was transformed into a song of triumph. Yet he still wanted death.

But life refused him this gift. It would not grant him this, the only thing he asked from fate. Instead it offered him new happiness and a new love—the love of a woman who was superior to his first and only beloved; but he would not accept it. He wanted only to keep faith. In the end he could resist no longer. He re-entered life, he who had been calling for death only a little earlier, he who eternally proclaimed that nothing is impossible for man, yet who, in reality, wanted only one thing—to achieve the very opposite of what he wanted. Even when the whole edifice of his life collapsed, nothing broke within him; he went forward to happiness as serene and resolute as he had previously been in readiness for death.

And when, at last, he stretched out his hand for life, when at last he overcame his cult of death, then the saviour he had once longed for came at last: death, which only a little while before would have been the jubilant crowning of his life, struck like a discordant blow. But, even now, how he died! His friends could not believe that death had really been so close at hand; later, they were convinced that he had no idea it was so near. Yet he drew up a new life-programme for the period of his dying; he carefully avoided anything that a sick man could not do to perfection or with absolute intensity; he lived only for what his illness could actually advance. Once he wrote: "Disease is certainly a most important subject for humanity. . . . We have as yet a very imperfect knowledge of the art of utilizing it." When, a few months before his death, he wrote to his friend Tieck describing his life, he said: ". . . so you see, it was a troubled time. I have mostly been serene." And Friedrich Schlegel, who sat at his deathbed, speaks of Novalis' "indescribable serenity" when dying.

5

Novalis is the only true poet of the Romantic school. In him alone the whole soul of Romanticism turned to song, and only he expressed nothing but that soul. The others, if they were poets at all, were merely Romantic poets; Romanticism supplied them with new motifs, it altered the direction of their development or enriched it, but they were poets before they recognized Romantic feelings in themselves and remained poets after they had completely abandoned Romanticism. Novalis' art and work—there is no help for it, it is a platitude but it is the only way of saying it—form an indivisible whole, and as such they are a symbol of the whole of Romanticism. It is as though, redeemed by his life, Romantic poetry became pure and authentic poetry once more after venturing forth into life and going astray there. In his work, all the tentative approaches of Romanticism remained mere approaches; the Romantic will for unity, a will which always, of necessity, remained fragmentary. was nowhere so fragmentary as in Novalis who had to die just as he was beginning to create his real works. Yet he was the only one whose life left something more behind it than a picturesque heap of rubble from which one can dig up a few glorious fragments and wonder what the edifice of which they were part was once like. All his paths led to a goal, all his questions were answered. Every ghost, every *fata morgana* of Romanticism acquired solid flesh in him, he alone refused to be lured into the bottomless quagmire by the will-o'-the-wisps of Romanticism; his eyes saw every will-o'-the-wisp as a star, and he had wings to follow it. He met the most cruel fate of all, but only he was capable of growing as a result of his struggle. Of all the

Romantic seekers for mastery over life, he was the only practical artist of the art of living.

Yet even he received no answer to his question: he put the question to life, and death brought the answer. To sing the praises of death is perhaps something more and something greater than to sing the praises of life: but it was not to find such songs that the Romantics set out.

The tragedy of Romanticism was that only Novalis' life could turn to poetry. His victory is a death sentence passed on the Romantic school as a whole. Everything the Romantics wanted to conquer sufficed for no more than a beautiful death. Their life-philosophy was one of death; their art of living, an art of dying. They strove to embrace the world, and this made them into slaves of fate. Perhaps Novalis seems so great and so complete to us today only because he became the slave of an unconquerable master.

1907

The Bourgeois Way of Life and Art for Art's Sake

THEODOR STORM

1

THE bourgeois way of life and art for art's sake: how much is contained within this paradox! Yet once it was not a paradox at all. How could anyone, born a bourgeois, even conceive of the idea that he might live otherwise than as a bourgeois? As for the notion that art is enclosed within itself and follows no laws but its own, once this was not the consequence of a violent refusal of reality. Art was there for its own sake just as any other kind of work, honestly done, was there for its own sake: because the interests of the totality, which were the justification and the root of everything, demanded that work should be done as though it had no other purpose but itself—that it should exist only for the sake of a perfection enclosed within itself.

Today we look back upon those times with nostalgia, the hysterical nostalgia, doomed from the start to remain unsatisfied, of sophisticated men. We look back with impotent nostalgia upon a time when one did not have to be a genius in order to approach perfection even from afar, since perfection was a natural thing and its opposite was simply ignored, even as a possibility: when the perfection of a work of art was a life-form, and works of art differed from one another only by the degree of their perfection. This nostalgia is the Rousseauism of the artistic consciousness—a Romantic longing for the unattainable blue flower, glimpsed in dreams, insubstantially fashioned from visions of form; a longing for the thing most opposite to ourselves; a longing for the great, holy simplicity, the natural, holy perfection to be born out of the birth-pangs of an ever-growing awareness, to be forced into life by the ultimate, gasping energy of a sick nervous system. The bourgeois way of life, which consists in cutting down the conduct of one's life to a strictly and narrowly bourgeois measure, is simply a way of coming closer to such perfection. It is a form of asceticism, a renunciation of all brilliance in life so that all the brilliance, all the splendour may be transferred elsewhere: into the work of art. Seen in these terms, the bourgeois way of life is a kind of forced labour, a hateful servitude, a constraint against which every life-instinct must rebel, a constraint which can be accepted only through an immense effort of all—in the hope, perhaps, that the ecstasy of the struggle will create that extreme intensity of feeling which the working of art demands. The bourgeois way of life, when it is like this, really consumes a man's life, because life should be its very opposite: splendour and brilliance, the rejection of all bonds, a drunken, orgiastic triumphal dance of the soul in the ever-changing grove of poetic moods. This bourgeois way of life is the whip that drives the life-denying man to work without cease. The bourgeois way of life is merely a mask that hides the bitter, useless pain of a failed and ruined life, the life-pain of the Romantic born too late.

This bourgeois way of life is only a mask, and like all masks it is negative: it is only the opposite of something, it acquires meaning solely through the energy with which it say "No" to something. This bourgeois way of life signifies only a denial of everything that is beautiful, everything that appears desirable, everything the life-instinct longs for. This bourgeois way of life has no value whatsoever in itself. For only the works which it brings forth confer value upon a life lived within such a framework and in such a form. But is this bourgeois way of life really identical with the nature of the bourgeoisie?

A life is made bourgeois first and foremost by the exercise of a bourgeois profession. But in the life we are talking about, can one speak of a profession at all? The impossibility of it becomes evident at first glance. It becomes obvious that the bourgeois order imposed on such a life is only a mask that hides a most self-willed and anarchistic preoccupation with the self, and that such a life adapts itself only in outward detail, with romantic irony and conscious life-stylization, to the outward form of its mortal enemy.

The bourgeois way of life and art for art's sake. Can these two mutually exclusive extremes coexist in one person? Can both be simultaneously lived, with equal seriousness and honesty, and be combined within a single human life? A life is made bourgeois first and foremost through the exercise of a bourgeois profession—through something which, seen by itself, is not so very significant; a profession in which success, however great, can never enhance the personality by the intoxication it produces, and a decline is noticed by two or three people at the very most. The true bourgeois mentality demands complete acceptance of all this, complete concentration on matters which may be trivial and insignificant and offer the soul no nourishment whatsoever. For the true bourgeois, his bourgeois profession is not an occupation but a life-form, something which—

independently from its content, as it were—determines the tempo, the rhythm, the contours, in a word the *style* of his life. Accordingly, the bourgeois profession is something which, in consequence of the mysterious interaction of life-forms and typical lived experience, must penetrate deeply into all creative activity.

A bourgeois profession as a form of life signifies, in the first place, the primacy of ethics in life: life dominated by something that recurs systematically and regularly, something that happens again and again in obedience to a law, something that must be done without concern for desire or pleasure. In other words, the rule of order over mood, of the permanent over the momentary, of quiet work over genius fed by sensations. Its most profound consequence, perhaps, is that such dedication can vanquish egotistic solitude: not dedication to an ideal projected out of ourselves and going far beyond the maximum of which we ourselves are capable, but, rather, dedication to something independent from and alien to ourselves, yet simple and palpably real for that very reason. Such dedication puts an end to solitude. Perhaps the greatest life-value of ethics is precisely that it is a sphere where a certain kind of communion can exist, a sphere where the eternal loneliness stops. The ethical man is no longer the beginning and the end of all things, his moods are no longer the measure of the significance of everything that happens in the world. Ethics forces a sense of community upon all men—if in no other way, at least through the recognition of immediate and calculable utility, of work done, however small it may be. The recognition of pure genius in one's own work can never be anything other than irrational. The workings of genius are always underestimated and overestimated at the same time because genius can never be measured against anything, whether interior or exterior.

In a life where only a productivity based on nothing but his talent can give a man weight vis-à-vis the world or support within himself, the centre of gravity always shifts in the direction of that talent. Life exists for work, and work for an artist is always an uncertain thing. Sometimes, as a result of hysterical effort, his sense of life can be raised to an almost ecstatic intensity, but this ascent to the heights has to be paid for by terrible nervous and psychic depressions later. Work is the purpose and meaning of life. Strong interiorization shifts the centre of life outwards, into the raging sea of uncertainties and incalculable possibilities; whereas ordinary, prosaic work offers security and solid ground. As a life-form, it causes a shift in the direction of life. The result of prosaic work is that the human value of the man concerned—his inner and outer weight—shifts to solid ground; it acquires permanence because the centre of gravity is displaced to the ethical sphere and to ethical values, i.e. to values where at least the possibility of permanent validity exists. Furthermore, such work never absorbs a man's whole energy; the life-rhythm which such work produces is, necessarily, of such a kind that life is the melody and everything else is mere accompaniment. When Theodor Storm went to see Eduard Mörike in Stuttgart, their conversation touched upon this question—the question of work versus life—and Mörike said that a poet's work "need only be so much that you leave behind a trace of yourself; but the important thing is life itself, and this should never be forgotten because of the work." Storm, from whose notes on Mörike I quote these words, reports that he said this "almost as though he meant it as a warning to a younger fellow-artist".

Mörike was a clergyman and devoted his later life to teaching, Storm was a judge, Keller used to describe himself, with some pride, as a "government clerk". When, in the correspondence between the country judge of Husum and the government clerk of Zürich, there was mention of the nervous condition of their mutual friend Paul Heyse, a letter sent from Switzerland to Schleswig contained the following passage: "Paul Heyse's condition is a mystery to me. He has produced a volume of the finest verse within the space of a year, and yet he is said to be continually ill. Perhaps such a suicidal rate of output is, precisely, the result of a disturbed nervous system. In that case my nerves are all right but my head's a little dull. Joking apart, I'm almost inclined to believe that Heyse is now paying for the fact that he has worked as a poet for almost thirty years without enjoying any change or distraction such as a post in government or teaching or some other profane occupation might have offered him. A man like that, who really devours the world, is bound to devour himself in the end. . . . But one must not say anything to him; it is too late!" The reply from Husum has a very similar ring: "On the subject of our friend Heyse, you have hit the nail on the head. Only a man of colossal health can stand a life's work which constantly calls upon the imagination and sensibility; who knows if Schiller, too, might not have made more of his life under other circumstances. . . ." This sounds as though health considerations alone made prosaic work a necessity—"homely work," as it is described by Storm, for whom it was so indispensable that he could not give it up even in old age, when he had retired with the happy thought of at last living wholly for his writing. And so he taught his daughters French and occupied himself with his small estate—perhaps in order that his life should maintain its accustomed healthy rhythm. It may look as though this were merely a matter of hygiene, but—as everywhere else—the posing of the question encompasses all answers: for Keller and Storm it seems to have been merely a matter of hygiene, but for others it led to the insoluble, transcendent tragedy of the relationship between art and life. A thing becomes tragic only when it is recognized as insuperable. A tragedy in the true, deep sense of the word can exist only where the opposing elements in an irreconcilable struggle have sprung from the same soil and are akin to one another in their innermost essence. Tragedy exists where there is no longer any sense in distinguishing between sweet and bitter, health and sickness, danger and salvation, death and life; where what is life-destructive has become as much of an indispensable necessity as that which is unquestionably good and useful. Storm's life was healthy and unproblematic; he always avoided the very possibility of tragedy. He saw the tragic kind of sickness against which one can and must protect oneself, just as one does—I cannot think of a more fitting comparison—against a cold or an upset stomach. All these for him are sicknesses which a healthy organism will throw off should the attempt to avoid them have failed. There is something strong and stubborn about such an approach to life, a hard, sure rhythm, a rugged energy. Once he wrote to Emil Kuh that even as a student he had sensed and felt that whatever might happen to him, or whatever he might allow to happen to himself later on, nothing could endanger the core of his life: ". . . that I could go to extremes without any fear of losing myself"; and in one of his poems he put it this way:

"If ever your heart weeps, make nothing of it.
Clink glasses, let them ring.
Nothing can kill a heart, you know it.
A heart's a strong and sturdy thing."

Nothing was ever problematic in Storm's life. The greatest pain assailed him, but he always found something solid inside himself to resist the pain. Storm was not a problematic man, and therefore fate could approach him only from the outside: if it was ordinary human fate, then it could be grappled with and conquered, but if it was more than that, then one had to stop and let it pass, head bowed in resignation, with a gesture of submission and composure. "You may have buried your very dearest," he wrote after his wife's death, "but life must go on, and soon you stand once more in the heat of the day, asserting yourself." He was religious in the sense that he felt all events to be interconnected, and he accepted this with happy resignation; he was religious without holding any specific belief, without becoming involved in the struggles and sacrifices of unreligiosity, although he lived at a time of great religious doubts. He was sensitive and responsive, the smallest outward impressions moved him deeply, but his sensibility could never influence the stolid, upright conduct of his life. His whole emotional world was intimately bound up with his homeland, yet it did not collapse when his country's annexation by a foreign power drove him into exile. His whole nature reached out for happiness, happiness was the very air he breathed, yet when after many years of happily married life he lost his wife he did not break down, though his sorrow was great and deep, and he succeeded in finding once more the happiness and warmth he needed. "However, I am not a man who is easily broken," he wrote to Mörike after his wife's death; "I shall not abandon any of the intellectual interests which have accompanied me until now and which are necessary for the maintenance of my life, for before me—as it says in a poem—lies work, and work, and work. And this work shall be done for as long as my strength lasts."

It is not easy to determine which of the two life-principles is here supporting the other: whether the simple, bourgeois, orderly way of life is supporting the equally calm and quiet certainty with which that life affects the soul, or vice versa. Only so much is sure, that the two are closely interlinked. Without a single moment's hesitation Storm chose a legal career although it had nothing to offer his inner life, and later on there was not a single moment in his life when he regretted the choice.

But we have not yet touched upon the crucial point of the problem —the point at which the bourgeois way of life connects with art. We have said that only the life's work gives meaning to a life; to preserve the fulness and strength of a life only has justification, sense or meaning if the cause for which one thus refuses to sacrifice that life is actually itself worthy of the greatest sacrifice. We are faced with a real paradox only when one of the faces of the Janus' head of a life is really the bourgeois way of living, whilst the other face is the hard struggle of rigorous artistic production. That world, the world of Storm and of those whose art he most admired and who most admired his own, is the world of the German aesthetes. Of the many groups of aesthetes in the last century, this is the genuine, truly German variety, the German l'art pour l'art.

We know of the almost Flaubertian torments with which Gottfried Keller gave birth to his works, often after labour pains lasting whole decades. We know how heavily the weaknesses and dissonances of the first version of *Maler Nolten* weighed upon Mörike, and how he sacrificed the richest and finest years of his life to the Sisyphean labour of producing a second version. Conrad Ferdinand Meyer's case is even better known. Storm, the "tranquil goldsmith and artificer of silver filigree", as Keller called him, may have produced his work with fewer torments, but his nature, like that of others we have mentioned, was that of a disciplined craftsman who makes no concessions. Perhaps this unsentimental, craftsmanlike, no-nonsense attitude was even more developed in him than in the others. His hands felt by instinct what material they ought to fashion and what form they ought to give it; he never made any attempt to transcend the formal barriers imposed by the potentialities and limitations of his soul. Within those barriers, however, he forced himself to achieve the highest perfection. Keller, a great and intensely consciously epic author, was always toying with the idea of writing a play; Storm would not let himself be tempted even into writing a novel.

Craftsmanship was the special feature of this kind of aestheticism. It was deeply and inseparably connected with the way of life which these men adopted and, with the primitive-bourgeois decency of craftsmen, carried through to the end. Their artistic practice and their way of life were equally simple, equally rectilinear, and this was what distinguished them from other aesthetes with their dreams of *ouvrier* perfection. Craftsmanship may have been Flaubert's ideal, but to be a craftsman could, for him, only be a sentimental idea (in Schiller's sense of the word), only a longing for an irretrievably lost simplicity. The craftsmanship of Storm, Mörike, Keller, the ballad-writer Fontane, Klaus Groth and others was, in the same sense, naïve. The goal of the former (the Flaubertian aesthetes) was to approach ideal perfection through superhuman effort, that of the latter (Storm, Mörike, etc.) was to achieve the consciousness of honest work well done—the consciousness that they had done everything in their power to create a perfect thing. For the former the accent was on work, for the latter on life; for the former, life was only a means of attaining the artistic ideal, for the latter perfection of work was only a symbol, only the surest and finest way of exploiting every possibility offered to them by life; a symbol of the fact that the bourgeois ideal—consciousness of work well done—had indeed been achieved.

This is why there was always a rather touching resignation about the way these men handed their works over for publication. No one was more clearly aware than they of the distance between something really perfect and the best that they themselves could do. But the awareness of this distance was alive in them with such immediate and regulated force that, actively, it played hardly any role at all. It was as though it had been expressed once and thereby settled for evermore, becoming the tacit recognition underlying everything that could be said later. The gentle humility of this tacit recognition always irradiated the gesture with which they allowed their works to go out into the world. For them, as for the craftsmen-artists of old times, art was—like everything else—an expression of life, and therefore a life dedicated to art involved the same rights and duties as any other human (bourgeois) activity. Hence the demands they made upon themselves were ethical, but they also had certain rights as men vis-à-vis work. The ethic not only demands craftsmanship but also raises the question of the usefulness of art. Keller thought of the possible pedagogical effect of his work as much as of its literary effect. Once, speaking about a subject chosen by Storm in which superstition played a certain role, he pointed out that this might be harmful in an age of bogus spiritualism. But at the same time he felt he had a right to give free play to all his little foibles (this is evident from the way he lovingly dwells on the minutest details), even at the risk of loosening the composition of a work. His underlying feeling was that his works, after all, were there for his sake, for the sake of giving expression to his energies; and since those foibles were part of him, they had to find expression like everything else. The process of work was decisive, not the result. Here the nineteenth-century artist's outlook is deeply and genuinely related to the outlook of the Middle Ages, that golden age of the Romantic nostalgia for craftsmanship. But the Romantics, just because they eternally longed for real craftsmanship, could never achieve it, whereas Keller and Mörike and Storm did achieve it in so far as it can be achieved in our time. The Romantics separated their longing from its object, or else their longing was, perhaps, only a symbol of the unbridgeable gap between them and it. One thing is certain (let it serve as an example here): Leibl came extremely close to Holbein, as close as any modern artist could come to him, whereas the English Pre-Raphaelites are as far as possible removed from the Florentines.

Poetry, more than any other art, is influenced by the spirit of the age. The fact that these authors were able to produce something which reminds us of the great art of the past—even if only as a faint glow cast by the work over real life—this fact, too, can be explained by historical and psychological factors. Many developments, especially economic ones, occurred in Germany later than in other countries, and many old social forms and ways of living were preserved there longer than elsewhere. In the middle of the nineteenth century there still existed in Germany, especially near the borders of German territory, towns where the old bourgeoisie was still as strong and lively as ever, that bourgeoisie which is so utterly different from the bourgeoisie of today. These writers sprang from the womb of that bourgeoisie, they are its true and great representatives. And they were aware of their role as representatives. I do not mean that they were intellectually aware of their situation but, rather, that historical feelings were for them life-feelings, life-factors with a practical effect on their lives; that homeland, family, class were for them the experience which determined everything else. What matters is not their love of all these things—after all, such love is to be found in others as well, and is even more obvious and striking in those others because the experience is less profoundly explored and therefore its form of expression is sentimental and full of pathos. No, the decisive experience of these writers, and most particularly Keller and Storm, was their bourgeois way of life. One might almost say that the overwhelming importance of Switzerland in the work of the one and of Schleswig in the work of the other was a consequence of the sensual, concrete nature of their fundamental attitude and perception. One may say this, if only because the lived experience of these writers meant no more than: "I come from such and such a place, and I am such and such a man"; and the consequence of this was that they were able to see genuinely and strongly only what grew on their native soil, and their view of men and of relations between men was dependent on the values which had grown from that soil. In their works, the bourgeois way of life assumes historic stature. In the works of these last great poets of the unbroken, old bourgeoise, a strong light with strong shadows is cast upon the most ordinary events of bourgeois life. In these works, produced as the old German bourgeoisie was beginning to become "modern", the old-fashioned interiors are still bathed in a fairy-tale, fantastic light. As these Rococo and Biedermeier interiors come gently to life, so also do their gentle, upright, simple, slightly narrow-minded inhabitants—even if only in recollection. In Keller it is his rich, fairy-tale-like humour that divests the most ordinary things of their ordinariness; in Storm they remain as they are, and the humour which surrounds them is barely noticeable: and yet these things show that his eye has lingered lovingly on them and is watching their gradual disappearance with melancholy—that he remembers everything he has received from these things, but is able to observe the decay with a quiet certainty which accepts the inevitable while weeping over it.

In Storm's world, this poetry of decay is not yet wholly conscious. (In Keller's world it is much more so.) His burghers still stride confidently along without feeling themselves or the bourgeois nature of their existence to be a problem. Even when a tragic fate befalls them, it seems as though it were only the fate of a single individual, as though only this one man were suffering such a fate; one does not yet recognize that the whole world is being rocked to its foundations. Everything still stands, despite misfortune and ill-fate, despite the fact that these men are truly strong only in their endurance, that their most virile gesture is that of seeing something pass fleetingly by—life, or happiness, or joy—and merely watching it pass, eyes darkened with unshed tears. It is a strength of renunciation, of resignation, the strength of the old bourgeoisie in face of the new life; and here Storm is a modern writer despite himself. Something vanishes, someone watches it pass . . . and goes on living, and is not destroyed. Yet the memory lives on for ever: something was there, something has gone, something might have been . . . once upon a time.

> I see your white dress flying by
> and your light, gentle shape.
> The scent of night flows sweetly from the chalices of flowers.
> I have thought of you, always, always.
> I long to sleep: but you must always dance.

2

Hard and tender, monotonous and full of nuances, grey and multi-coloured: out of the fusion of all these, Storm makes his world. The North Sea hurls its waves against the coast, the sea wall can barely protect the land against the gales of winter, but the pure air and, still more, the heavy mist lend softness to the sandy beaches, the meadows, the towns, dispensing a simple, monotonous tranquillity over everything alike. Meadows, pastures, small islands in the sea, nothing really beautiful as far as the eye can see, nothing to capture the eye at first glance, nothing to sweep one off one's feet. Everything is simple, quiet, grey and monotonous. Only a native's eye can find beauty in such a place; only a native ear can hear the tale of deep and great experiences told by every tree and every shrub—only a man who has known that slow darkening of the shadows or that timid redness of an evening by the sea at crucial moments of his life. The little towns with their simple, uniform, old German houses, their simple little gardens, their simple rooms stuffed full with objects inherited from grandparents or even more remote ancestors, are just as quiet and just as monotonously grey. But even the greyness of these houses and these rooms is refracted into a rainbow of a thousand colours in the eye of the native to whom every cupboard has many stories to tell about what it has seen and heard in the course of its long life.

> On a grey beach by a grey sea
> the town lies apart
> the sea-mist rests heavy on the roofs
> and through the stillness of the air
> the sea roars round the town.

> No forest sounds, and in May
> no birds trill ceaselessly.
> Only the migrant goose with its harsh cry
> flies through the autumn night.
> Grass flutters on the beach.

The people, too, resemble the landscape within which they move. At first glance one might think that there are no differences between them. Strong and simple, blond, striding confidently along: thus the men. And dreamy, even quieter and even fairer, such are the girls and women. It seems as though the tranquil sun of childhood idylls must shine on everyone alike; as though the same small joys and gentle sorrows must bring forth the quiet, monotonous folk-melody that accompanies all growth in such a place; as though everyone here must have the same fate; as though man and fate approach one another at the same pace, both with the same simple, firm and confident certainty, before the encounter and at the moment of encounter; but that, after man and fate have met, the man must show the same spirit of sacrifice, the same strength in order to continue striding quietly along, to resign himself and count his blessings, to remain upright—the same unbrokenness in the face of every blow. In the grey air of Storm's world, the hard outlines of the shapes of men and destinies merge greyly into one another. Often it appears as though in all his stories and poems he were speaking about the same thing: fate dealing its blows, strong men who survive their fate and others, a little less strong, who are destroyed. But every time the strongest and finest riches of the soul flow from the wounds dealt by fate. Every destiny appears to be the same because the people are so taciturn and the life-gestures of each so deeply akin to those of the others. But one need only step back a little—for a different reason, in fact exactly the opposite, from why one steps back from a painting—and the monotony of this life disappears. Then one sees that every person and every event is only part of a symphony which, unintended perhaps and certainly unspoken, rings out from the totality of people and events; as though every separate thing were only a ballad or a fragment of a ballad, an element of that whole from which a great epic shall one day be made, the great epic of bourgeois life.

Such an epic, if ever it is written, will speak of a quiet and confident strength. There will be no events in it, or, at any rate, the events will have no importance: the only thing that such an epic will really describe will be the way that people regard those few events that befall them. The things which befall them, not the things they do. In this world, deeds play a small and insignificant part; men anyway only want to do what they are allowed to do, and their firm confident stride takes them only to the goal they were anyway meant to attain. Everything that determines the course of life, everything that throws up tormenting doubts and causes deep pain, all this comes always from the outside, it only *befalls* people; they themselves do nothing to conjure it up, and, once it has happened, they fight against it in vain. Value, which creates differences between human beings, is revealed in the response of each to the inevitable. Fate comes from the outside, and inner strength is powerless against it; but just because of this, fate must stop on the threshold of the mansion in which the soul dwells, and can never enter it; fate can destroy these people, but can never break them. That is the real content of the resignation which is usually described as the essence of Storm's poetry. Storm was strongly opposed to the view that tragedy presupposes guilt. Not only his chosen subject, but also the very essence of his world-view contain much that is reminiscent of the tragedy of destiny, e.g. the idea that every unforeseen and incalculable detail may prove decisive in a life. But Storm stopped at the mere possibility of this; he did not regard life as a chaotic play of incalculable accidents. There is only a possibility, for him, that life may take such a form; and nothing, no inner or outward choice, determines whose life, when, to what extent, shall take such a form—only accident, only the accidental concatenation of accidental circumstances can decide this. Then there is no help, one has to make the best of it, fighting is of no use, one must accept the wealth of sorrow that will enrich one's soul.

In this world, then, fate has a force which works mechanically and admits of no outward resistance. Yet fate is not a mystical, otherworldly power, not the intervention of higher forces in ordinary life. Storm's world is the world of everyday life; as Kuh once said, his poetry is that of "holy everyday". Fate for him is nothing but the power of simple human conditions, the power of human thoughts and human contracts, of prejudice, of habit, of moral commandments. In Storm's world there are, in a man's soul, no inner struggles between contradictory forces. Duty—that which has to be done—is determined in advance, and for ever, with a certainty that excludes any controversy, and doubt can at most exist concerning its point of application. Fate alone, outward circumstances independent of the will of man, can place a man at a crossroads; but even then there is no real sin in this world. Storm's characters are incapable of evil. It is not that every person in this world is proof against the very possibility of evil; but ethics for everyone in this world is a natural life-function like breathing; an unethical action is therefore *a priori* impossible. Thus it is that the greatest misfortune occurs when the irresistible power of circumstances forces a human being to an action which his own moral sense condemns—and in Storm, moral sense is infallible. Yet there is no tragedy—at least not in any outward sense. Although the verdict of ethics is harsh and irrevocable, the force of every man's moral sense is at the same time so great that it keeps intact every man's essential nature despite everything that may befall him. It has befallen him, and with manly courage he stands aside from the path of happiness, with courageous composure he suffers for something he really could not help, and not for a moment does he seek to throw off the consequences of his "action". But at the same time he feels that he has done nothing, everything has been done to him, and everything within him remains intact; something remains in him that no outward force can touch.

This is the power that the consciousness of duty done assumes as a life-form, a world-view that still preserves its old, universal validity with all the effect of a categorical imperative—even if the naïve faith, the confidence that doing one's duty makes some small difference to the course of events, has been lost long ago. The world goes round somehow, something makes it go round, who knows what or why or what for? Why ask when there is no question, why knock on doors that will remain shut forever, why deceive your soul with the old, comforting, brightly coloured lies? To do your duty: that is the only sure way of life. There is a character in one of Storm's poems—an old man on the threshold of death—whose mood is a perfect expression of this attitude. The old man stands in his room which is filled with mementos of a long and happy life. A thousand small signs tell him that the end has come, he hears bells ringing in the distance and he knows that the sound of these bells means positive hope to many people.

"They dream," he softly says.
"These coloured visions are their happiness.
Yet I know it's the fear of death
That breeds such visions in the human brain."
He stretches out his hands in deprecation.
"Whatever I've done wrong, there is one fault of which I'm free.
Never have I surrendered reason into captivity,
Not for the sake of the most glittering temptation.
As for the rest: I wait with patience."

The important thing here is the gesture, not the content. Storm's lack of religion was in fact profoundly religious. Here, in the face of death, where no struggle is possible, the quiet strength is to be clearly recognized with which a man must look destiny in the eye; at other moments in life, when objectively the outcome of the struggle is not so clearly determined in advance, it is our weakness that is perhaps more evident. Just as, in the relationship between man and destiny, it is difficult to distinguish between what is inside and what outside, so it is difficult to distinguish between weakness and strength. A strength turned inwards usually appears outwardly as weakness because the world-sense of these people is so profoundly unified, the moral laws which support their lives so unshakeably strong, that they react to brutal events coming from the outside with the same immediately ethical attitude as they would to events coming from inside themselves, and this is also why they can fuse these events inside their souls. This power of fusion is the essence of their strength; their weakness is that—in most cases—even the strongest manifestations of life must wait for something to impinge upon them from the outside, and only very rarely do they go out themselves to meet the challenge. For the same reason they only very rarely come up against something that can be fought victoriously.

It goes without saying that these are only the broadest frontiers of these people's world. But just because these frontiers are completely unassailable, they are never actually staked out anywhere, and their full implications are never carried through to the end. Storm's sense of values, and especially that of certain of his characters, has much in common with the world-view of Hebbel, his compatriot, as expressed in the character of Meister Anton. But Storm, being less clear-sighted and less rigorous, is not as urgently aware of the decay of the world he describes; at the same time, because he attaches less importance to specific opinions and value-judgements than to the entire sum-total of a life, he avoids Meister Anton's ruthlessly doctrinaire narrow-mindedness. Nor is another kind of life, another world more powerful than the one he knows, to be found anywhere in his work. He sometimes portrays people who lead a very different kind of life, but even these do not provide a clear contrast to his typical characters. The greatest contrasts reveal themselves in people's actions: one man behaves decently, another does not; one is reliable to the extreme, another absolutely irresponsible and frivolous; for one, the prize of life is order and a secure sense of work well done, for another the momentary enjoyment of superficial pleasures at any cost. These contrasts could be carried on to infinity, and yet there would remain one sphere in which the extremes were in perfect harmony with one another: the sphere of ethical evaluation. Ethics rule Storm's world with such power that even the man who does not act ethically, *feels* ethically—only he is weak, he has not the strength to live in the way that his innermost feeling prescribes. If ever we meet a character whose feeling does not fit into this world, he is a completely grotesque case bordering on the pathological, a bizarre curiosity.

A mood of eternal transience, a mood of acceptance of the law of decay, a tender, forgiving love accompanies every downward step. Weakness, like strength, is given to man by nature; one who is strong, honourable and dutiful is not so through merit but through grace, and the same is true of the opposite. To be a good man is not a merit. Perhaps it is luck, but only perhaps, since for actual life it is without consequence. In any case it is a refinement: it creates an aristocracy, it creates distances between men. It creates the most securely established aristocracy of all, an aristocracy so sure of itself that it cannot know either pride or harshness but only a gentle forgiveness and understanding of those who are made of different, inferior stuff.

> One man asks: if I do this, what will come after?
> Another only: am I doing right?
> This is what makes the difference
> Between the free man and the slave.

The atmosphere of Storm's world results from this fusion of dryness and sentimentality. The events are as simple and ordinary as possible, and the people in whose lives these events occur are neither unusual nor interesting. They are simple German small-town dwellers, ranging from the petty bourgeoisie—sometimes the working class—to (again only sometimes) a few old Patrician families. Everyday life flows quietly on until, suddenly, doom strikes, but even then the same life goes on, and nothing happens except that a few lines are etched upon a face that was young before; the collision with fate has done no more than throw someone off his life's course, but now he leads a life somewhere else that obeys the same sure rhythm. Only a very few men and women, made of weaker stuff, perish completely and irretrievably.

Sentimentality, however, plays no part in the actual course of events—this is the logic of Storm's whole development—and does not even blur the hard edges of events; what is sentimental is only the way that, in retrospect, the memory of these events lingers on in these people's souls. The sentimentality lies in their being moved by their recognition of the workings of destiny. Its artistic significance is that it accompanies the harsh *staccati* of events by softly melodious *legati*, dissolving tragedies into requiems; and its human significance is that it protects the unerring certainty of ethical evaluations against short-sighted judgements.

The mood of Storm's idylls is similar to that of his tragedies; their beauty grows from the same root. This is true even of the simplest, smallest interior scenes, the small pictures which convey nothing more than the intimate, exquisite mood of an old room filled with old furniture, where the telling of long-forgotten stories is the barely audible theme of the variations which Storm is playing, and where the purpose of the whole is no more than to make the atmosphere of that simple room perceptible to the senses. The basic mood is the same everywhere: a sense of organic growth, a sense of the natural interaction of things, a sense of resigning oneself to the necessity of movements produced by that interaction, a recognition of the impossibility of grading things according to their greater or lesser importance. A sense of history becomes a sense of life. The mood of these rooms recalls old Dutch interiors, but here everything is more atmospheric, more lyrical, more sentimental. What, in Dutch painting, was a sure awareness of naïve and happy vitality, here becomes a conscious enjoyment of fading beauty. The mood of these rooms includes, with a certain gentle pedantry, the awareness that they have already half-vanished and will soon disappear altogether; the sense of history bestows not only a flower-like beauty on everything, but also the melancholy yet ungrieving reflections of ineluctable decay. By allowing the natural course of events to become conscious, Storm's historical sense brings it close and at the same time removes it to a certain distance; it makes the attitude towards that course of events more lyrical and more subjective, and at the same time surrounds it with the cool air of purely artistic enjoyment.

These interiors, however, only form the background to most of Storm's short stories; it happens only occasionally that the background detaches itself from the rest and becomes its own purpose, an image enclosed within itself. On these occasions the mood of such interiors is—for purely formal reasons—an idyllic one. But besides these, there are a number of other short stories by Storm which are idylls by their actual content—where this basic mood is conveyed, not only by his gentle glance lingering on the old furniture, not by the fact that the whole image consists only of that glance, but also by the course and content of the events depicted. The mood of a departing storm—sunshine after a cloudburst—is the tone of these short stories, and this is the root of their inner kinship with his tragic tales. In both, storm-clouds pile up above the heads of the people portrayed, and in both the characters await the thunderbolt with the same feelings—except that in the one case the lightning strikes, and in the other not. Happiness comes from the outside, just as unhappiness does; it comes from somewhere, and enters where there are souls with whom it can find a beautiful home. But it knocks where it chooses, and among all those who are worthy it selects at will the ones with whom it will decide to stay. And so in these idylls, just as in the tragedies, there is a sense of events willed by fate. Some-times nothing at all comes to disturb the melody of idyllic happiness, and the fateful mood of the tragedies can be detected only in the passive abandonment with which the characters portrayed let them-selves be borne upon waves of happiness.

Tragedy and idyll: between these two extremes every drama that occurs in Storm's world is played out, and the way in which the two merge into one another creates the special atmosphere of all his works. Absolute uncertainty of life in all its externals, unshakeable solidity where the point at issue is the soul—that is their essential, deeply bourgeois feature. It is the life-mood of a bourgeoisie that is just beginning to feel insecure; in this life-mood, the great old bourgeoisie that is in process of disappearing becomes historic, deeply poetic in the work of its last, still unbroken poet. This life-mood permeates all his works—even those which, out of love for older styles, go back to still remoter times and in which, for this reason, we sense something of a pure artistic structure.

The world of Storm's poems is even more definite and the world of the life-feelings expressed in them still purer. The people, or shadow-images of people, whom we project behind the poems, are still more exquisite; the motives which move them are deeper, the tragedies they experience are purer. This is undoubtedly a question of form. The nature of the people in Storm's world is such that it is best expressed through some manifestation of life touched off by fate—that is to say, through their mood. Actions, facts, events, everything external is, to tell the truth, quite superfluous—it is necessary only because, as Storm once wrote to Kuh, there are subjects which demand broader references than pure lyricism allows. But just because this is so, Storm achieves, in certain poems where these broader references are not called for, a complexity and purity of form-giving which his short stories could never attain. Only poetry can give fully adequate expression to the quiet, simple interiority of the people he usually describes (perhaps we may say to his interiority). These people and their creator are much too tranquil to throw them-selves head over heels into the turbulent stream of events, and much too simple for an analysis of their soul, revealing all its hidden depths and deepest secrets, to succeed in disclosing wonderful, unimaginably beautiful soul-landscapes. The true beauty of this world and its inhabitants is the lyrical description of a quiet, warm, simple life mood; and its genuine, truly perfect form can only be a completely tranquil, completely simple lyricism. Such lyricism, just because it is simple, embraces all subtleties more purely and more powerfully than the short story, which would at first glance appear more suitable for the purpose, but whose form demands projection into external facts

or resolution by analysis. The world of Storm's poetry is built somewhere between the two, refusing the formal demands of either.

> You bit your lips till they were sore and bleeding.
> You wanted this, I know it well, because my lips once covered
>   them.
> You let your fair hair be bleached by burning sun and rain :
> You wanted it because my hand had once caressed it.
> You stand all day over the stove in the heat and smoke.
> Your delicate hands are all raw.
> You want it thus, I know it well, because my eyes once lingered
>   on them.

3

Storm's literary forms were the lyric poem and the prose narrative,
or, more precisely, the lyric poem and the short story. He never let
himself be moved even to experiment with other forms. His development continually enriched his capacity for insight, and this, quite
unintentionally, brought his short stories close to the novel's domain.
Keller, who refused to recognize a difference of principle between the
novel and the short story, often advised Storm to practise less
simplification, to leave out less, not to distance his themes so strongly,
so that the same themes, allowed to spread out in a natural way,
might become novels. In this matter Storm refused to listen to his
friend's advice and stuck always to his chosen short story form. But
it is true that his concept of the short story comes close to the old
notion of the novel and is, in many respects, the opposite of the old,
authentic short story. In a foreword which has been suppressed,
Storm makes a polemical attack on the old definition whereby the
short story is the brief recounting of an event which is made gripping
by its unusual nature and has a surprise climax. He maintains that
the modern short story is the most rigorous and rounded form of
imaginative prose writing—sister of the drama, capable, like drama,
of expressing the most profound problems. Since poetic drama has
been driven off the modern stage, the short story, he says, is destined
to take its place.

Here Storm anticipates the modern impressionistic development
which completely interiorizes the short story, filling the old framework exclusively with inner content; he anticipates the transformation which, in its ultimate consequences, dissolves all strong
construction, all forms, into a low-toned, delicate, vibrating sequence
of psychological nuances. The modern short story—as a characteristic
example I would point first and foremost to those of Jünger Jacobson

—transcends the short story's possibilities by its content. The theme becomes more delicate, deeper, broader, more powerful than the old form would allow, and for this reason—although at first glance this appears paradoxical—these short stories are less deep and less subtle than the simple old stories used to be. For their subtlety and depth depend solely on their raw, unprocessed material—on the nature of the characters portrayed and their destinies, and on the fact that these are closely akin to the life-feelings of modern men. The nature of the short story form is, briefly, a human life expressed through the infinitely sensual force of a fateful hour. The difference in length between a novel and a short story is only a symbol of the true, profound, genre-defining difference—namely, that the novel gives us the totality of life by its very contents, by inserting its hero and his destiny in the full richness of an entire world, whereas the short story does this only formally, by giving form to an episode in the hero's life in such a strongly sensual way that it renders all other parts of his life superfluous. When the content of the short story becomes very deep and subtle, this on the one hand robs the decisive situation of the story of its fresh, strong sensuality, and, on the other hand, shows its characters in such a many-sided way and in so many relationships that no single event is capable of expressing them completely. This creates a new artistic genre, an absurd one like all those which result from modern development—a genre whose form is formlessness. This approach cannot deal with more than a few episodes in a human life; these episodes can no longer become symbolic, as they were in the old short story; and the whole is not strong enough to form an all-encompassing universe rounded in itself, like the novel. Hence these short stories are rather like scholarly monographs, or, still more, like rough drafts for such monographs. Their nature is antagonistic to art—even when their means are truly artistic—because the whole can never release a feeling independent from the concrete content and created by the form alone—a feeling which, therefore, cannot be altered if we change our opinion of the content. The effect of these works, like that of scholarly works, is based wholly and entirely on content, on that essentially scientific interest which the new observations contained in them can arouse. These writings (and this is the test, not the proof, of my remarks) lose their meaning when their observations get out of date, or even when they become universally known and lose the charm of novelty. But the crucial difference between a work of art and a scientific work is perhaps this: the one is finite, the other infinite; the one closed in upon itself, the other open; the one is a purpose, the other is a means. The one—we are now judging by consequences—is incomparable, a first and a last, the other is rendered superfluous by a better achievement. To put it briefly, the one has form and the other has not.

Storm must have sensed this danger somehow and this, no doubt, is why he so cautiously steered clear of the novel—as though he knew in what way he fell short of being a real, great novelist and why his themes were, of necessity, short-story themes which could not and should not be expanded into a novel. When Emil Kuh once called his short stories classical, he disagreed. "Surely," he wrote, "to be classical, a writer's work must reflect in artistically perfect form the essential spiritual content of his time . . . as for me, I'll have to content myself with a box well to the side of the stage." The remark touches, if only indirectly, upon the question of style. Storm's view of the world could not embrace the immense richness of life, as the novel form demands; he saw only episodes, only short-story subjects. But his way of seeing was too subtle, too interiorized to find expression in the old, simple, strong short-story form—the old form where nothing exists but facts and outward events, where, as Friedrich Schlegel said of Boccaccio, the deepest and most subjective moods are expressed purely through the mediation of sensual images. In Storm's first short stories, his purely lyrical interiority, still concerned only with the vibrations of the soul—his interiority which at that time still found free and direct expression—did in fact break down and destroy the form. "Here and there . . . one might perhaps wish for more individual definition," said Mörike, cautious and considerate as ever, of these early stories. The later stories set out to express the richest possible inner life, the entire soul-content of one or several characters, but always in such a way that these contents, having organically entered the epic form, actually extend and enrich it; nothing crudely direct is left behind; nothing, in these later stories, has significance from the point of view only of content.

Thus the form leads back once more to the question of the relationship and interaction of the internal and the external. The make-up of Storm's soul helped him to achieve artistic synthesis. On the one hand, his interiority was not yet so morbidly intense as that of today's writers; he had no compulsion or wish to trace every mood to its innermost roots within the soul; as Kuh said, he always stopped before the last gate but one. On the other hand he did not see outward events either with brutal harshness or with vigorous sensuality. The two elements were not so far removed from one another that they could not be welded into organic unity.

Storm achieved unity of tone through unity of delivery, epic form through the use of direct narration, that most ancient form of the epic which defines its very condition of existence. Almost all his short stories are placed within a frame—that is to say, it is not he himself but a narrator specially invented for the purpose who tells them from memory or reconstructs them from old letters or chronicles. If ever Storm does tell the story himself, he seems to be drawing every detail from his own memory, to be telling someone else about a curious happening in his own life. In this way he attempts to revive the old tradition of story-telling (Keller and Meyer did this too) or to re-create the original nature of the short story by artificial means. For Storm this was more than just an interesting method; the importance of oral delivery, that modest relic of true epic culture, cannot be over-estimated. Oral delivery was for him the touchstone of success in conveying the mood he wanted to create. But this method only intensifies the effect produced by placing the story within a frame; its real significance goes beyond achieving the harmonious directness of the narrative tone. To put it briefly, it is perhaps this : a distance is created from which the conflict between the internal and the external, between action and soul, is no longer visible. Memory, which is the typical form of narration within a frame, does not analyse events; it is rarely aware of the real motives underlying events, it never expresses events as a sequence of slight, almost imperceptibly changing vibrations of the soul. It follows from this that events are narrated in the form of vivid, sensually perceived images or fragments of dialogue—which nevertheless contain every-thing the author wants to convey. Memory and the natural technique of narration from memory leads to another, equally strong and sure epic form : the ballad. The ballad element compensates for whatever Storm's short stories have forfeited of their true quality as short stories. By excluding all analysis and preserving their full sensual power and symbolic significance, it prevents their becoming extended into novels; but the distancing which is thus achieved counteracts the fragmentariness of the events and their excessive harshness com-pared with the sensitive inner life of the characters. These vividly seen pictures fit together with perfect harmony because the narrator remembers only those aspects of the events which united them into a whole—only what has become the centre of the structure. And, lastly, this technique also makes for more sensual characterization because memory retains only what is visible and audible in the characters, and whatever is typical and general in them is built up slowly out of these sensual features. Storm's technique of charac-terization is the opposite of that of more modern short-story writers, who begin by establishing the grey background and the common and humdrum features of the characters, and then detach them from that background by a highly (too highly) nuanced refinement of the central theme. If, therefore, the content of Storm's short stories falls short of the breadth of the psychological insight shown by later practitioners of the genre, his psychology can be said to have been wholly transmuted into form, whereas the richer world of the moderns still remains, to some extent, unprocessed.

Yet even this proves that Storm stood at the end of an era. A single generation later his psychology would already have seemed superficial and his world-view a rejection of reality. A single generation later hardly anyone still remembered the simple, vividly perceived conditions which form the background to his stories; an author whose perception of life remained at Storm's level would now read like a family chronicler. At the same time, any attempt at closer analysis or at confronting more profound problems would have endangered or actually upset the precarious balance of Storm's type of short story.

Storm's stylistic solution did not follow directly from the essential nature of his themes; it was drawn from his purely personal ability to bring together a thousand opposing tendencies and to establish a delicate and infinitely cautious balance among them. For all its formal perfection, Storm's epic work is not an *art robuste* like, for instance, Maupassant's. He is truly the "quiet goldsmith and artificer of silver filigree" of the modern short story, and the description defines both the upper and the lower limits of his importance. He marks a watershed; he is the last representative of the great German bourgeois literary tradition. Nothing is left in him or in the world he depicts of the great old epic, such as Jeremias Gotthilf still achieved, yet the atmosphere of decay which engulfs his world is not yet strong and conscious enough to become monumental once more, as is the case with Thomas Mann's *Buddenbrooks*.

The fact that Storm is the last of a line is still more evident in his poems. He represents the peak and the end-point of the development of German bourgeois lyric poetry which grew from the soil of the folk-song. This development began with Günther, and all of its threads, by way of Goethe and Romanticism and everything that came out of Romanticism, notably the twin poles of Heine and Mörike, converge on Storm. But whereas in his short stories, however tentatively, he is looking for a transition to something new, in his verse he abides rigorously by the old form and rejects not only all experimentation but also every effect which is not strictly lyrical. Yet in his poems he found not only a purer and stronger but also a more complex, more nervous, vibrant and modern expression for his perception of life than he ever did in his short stories. I believe that these two facts are not really contradictory, because the theoretical reasons for both are only the concomitants of the interrelationship between form and feeling. Storm's uncompromising dogmatism vis-à-vis his poetry was simply a sign of his strong sense of security in that medium, just as his more conciliatory attitude towards the short story, his willingness to go beyond the old concept of the genre, was a symptom of his inner insecurity as a short-story writer. The reasons —both the poet's and the short-story writers' reasons—are not hard to understand, and many of them have been outlined already in this essay. In lyric poetry there are none of the dissonances of the outside world which determines the face of men, and none of the dissonances of Storm's way of comprehending and evaluating that world. Lyric feeling can express itself purely and directly. And this lyrical reflection of events was for Storm—even as a short-story writer—the decisive experience.

The essential feature of Storm's lyrical form is that it makes full use of all the great values of the past: extreme economy of expression; an almost impressionistic reduction of images and metaphors to the barest essentials, the barest hint; a narrowly limited vocabulary with sudden sensual highlights; and, most especially, an extraordinarily subtle, deep and unerring musical quality. A musical quality which a long poetic development, running parallel to the development of music, had refined to a point where every modulation of tone was a conscious effect; a musical quality which, for this very reason perhaps, must always remain strictly within the limits of song. All such poems are capable of being sung; this possibility remains open at all times; and this defines the limits of the power of melody, which attempts to express the soul by purely acoustic means. (It goes without saying that the condition and principle of this style is not that the poems are actually sung, but that they can be sung.)

Storm the poet is in every sense the last representative of this development. All the simple motifs had been used up long before; more than that, Mörike had developed the imagery of language to the point of preciousness and Heine had virtually destroyed the form by mixing intellectual values with pure mood. Storm took up the new values of both and reinserted them into an absolutely simple and strict old form. But such simplicity was in his case already a conscious stylization, the last decorative flourish of a great development; his verse, with its deliberately primitive simplicity, is the final sharpening of all the already blunted possibilities of the past—so that at the next attempt the point was bound to break. After him there could be nothing but empty, frivolous mannerism. When Storm is at his best, his deeply melodious, softly atmospheric, yet Nordically severe verse is as yet quite free from mannerism. Hardness and sentimentality combine in these poems as irony and sentimentality combine in Heine's, but here the two merge together and do not, as is often the case with Heine, confront one another in such sharp contrast that the effect of the poem is destroyed.

Across the heath my steps ring out
dully the earth echoes under my feet
autumn has come and spring is far
was there ever a time when I was happy?
Brooding mists float on the air
the grass is so black and the sky so empty.
If only I had not walked here in May!
Life, love, how both have flown away!

A courageous, resigned, austere life-mood: such is the poetry of the last poet of the bourgeoisie, great after his own fashion.

1909

The New Solitude and its Poetry

STEFAN GEORGE

I

L'IMPASSIBILITÉ! No one who aims at something more than sharing Everyman's little joys and miniscule sorrows, no one who refuses to join in the bustle of a provincial market-place and to become absorbed in the exciting problems discussed there—no one can escape being labelled with it. It threatens everyone whose soul is not totally dedicated to the commonest things, everyone who does not carry his heart on his sleeve, and especially everyone who persists in viewing art as serious work—a poet who wants to produce poetry that is self-sufficient, poetry from which no way leads outward, which demands nothing from the reader but that he read it. This is why Goethe's Tasso and Orestes, torn as they are by hysteria, nevertheless seem to us cold as marble. Even Baudelaire's sobs were doomed to remain unheard, simply because he had the skill to find good adjectives to express his torments. Today, after Grillparzer and Hebbel, after Keats and Swinburne, after Flaubert and Mallarmé, it is Stefan George's turn. Today he is the "cold" poet who is "far from life", who "experiences" nothing, whose verses are like beautifully polished crystal chalices admired by fellow craftsmen and gaped at in bewilderment by the many, yet which really mean something to a very few.

What does it signify, this *impassibilité*, this coldness of which we hear so much and so often? A reaction that recurs frequently must have deep foundations in the soul, that much is certain. But it is equally certain—a thousand documents are there to prove it—that something which seemed cold and offensively objective yesterday already begins to reveal its hidden lyricism today, and perhaps by tomorrow many people will think it too mild, too confessional, too subjective, too lyrical altogether. These concepts fluctuate rather like those of Classicism and Romanticism, of which Stendhal said a long time ago that everything has at some point been Romantic and everything at some time becomes Classical: Classicism being the Romanticism of yesterday and Romanticism the Classicism of tomorrow. In the same way one might say that there are only temporal differences between *impassibilité* and subjectivity—in other words, these are categories of history or evolution, but not of aesthetics. Is this true? What happens, I believe, is that the reader compares his own feelings about life with what the poet (as the reader thinks!) feels about his own self-created world. This attempt at identification reveals certain differences of temperature, and the reader projects these differences into the poet. In this way any poet must appear cold who, for example, regards the end of a life or of a cause as necessary or useful or not wholly regrettable, because he sees it as part of a causality which his public does not yet spontaneously feel; and he must immediately cease to appear cold when things which at first, in isolation, struck the reader as shocking accidents or blows of fate, come to be felt by him as natural necessities, generally recognized and felt as such from time immemorial. This happens with every change of feeling. But it is not the standpoint of art. Art is suggestion with the help of form. There does not have to be agreement between writer and reader; indeed the absence of agreement cannot diminish the effect of somthing which has been written with real suggestive power, or rather, it need not always diminish that effect, but it can—and always does—modify it. Hence the question does not touch upon the value of the work but rather upon its situation in society. It is the history of the passage of a written work from Romanticism to Classicism, from bizarre strangeness to sublime simplicity, from naturalism to stylization, from coldness to warmth, from exclusivity to popularity, from the impassive to the confessional (or vice versa)—rather as the sun rises in the morning, reaches its zenith at noon and sets again at night. We may yet live to see Madame Bovary in the hands of students of educational establishments for young ladies; Ibsen may, in a not too distant future, take the place of Schiller in adult education literature courses; and—who can tell?—Stefan George's poems may some day, for all we know, become folk-songs.

George's coldness, then, is due to the contemporary reader's not knowing how to read, combined with a whole series of sentimental attitudes, many of which have been proved superfluous. He is cold because the notes he strikes are so delicate that not everyone can hear them; because his tragedies are such that the average reader of today does not yet feel them as tragic, and therefore believes that the poems in question were written only for the sake of their exquisite rhymes; because the sentiments expressed in ordinary poetry play no part in his life.

One day, perhaps, despite all this, his poems may still become folk-songs.

Perhaps. But the impenetrable *odi profanum* is not always only the historical, or accidentally determined, fate of a poet; more often it is due to an interaction between the poet's individuality and the conditions of his time which is so intimate and so profound that it actually determines the ultimate and crucial formal problems of his work. The passage of time or changes in popular feeling can never alter an exclusivity of this kind.

There are writers whose isolation in their time is only a matter of content, and there are aesthetes; or, to be more precise, there is a sociological and a psychological variety of art for art's sake. By saying this I am, of course, defining only the two extreme poles between which there are thousands of nuances. Who is an aesthete? Goethe sensed this problem—he was perhaps the first to sense it—and talked about it in a letter to Schiller, as follows: "Unfortunately some of us moderns are sometimes born poets, and we struggle and sweat . . . without rightly knowing what we're supposed to do; for specific directions should, if I am not mistaken, come from the outside, and occasion should determine talent." It may even be superfluous to add: an aesthete is someone born at a time when a rational sense of form has died out, when form is regarded as something which has been ready-made from history and which may, therefore, be convenient depending on personal mood; the aesthete cannot fit into this scheme of things and is willing neither to take over unchanged the forms created to express the inner state of others, nor to recite his own feelings without any form at all, a practice dear to every inartistic era; he constructs his own "specific directions" for himself, so far as he is able, and creates out of himself the conditions which determine his talent.

George is an aesthete within this definition, the only definition that has any meaning at all. He is an aesthete, and this means that no one today has any use for songs (or rather, only few people have any use for them and even for these people this use is quite tentative and vague); and so he must find within himself all the possibilities of song that would act upon the unknown, ideal reader, who perhaps does not exist anywhere. He must find within himself the form for the poetry of today. And although this, however true it may be, tells us nothing really decisive about his nature as a poet, it does perhaps clear out of the way a few of those empty phrases that are bandied about in connection with his name. I fear I may be writing, at least in part, for readers who until now have only heard such things about him, and have perceived nothing else in his work.

2

Stefan George's songs are songs of travel, stations on a long, apparently endless road which pursues a definite goal yet, perhaps, leads nowhere. All of them together form a great cycle, a great novel, supplementing one another, explaining one another, reinforcing, modifying, emphasizing, refining one another. Yet none of this is intentional. They are like Wilhelm Meister's wanderings, and perhaps a little like *L'Education Sentimentale*, but constructed entirely from the inside, purely lyrically, without any adventure or event. The only events they show are reflexes of the soul; the soul's enrichment, but not the sources of the riches; the going astray, not the possible point of arrival; the torment of parting, but not what it might have meant to walk side by side with another; the tempestuous joy of a great meeting, but not whether the meeting led to an organic union; only the sweet melancholy of recollection and the intellectual ecstasy, full of a bitter joy, which is born of the contemplation of transience. And loneliness, much loneliness and solitary journeying. The route leads from solitude to solitude, past human companionship, through the transience of great loves and back to loneliness, and then once more, along a new path, to new solitudes that are always higher, more final, more cleansed of sorrow.

> Scarcely had you laid the trowel down
> and looked contentedly at what you had constructed:
> every building was for you but the threshold for the next
> for which not a single stone had yet been cut
>
> to you fell a portion of flower seed
> garlands you wove and danced on the moss
> and when you looked towards the next mountain ridge
> you chose your fortune on the other side.

or better still:

> So long as a coloured haze still lit the mountain
> I had no trouble finding the way
> many voices were familiar to me in the woodland.
> Now everything is silent on the grey evening path.
> There is no one walking who even for a little way
> Might offer me some hope, desire, or comfort, however small.
> No other wanderer walks in quite such darkness.

What, then, are Stefan George's tragedies? The poems draw only the imaginary portrait of the poet, and the answers they supply are only symbolic: they give a platonic idea of the tragedies, free from all empirical reality. George's lyricism is very chaste. It reproduces only the most general and symbolic experience, thus robbing the reader of any possibility of recognizing intimate signs of life. Of course a poet speaks always about himself—how else could songs be ever made? He tells everything about himself, the deepest and most hidden things, and with every confesion he becomes that much more mysterious to us and wraps himself that much more in his solitude. He casts the rays of his verse upon his life in such a way that only the play of light and shade entertains us and no contour ever becomes visible in the flickering chiaroscuro. Every poem is a fusion of concrete images with symbols. In the past—one need only think of Heine, Byron, the young Goethe—the experience was concrete and the poem typified it and made a symbol of it. The accidental, the thing that happens only once, whose course was easy to reconstruct from the poems, grew in front of our eyes into an event of general significance, a value which mattered to everyone. The experience was palpable, its representation typical, the event individual, the adjectives and metaphors general. These poems were abstract descriptions of certain landscapes or stylized adventures of well-known people. George typifies the experience before there is any question of making poetry. In the introduction to one of his volumes of verse he writes: "The experience has undergone such transformations through art that it has become insignificant for its creator himself, and for anyone else to 'know why' would be confusing rather than illuminating." But to express this experience which has become absolutely typical, which is for ever detached from the poet's person, which has been distilled a thousand times, he has words of wonderful momentary power, swift, sudden and delicate, softer than rustling leaves. His landscapes do not exist anywhere and yet every tree and every flower is real and the sky glows with unique, never-to-be-repeated colours at a certain specific hour. We do not know the man who wanders through this landscape, but within a single moment we see a thousand minute fluctuations in his innermost being, only to lose him out of sight the next instant and never to see him again; we do not know who it is he loves, why he is suffering or why he is suddenly jubilant, yet we recognize him better at that moment than if we knew everything that had ever happened to him. George's technique is the impressionism of the typical. All his poems are symbolic snapshots.

> . . . When through the blazing vermilion of foliage
> and the green-metal trunks of black pines
>
> we visited this tree or that; silent guests
> walking apart in loving discord
> each listening secretly among the branches
> for the song of a dream not yet come. . . .

In these poems there is the cry that bursts out involuntarily through clenched lips, the ultimate confession that is whispered with head averted in a darkened room. They are completely intimate and yet they keep their author at an immense distance from us. They are written as though the reader, together with the author, had experienced every detail of what has gone before and can now anticipate together with him what will happen next; as though the author were talking to his best friend, the kind of friend that exists only once in a lifetime, a friend who knows everything about his life, who understands the gentlest hint and who might almost be offended if he were told any facts, yet who just for this reason is most interested in the smallest concrete detail. (George's earliest lyrics were intended for a very general, not initiated reader.) This is why these poems can only speak of the most personal things, only the most profound things which change every minute; this is why George's poetry can finally—more finally perhaps than any poetry before it— transcend the atmosphere of "she loves me—she loves me not" and express only the most delicate intellectual tragedies.

> My faithfulness forces me to watch over you still
> the beauty of your suffering makes me sing.
> My holy aspiration is to become sad
> so that I may more truly share your sorrow.

George's songs really express the same feelings, and are written to satisfy the same needs, as intimate plays and lyrical short stories. In a very strict sense they are perhaps—in large part—not poems at all but something new, something different, something which is just now coming into being for the first time. I believe that poets who write like this—George and certain French, Belgian and Dutch poets —have come closest to the new poetry towards which poets of every persuasion are moving today, and for the sake of which they have rejected all the tried and tested effects of poetry and destroyed the poetic forms which they, more than all others, regarded as sacred. What has happened? In a sense we have already said it: we no longer attach any decisive importance in our lives to grand tragedies and vigorous, unbroken feelings that oppose one another in categorical contrasts—as though these were for the most part too loud for our organs of perception, just as ours would perhaps have been too soft for our fathers'. Our life today is shaped in such a way that glances which no one has noticed or words which have been let fall without being heard or understood are coming to be the forms in which souls communicate with one another. It is as though the process of their intercourse were softer and yet more rapid, and the contrast area larger and rougher and more broken. The whole large and complex apparatus of almost all today's plays and short stories is there only to prepare for one such moment, such a meeting or parting. We listen to people talking with one another for long periods in ways that seem unnecessary and unimportant and tiresome—until suddenly we hear music and the sound of the soul's profound desire (for what comes into being here is lyric poetry, after all), only for it to cease immediately afterwards, whilst we wait nervously and impatiently for the return of another such moment. People hate one another, destroy and kill one another, and at the end, on the Golgotha of the great destruction, there rings out from an immeasureable depth the bell-like word of eternal unity and eternal separation. . . . The new songs give us nothing but such moments, rejecting all tiresome preparatory mechanisms. Therefore their technique is more uniform and their effect more direct than those of anything similar being produced today. Intimacy and sensualization: the intimate drama and the lyrical short story ought to bring these opposite poles together; the lyric poetry being born today is capable of uniting them truly and completely, allowing each to stand without dissonance.

What is the essential nature of this new lyric poetry? We have already defined a good deal of it; let us try now to sum it up in a few sentences. Technically speaking, as with music, it consists in the dominance of the accompaniment over the solo voice. What does this mean? The old lyric poetry was *occasional poetry* (Goethe described it as such), and, for that very reason perhaps, its form was the most typical, the simplest, and the one that spoke most directly to the masses: the form of the stylized folk-song. Lieder music, the necessary correlative of these new folk songs, came into being as the paradoxical complement to this paradoxical development—necessary because this form is determined by imaginary singing, and therefore can achieve ultimate perfection only if it is actually sung. And today we cannot any longer imagine these folk-songs without that music; whatever we may perhaps feel to be lacking in a poem by Heine or Mörike has been added by Schubert and Schumann, Brahms and Wolf: what has been added is the metaphysically great universality of the experience, everything that is typical about it and that goes beyond the purely personal. The essential nature of the new poetry is to render this accompanying music unnecessary, to endow the combinations of vowels and consonants with tones in which we shall hear what may not be expressed for a long time yet or perhaps never at all, what cannot be expressed in words but only aroused from sleep by the sound of words in the soul of every reader. The new lyric poetry makes its own music, it is text and sound, melody and

accompaniment all at the same time: something closed within itself
and needing no further addition.

> Softly still in the rising year
> for you the scented garden laughs
> ivy and speedwell plaited
> in your streaming hair

> The wavy corn is still like gold
> no longer quite so high and rich perhaps
> roses still greet you kindly
> though their brightness has paled a little

> let us not speak of what we cannot have
> let us vow to be happy
> even if no more is to be granted us
> than to walk round once more together.

It had to happen like this. Those earlier folk-songs became final
only when they were sung: but who, today, could write such music
for us? The quality of those songs was such that it could move many
hundreds of people in a concert hall at the same time; today we feel
nothing at the same time as anyone else, and if something does touch
many of us simultaneously, it touches only a large number of isolated
beings. A mass feeling can scarcely develop out of such a general
mood. The new songs were, in the ideal sense, written for just one
person, and only person can read them, withdrawn and alone.
Heine's songs, as they are sung at concerts, have never offended
anyone's sensibilities; the new songs one can bear to hear only from
someone very dear and very close.

There is no question of coincidence here; it cannot be coincidence
that English lyric poetry, great and wonderfully musical as it is—for
all that it has never been set to music and would surely reject such
treatment completely—is only just beginning to meet with serious
attention on the continent of Europe. Nor can it be a coincidence
that English poetry and French poetry together have completely
and definitively destroyed the German folk-song tradition, which had
already become sterile; that the poems written by Goethe in his old
age, anticipating all our modern developments, were never as much
admired as they are today; that poets who in their own time were
rejected as unmusical and unlyrical—Brentano, Hebbel, Conrad
Ferdinand Meyer—are beginning to be discovered and appreciated.
Nor is it a coincidence that the German *Lied* has broken through the
churchy solemnity of its Parnassian rhythms and, by so doing, has

helped the birth of a new, more intimate poetry—a poetry which is related to the older English and more modern German styles.

Intimacy and sensualization: this contrast is the technical expression of the psychological problem of closeness and distance. We have seen how George's poems are formed in a technical sense; and what we have said so far makes it clear that such placing of opposite poles emerges from the verse-reading technique of the solitary reader. Why it had to happen like this is difficult to judge, and is more than a purely technical issue. The solitary reader's reading method helped to determine it, but the loneliness of the man of today demands that the elements should be mixed in this particular ratio. Closeness and distance: what is the meaning of the relationship between these two? From the standpoint of human relationships it means the rhythm which the alternation of telling and not-telling creates. Today we tell everything, we tell it to someone, to anyone, no matter to whom, and yet we have never really told anything; other people are so close to us that their closeness tranforms what we have to give them of ourselves; yet they are so far from us that everything becomes lost on the way from us to them. We understand everything, and our greatest understanding is a rapt marvelling, an incomprehension intensified to the point of religiosity. We long passionately to escape from our tormenting loneliness, yet what is closest to us are the subtle pleasures of eternal solitude. Our knowledge of humanity is a psychological nihilism: we see a thousand relationships, yet never grasp any real connection. The landscapes of our soul exist nowhere, yet every tree and every flower in these landscapes is concrete.

3

What, then, is the nature of Stefan George's tragedies? In a word, they are the tragedies of Professor Rubek—except that they are unspoken; generalized in the sense that Rubek's fate—his withdrawal from life—is today the fate of every man, that the tragic dilemma of art and life is thrown up every minute of all our lives. The eternal leavetaking of the epilogue, the eternal inability to depart, but purer, deeper and more true, without the dusty legend of the one and only beloved; always living through the same thing, with every tree, every moonlit night, every passing sympathy, always in a different way and yet always the same: forever wanting to belong somewhere, yet honest enough to face the ancient sadness of never belonging anywhere.

The man of George's songs (the poet, if you like, or better still the profile that emerges before us out of the totality of these poems—or, best of all, the man whose life-contents seem to be expressed in these poems) is a lonely man detached from all social bonds. The content of each of his songs and that of their totality is something that one must understand, yet never can : that two human beings can never become one. And another thing : the great search, along a thousand paths, in every solitude, in all the arts, the search for human beings like ourselves, for a communion with simpler, more primitive, unspoilt beings.

Dancing hearts whom I admire and seek out
Gladly abasing myself that I may not disturb your amusements
You who move me, you light ones, you who fulfil me,
You whom I admire so much that you yourselves have to smile
                                        in astonishment,
You who sweep me along in your friendly crowd,
You must never know it is only my disguise that resembles you
Light hearts, who treat me as a friend :
How far you are from my throbbing heart !

Nature itself is somehow strangely distant from this imaginary man of George's songs, the man we have to postulate. Nature is no longer the kind mother who shares her sons' joys and sorrows. Nature is not even the romantic background to such feelings. And although it is entirely true that without the tawny leaves of an autumnal garden that meeting between souls may never have occurred— though we know that a moon and its greenish gleam may have determined a whole life—yet these men are alone in nature, and their solitude is deadly and beyond all salvation. A communion of souls exists only for the brief moment of holding hands—a communion between one human being and another, only as a fulfilment of a wish, anticipated in the mind, just one step nearer to one another, just a moment more spent in one another's company . . . and then the folly of belonging together is over and done with.

Yet this is a poetry of human relationships—of "inner sociability", to use George's own apt phrase. It is a poetry of friendships, of the meeting of souls, of intellectual companionship. Sympathy, friendship, sentimental attachment and love all merge together in it; every friendship is strongly tinged with eroticism, every love is profoundly intellectual. And when there is a parting, one knows that something is no more—but never what it was that has now ceased to be. George's immense discretion is almost symptomatic, a symbol of the inseparable fusion of feelings in our time. Perhaps it is the fault of the technique he uses that we do not clearly see what is happening, or to whom; and yet, perhaps, the whole purpose of the technique is to conceal these things, for even if we saw, we should not really understand.

Here is the poetry of modern intellectuality, an expression of its highly specific life-feelings and moods, no longer setting out—by being popular and simple—to express the "universally human" aspects of modern intellectuality. Yet it is not intellectual poetry; it is not "modern" in the superficial sense. The props of modern life play no part in it (as they often do in Dehmel's poems), and no intellectual duels are fought out between conflicting world-views. George's songs describe how the new soul reveals itself in all its minutest expressions, as well as in those which belong to the life of the sentiments. In this George is neither revolutionary nor experimental; so far as content goes he does not extend by a single inch the areas occupied by lyric poetry before our time. But he is able to give purely lyrical reflection—in the old sense—to life-phenomena which, perhaps, could not have been expressed in verse before.

The direction of his development leads more and more directly and more exclusively to this point. The poems which have followed the phantasmagorical fairy-tale landscapes and sultry hanging-gardens of his earliest work have been increasingly simpler and more austere, using an ever greater economy of means. There is a kind of Pre-Raphaelitism in this development, not the Pre-Raphaelitism of the English but the really primitive, really Florentine kind: a Pre-Raphaelitism that does not make austerity piquant but adopts austerity as the basis of its stylization; one for which primitivism is an artistic ethic, so that it is incapable of even noticing beautiful things if they are harmful to the composition; one which uses the airy lightness and the fragile stiffness of its lines to infuse spiritual life into itself; one which, however consciously or calculatingly, is willing to contain life within itself only by means of a puritanical technique, and would rather give up that life altogether than forgo its snowy, sometimes perhaps rather starchy, purity.

There is something deeply aristocratic in Stefan George's poems, something that keeps out every lachrymose banality, every super-ficial sigh, every cheap sentiment by a scarcely perceptible glance, a barely sketched movement. In George's poems there is virtually no complaint: it looks life straight in the eyes, calmly, with resignation perhaps, yet always courageously, always with head held high. In them we hear the final chords of all that is best in our time: Shaw's Caesar meeting the world with a steady glance; the gestures with which Hauptmann's Geyer and Kramer, his Wann and his Charlemagne conclude the play; and most of all the handclasp of

Allmers and Rita, left alone at the edge of the fjord when the stars
have already risen and the lost Eyolfs, both Eyolfs, the Eyolfs
they never possessed, have vanished for ever. A fine, strong,
courageous farewell, after the fashion of noble souls, without complaint or lamentation, with broken heart yet with a firm tread,
"composed" as the wonderful, all-comprising, truly Goethean
expression has it.

> How timidly your fingers weave the tired stems !
> This year will give us no more flowers
> No pleading would bring them here;
> One day perhaps another May will bring us others.
>
> Release my arm and stay strong;
> Leave the park with me before the parting ray
> Before the mist from the mountain spreads over.
> Let us depart before winter drives us away.

1908

Longing and Form

CHARLES-LOUIS PHILIPPE

Ma, poiché la piacque di negarlo a me, lo mio signore Amore, la
sua mercede, ha posta tutta la mia beautitudine inquelle che non
me quote venir meno.

La vita nuova. XVIII

1

L ONGING and form. They always say that Germany is the land of
Sehnsucht, of longing, and German longing is so strong, they
say, that it destroys all form, so overpowering that one cannot
express it except by stammering. Yet people talk about it all the
time, and its formlessness is constantly remoulded into a new,
"higher" form—the only possible expression of its nature. Are we
not justified in asking (Nietzsche understood the question very
clearly) whether this formlessness of longing is really proof of its
strength or, rather, of an inner softness, a yieldingness, a never-
endingness?

I believe that the relation is most clearly summed up in the difference between a typically German and a Tuscan landscape. It is
perfectly true that many German forests have something nostalgic,
something melancholy and sad about them; yet they are homely and
inviting. They are airy, their contours are gently blurred; they suffer
patiently whatever may happen inside them or may be done to them;
one can make oneself comfortably at home inside them, one can even
pull one's notebook from one's pocket and—to the accompaniment of
a nostalgic rustling of leaves—write poetic songs of longing. But the
landscape of the South is hard and resistant, it keeps you at arm's
length. A painter once said: "It has already been composed before
you ever get to it". And you cannot enter into a "composition", you
cannot come to terms with it, nor will it ever give an answer to
tentative questions. Our relationship to a composition—to something
that has already taken form—is clear and unambiguous, even if it
is enigmatic and difficult to explain: it is that feeling of being both
near and far which comes with great understanding, that profound

sense of union which yet is eternally a being-separate, a standing-outside. It is a state of longing.

In such landscapes the great Romance poets of longing were born, they grew up in it and they became like it themselves: hard and violent, reticent and form-creating. All the great forms and form-givers of longing come from the South: Plato's Eros, Dante's great love, Don Quixote and the scorned heroes of Flaubert.

Great longing is always taciturn and it always disguises itself behind many different masks. Perhaps it would not be a paradox to say that the mask is its form. But the mask also represents the great, two-fold struggle of life: the struggle to be recognized and the struggle to remain disguised. Flaubert's "coldness" was soon unmasked, it is true; but did not Beatrice become pure symbol, and did not the longing of Socrates become a philosophy of longing?

The questions are posed most clearly in the *Symposium*. Who is the lover, and what is loved? Why does one long for something, and what is the object of longing? None of Socrates' friends understood him on this issue, although he formulated the great, crucial difference in clear words, leaving nothing unsaid. "Love empties us of the spirit of estrangement and fills us with the spirit of kinship." Aristophanes found the most telling image to express it: once, all living creatures were double what they are today, but Zeus cut them in half and they became men. Longing and love are the search for one's own lost other half. That is the small, the fulfillable longing. Men who belong to the tribe of this myth can find their other half in every tree and every flower; every encounter in their lives becomes a wedding. But whoever has glimpsed the great duality of life is always with another, and for that same reason always alone; no confession and no complaint, no devotion, no love will ever make one out of the two. Socrates understood this when he said that love lacks beauty and goodness; longing alone can give beauty—the beauty of another.

Eros is in the middle: one never longs for what is foreign to one and never for what is already one's own. Eros is a saviour, but redemption is a vital problem only for the unredeemed—only for those who cannot be redeemed. Eros is in the middle: longing makes a link between those who are unlike one another, but at the same time it destroys every hope of their becoming one; becoming one is coming home, and true longing has never had a home. Longing constructs its lost fatherland out of vivid dreams dreamed in ultimate exile, and the content of longing is the search for ways that could lead to that lost home. True longing is always turned inward, however much its paths may lead across the external world. But it is only turned inward; it will never find peace inside. For it can create even its most profound self only through dreams; it can search for this inner self in the infinite distance of its own dreams, as something alien and lost. Longing can create itself, but it can never possess itself. The longing man is a stranger to himself because he is not beautiful, and a stranger to beauty because it is beautiful. Eros is in the middle: he is truly the son of wealth and poverty. "*L'amour*," says Charles-Louis Philippe's Marie Donadieu, "*c'est tout ce que l'on n'a pas.*"

This was Socrates' confession, clearer and more frank than his last words about offering a cock to Asclepius. Yet the revelation was a new way of concealing. Socrates could never keep quiet. He was vulgar: a sentimental man, and a dialectician. Therefore he "wrapped himself in names and expressions like a wild satyr in his pelt". His discourse never fell silent, nothing ever clouded its transparent clarity. Socrates was never monological. He went from one group of discoursing men to another, always speaking or listening to others. His whole life seemed absorbed in the dialogical form of his thinking. And when he fell silent for the first time in his life—after he had emptied the cup of hemlock and his feet had already begun to grow numb—he wrapped himself in his cloak. No one saw the changed face of Socrates: Socrates alone with himself and without a mask.

But what was hidden behind his words? Was it the recognition of the ultimate hopelessness of all longing? There is much to support this—but Socrates never said it. No word, no gesture ever betrayed where, in his humanity, lay the source of his philosophy of longing. He had become a teacher and prophet of longing, analysing its nature with wise words, arousing longing everywhere he went with the ironically tempting pathos of his discourse, and always and everywhere denying himself any fulfilment. He loved every beautiful youth in Athens and he aroused love in every one of them, but he deceived them all, too: for his words seduced them to love, but then he led them towards virtue, beauty and life. Hopelessly, each one of them longed for him, and his own hopeless longing burned for every one of them.

Love always leads somewhere beyond itself: "it's object," says Socrates, "is to procreate and bring forth in beauty". It was towards this high point that he had forced his life, and towards this that he seduced and deceived the youths of Athens. Through him, they ceased to be objects of love and become lovers; and the lover is more divine than the beloved, because his love, being a way towards self-perfection, must always remain unrequited. "They are," said Schiller of the objects of human longing, "what we once were; they are what we are to become once more." But the past—that which has been lost to us—has become a value because we create what has been lost to us, a way and a goal, out of its never-having-existed; this is how longing rises above the goal which it has set itself, and this is how it ceases to be bound to its own goal.

Longing soars higher than itself; great love always has something ascetic about it. Socrates transformed his longing into a philosophy whose peak was eternally unattainable, the highest goal of all human longing: intellectual contemplation. By advancing thus towards the ultimate, insoluble conflict, his longing became free from conflict in terms of real life: love—the typical form of longing—became a part of the system, an object of his explanation of the world, a symbol of the way in which the world hangs together; Eros ceased to be the god of love and became a cosmic principle. Socrates the man disappeared behind his philosophy.

But it will always be denied to men and poets to soar as high as this. The object of their longing has its own gravity and its own self-demanding life. Their soaring is always tragic, and in tragedy hero and destiny must become form. But, in tragedy, only hero and destiny can do this, and hero and destiny they must remain. In life, longing has to remain love: that is its happiness and its tragedy. Great love is always ascetic, whether it raises the object of love to supreme heights and by so doing alienates it from itself and from the lover, or whether it merely uses that object as a springboard; whereas petty love abases love and causes mutilation, which is another form of asceticism. Great love is the natural, the real, the normal kind of love, but among living human beings it is the other kind that has become normal: love as silence and repose, love which cannot and will not lead to anything else. Marie Donadieu says: *"L'amour c'est lorsque l'on s'assied le dimanche soir et tout cela vous suffit."* It is the struggle between sacred and profane love. In life, longing has become love, and now love is struggling to be independent from longing, its lord and begetter.

The love-struggle between man and woman is merely a mirror-image of this struggle. An impure and distorted mirror-image; yet the truth lies precisely in the distortion. If we could see the truth clearly and purely in human beings, love itself would be killed. Great love would then be without an object, it would become pure longing —whilst petty, profane love, whatever its object, would then simply be a resting-place. The love of a woman is closer to nature and more deeply tied to the nature of love: sublime and vulgar love, sacred and profane love coexist inseparably within her. A woman in love is always full of longing, but her longing is always practical. Only a man sometimes knows real longing, and only in men is longing often completely dominated by love.

In this struggle, love is stronger than longing; indeed, what arouses longing is generally a weakness—but one which is unaware of its roots and feels itself to be a weakness for that reason alone. It seems to it that it cannot hold on to anything, and it realizes only rarely that it does not want to do so. But Socrates held Eros to be a sophist and a pholosopher; and Philippe says somewhere, very simply and beautifully: *"ceux qui souffrent ont besoin d'avoir raison"*.

The two kinds of love confront one another in Philippe's novels when two men are struggling to win the same woman. (Within the woman herself they have become one to such a point that no struggle is possible.) A pimp and a young student from the provinces fight the first great battle. They fight it over a prostitute. The outward contradictions of the situation are rendered sensual by being made extreme: the object of the two men's love is accidental, yet they are bound to it, and the woman is so pliant, her gift for love is so great, that she would be able to adapt herself to either kind of love. It takes a long time before the contest occurs, but when it comes it takes only a moment. It is purely a question of force, of determination to possess, and so the outcome is never really in question. The pimp need only lift a finger, and although the harlot has begun to be attracted to the other kind of life through the other man's slow, attentive love-making, she nevertheless follows without protest. The student remains alone and in despair: *"Tu n'as pas assez de courage pour mériter le bonheur: pleure et crève!"*

The balance of forces is always the same. In Philippe's last completed novel it leads to a tragically grotesque episode. A quiet, sensitive man loves a quiet, pure girl. Their love for each other matures slowly in a beautiful idyll under the roofs of Paris, white on white, without embraces, without even the touching of hands. She has never known anything in life except hard work; and he wants to lead her slowly towards love and happiness. But it is enough, just once, for another man—a stronger and a simpler one—to have an hour to spare, and one girl's senses, aroused by the other kind of love, submit without resistance to the other man's strong embrace. Here again there is no struggle and the outcome is decided at the moment when simple, profane love makes its appearance on the scene. But the defeated lover's reaction is different. He no longer feels his defeat as a personal failure; for him it represents the total vileness of life where the victory of filth over purity is a foregone conclusion. Philippe expresses this feeling with superb, almost Greek, sensual simplicity. When the hero learns what has happened from the seducer himself—who is his friend—he, though usually a fluent and intelligent speaker, is left speechless. He leaves the café where the conversation has taken place—and is sick in the street outside.

Between these two books Philippe wrote *Marie Donadieu*, his book about love. It is the same conflict once more, but richer and subtler. The conflict is the content of the whole book. The confrontation, the moment in which it is decided who shall possess the woman, is perhaps the most strongly depicted, yet it is only one moment among many. The real issue is something else—the self-realization of the higher form of love, its ability to pass over the other kind, its transformation into longing. Every point this book makes is needle-sharp. Once more there are two friends struggling over a woman, but this time they are both men of sensibility and distinction, men who entertain a faint, unspoken suspicion concerning the human value attached to love, men who, at the very moment of their struggle with one another, are still able to feel a certain solidarity with each other. "Do you believe," says Raphaël, the simpler and stronger of the two, to his friend Jean Bousset when they are taking leave of one another, "do you really believe she is suffering? She is suffering less than we are."

Jean understands love, but Raphaël understands the woman. When Jean, long before he falls in love with Marie, visits Raphaël and Marie for the first time, he understands the nature of love through them. "*Je sais,*" he thinks, "*que ce n'est pas toi, Raphaël, qu'aime Marie, pas vous, Marie, qu'aime Raphaël, mais vous aimez je ne sais quelle part de vous même, la meilleure et la plus profonde, qui se mire dans l'autre et y multiple son image. Car l'amour est l'étendue et la multiplication.*" He has recognized the nature of his own love. But he does not know it and could not know it before Marie came into his life and had to leave it again. All he has recognized is his own life. Seeing Raphaël and Marie that day, he thinks: "You are happy, you are rich, but I am alone and trapped and there is no way open to me. There is the anchorite's way, the adventurer's way and the lover's way—but which of these have I chosen? Am I not a cripple because I have not chosen to travel along any of them?"

He does not yet know that his way is the unity of all three. He understands nothing about Marie and Raphaël and the relationship between them; he delivers himself of fine and clever monologues; but he is not clever enough to realize that his words are bringing home to Marie, for the first time in her life, that she has a soul and that no one has yet recognized it. The moment at which his words take possession of her flashes by without his noticing it—and for that reason without her becoming aware of it. They would never have found the way to one another if sheer accident had not willed it. But Raphaël sits with them, calm, smiling and serene; he loves his friend and his friend's conversation entertains him. Everything for him is simple and clear, that is why he uses few words and regards talking as a waste of time. For him it is something else that matters, something simpler and truer than the poets with their longing can conceive. Jean can talk beautifully, and great truth is in his feelings; but Raphaël's truth has weight, whereas Jean's is incorporeal and evanescent.

This weight is enough for decision, but not for anything more; and a life is more than a decision, even if it is weaker. Raphaël possesses Marie, she belongs wholly to him; only when he is absent can there be love between Marie and Jean. But Raphaël only has to appear and say to her, simply and calmly, "Come with me", and she will go with him unresistingly and Jean will unresistingly let her go. Raphaël says gently to Jean: "You talk and think and believe that it is enough if the truth is on your side. But women are children, you know; one must not be angry with them." And Marie follows Raphaël as if it were the most natural thing in the world to go with him; just as, years earlier, as a young girl, she gave herself to him, the first man in her life.

Yet she has always been unfaithful to Raphaël, whereas her love for Jean gives her purity. Whole areas of the soul which she never knew before are opened to her. Before Jean appeared in her life, she was a little animal, fluttering and fair—out for adventure, tasting everything, enjoying everything, without faith or true devotion—and Raphaël was only the harbour to which she always returned. What Jean understands through thinking, she knows through experience: that love is not pleasure but cognition; but she will never be able to distinguish between pleasure and cognition, and for him it will always remain a concept in the mind. Both have the same unity, but their two unities can never meet; he will remain an ascetic at the very height of pleasure—although, perhaps, a connoisseur, an Epicurean of asceticism—whereas for her, intellectual recognition will always be an empty thing because she recognizes only consciously, in order that one day she may not need to recognize any more. She is perhaps the only woman in his life and will perhaps always remain so, and yet he is unfaithful to her in the midst of their most passionate embraces. She was faithful to him before she ever knew him, when she was still being unfaithful to Raphaël with every chance acquaintance.

He has awakened her soul: no, he has given her a soul. She flutters no more; her soul spreads out its wings, beautiful and calm. He has given her purity and longing, and this longing—the great. wonderful, practical longing of woman—flies after the possession they have lost. Just as longing makes Indian shepherdesses imitate the words and movements of Krishna in their dances and songs, so that they may, in that way at least, feel at one with him, so the rhythm of his thoughts flows through her small, blonde, foolish head. When she returns to him she brings his words back to him on her own lips: she wants to win him back with his own weapons.

But he rejects her love. For him she was only a school of self-recognition; she has served her purpose and can go on her way. Only the man is recognized in love: the woman recognizes him, and he recognizes himself; she will never be recognized. A few months after the great separation Marie returns to Jean once more. But he tells her that it is too late. By going out of his life she has given him a new loneliness. He has always been lonely, but this is a new loneliness altogether. A more bitter, more painful one than before: the loneliness which follows after being with another: disaffection. He has remained alone with himself and the world; he has learned to experience himself and the world, and he knows now what is given and what is denied. He tells her simply and clearly of his great new discovery which will separate them from each other for ever: "Ah, il y avait bien autre chose que toi dans le monde." He says it to her and she sits on his lap and embraces him; her whole soul and her body are fighting for this, the only good, which she has recognized at last. Practised and clever, she slips off her blouse, she throws her naked arms round his neck, he sees and feels her breasts. But he stands up and goes to the window. It is too late. He is already living in another life—living life, he calls it, quoting Dostoevsky—the only life that is real to him. His love has become longing. He no longer needs a woman. He no longer needs love.

He does not say it in so many words, but every intonation betrays it: she has become the only woman in his life. He is a petty bourgeois in Paris, not a troubadour; perhaps he will never mention her name again. But every word and every action in his life will be an unspoken poem to what she has given him: she who came into his life and then left it again: she who took away his loneliness and then returned it to him. His new happiness, which he tries to explain to her in wordy, incoherent speeches, is the same as Dante's indestructible happiness after Beatrice refuses to return his greeting: "In quelle parole che lodano la mia donna." The difference is that he has never said it and never wants to say it.

Longing has made him hard and strong. He who lets her go on her way, speechless and weeping, crushed and trembling with pain, now has the simple strength needed for renunciation. The strength needed to be harsh and unkind. For he has destroyed her life.

3

Poverty forms the background to all these books. In them, poverty is truly—and not symbolically, as in the discussion about Eros—the mother of longing. Charles-Louis Philippe is the poet of the poverty of the small-town petty bourgeois. Such poverty is first and foremost a fact, simple, hard, unromantic and incontrovertible. But that is just what makes it transparent and shining. The people he writes about long to get out of their poverty, they long for a little freedom and sunshine, for something vaguely great which, even in their dreams, already has the sweet, small format of their world, something that can only be described as "living" and which, in the matter-of-fact directness of their language, means a little more money or a better job. Yet this longing is unfulfillable, and therefore it is a true longing. For the poverty of these people is not external; they are not poor because they were born poor or have been impoverished, but because their soul is predestined for poverty. Poverty is a way of seeing the world: a confused longing, expressed in clear words, for something different, and a much deeper love of what one would like to leave behind; a longing for colour in the grey monotony of life, and at the same time the finding of richly nuanced colours in that very monotony of the immediate environment. An eternal going back. It is the destiny of all Philippe's heroes; they want to get away and it looks as though they were going to succeed, then suddenly there is an impediment and they come back. Is it a matter of external causes? I do not think so. I think they want to give up even if they are not conscious either of the goal or of their reasons; something in them loves their poverty and their oppression—just as Jean Bousset, in love, loved his loneliness—and the external impediment is transformed internally into an insuperable barrier. This is how Philippe defines a poor man: *"celui qui ne sait pas se servir du bonheur"*. But their going back is circular: the home they find again has meanwhile become different. They are no longer at one with it, they love it deeply and tenderly and are loved in return, but in the last analysis they have become strangers to it and their love will never be understood nor requited. From now on something in their life remains permanently open and in a state of flux: their social position has become a state of longing.

This giving up, too, appears as a weakness, but it grows into a rich and happiness-bestowing world-view which can draw great treasures from its mature finality and yet is always conscious that it is only a surrogate. *"Les maladies sont les voyages des pauvres"*, says Philippe, and the phrase perhaps expresses most clearly the twin aspects of the condition of poverty, its inner wealth and outward weakness. It is a genuine and profound Christianity; here, Christianity has returned to its true beginnings and has become an art of living for the poor. Yet it is completely earthly, completely corporeal and life-affirming. Thus Chesterton's paradox that Christianity is the only framework in which the pleasures of paganism have remained alive becomes still more paradoxical and yet quite natural and simple. In Philippe, Christianity is not just a framework—it becomes paganism itself, and renunciation and pity are transformed into the joy of living. These new Christians are not seeking the salvation of their souls, they are seeking themselves or their happiness, or both. But their ways and means are profoundly in harmony with the nature of Christianity. Late paganism and early Christianity intersected and intermingled even in times when they were no more than historical facts; as timeless forms of feeling they can never be mutually exclusive. Action and love have become gentle and contemplative, and goodness is conscious and yet naïvely pleasure-seeking. "En ce temps-là," says Jean Bousset speaking of the past, "on était un guerrier. Aujourd'hui c'est le temps de la vie."

As a result of this there is an idyllic element in all the life-manifestations of these people. The small-town novel Le Père Perdrix is the most typical in this respect. An old workman is forced by life to adopt an idyllic way of life. He is incapable of working and so spends his days sitting on a bench outside his house. He plays with children, sometimes someone sits down beside him for a little chat, most often it is Jean Bousset (whose youth is described in this book). There is a great and profound silence around the old man who throughout his long life could hear nothing but the noise of his own work. At first he finds this silence around and inside him disturbing and tedious, but little by little he becomes accustomed to his new way of life and finds it enriching and beautiful. This is a small-town idyll; its real hero is silence, and silence unites and holds together the different lives described. One day the old man's children come to visit him— they are all married and live far away—and once the petty-bourgeois-proletarian fear of overspending has been overcome, there is a great feast. Everything is purely idyllic. The setting is petty-bourgeois and poor, but a pagan gaiety and self-oblivious enjoyment dominate the scene. The way these people eat and drink, their total absorption in physical well-being, is described with a firm, robust charm not unlike the description of the procession of Adonis in Theocritus.

But . . . because of this feast, the old man forfeits his right to a poor man's pension. Everything is purely idyllic. But . . . Jean Bousset, still a naïve dreamer at this stage of his life, loses his job and his career because, just this once, he speaks up for the workers. Jean Bousset obtains a small post in Paris and takes the old man whose wife has died in the meanwhile, to live with him. Now the two of them live together in the attic of a Paris hotel, the old man and the fair-haired youth. Everything is peaceful and beautiful and idyllic. But the old man feels that he is a useless burden to his friend—and, silently, he tiptoes out of his life.

Philippe regarded such an attitude as a weakness; he wrote to a friend that he had wanted to describe *"une résignation con-damnable"*. His conscious admiration went to the strong ones, the self-reliant ones, the ones who do not give up. He always let them win—yet Jean Bousset, who is the best of the weak ones, does not want to win, and the others, too, are made richer by their defeat than the winners by their victories. May we not conclude, then, that Philippe's love of the strong ones was in itself a form of longing?

His art draws its power and richness from this struggle against his own sentimentality. He wants to come out on the side of pure strength, even when this strength expresses itself in terms of depravity and vice—and he ends up with a profound sympathy with every living creature, a sense of brotherhood towards every man and woman. His cult of the strong hero is transformed into Buddhist pity—a Christianity without damnation, a Christianity wholly of this world. The world is hell and purgatory and heaven, all at once, and every man dwells in each of these kingdoms. *"Ce n'est rien, Seigneur. La faim des tigres ressemble à la faim des agneaux. Vous nous avez donné des nourritures. Je pense que ce tigre est bon puisqu'il aime sa femelle et ses enfants et puisqu'il aime à vivre. Mais pourquoi faut-il que la faim des tigres ait du sang, quand la faim des agneaux est si douce?"*

The same feeling, however, helped him to defeat his own sentimentality. The harshness of life is for him the natural condition of life. The life-affirming, joyful mood of his idyllic scenes is "yes . . . despite everything". His novels are never cowardly. Every one of his idylls is set against a background of danger threatening them from the outside; without such a background, the pure radiance of their untroubled serenity would become monotonous and dull. But the life-sense of most idyllists is too weak to stand the sight of real danger; when they describe their beautiful worlds of quiet happiness, they are escaping from the dangers of life, not incorporating those worlds magically into the harshness of reality. That is why danger or the threat of danger in their works is always purely decorative, external and without gravity (one need only think of Daphnis and Chloe or of the *pastor fido*). In Philippe's novels, too, danger always strikes from outside; his idyllic scenes are pure, harmonious and without inner discordance. But the cruel harshness which reigns outside is their constant precondition, their eternally unchanging background, often their very source. In all his books, this outside force is poverty. In *Bubu de Montparnasse*, a novel about prostitutes and pimps, it is also syphilis. The relationship between the student and the little

whore—a relationship which is convincingly beautiful and pure—
begins when he catches syphilis from her. The disease brings them
together. He feels excluded from the healthy, happy environment of
his parents' home: must he not give his love to the only one still
left to him, the very one who has caused his expulsion?

Philippe wanted to get away from his world of gentle pity. He
aspired to a harder, more rigorous world, and the ways which led
there were to be ethics and work. His ethical sense was always very
strong; even the abject Bubu is a product of it. When Bubu learns
that his mistress is ill, he wants to abandon her, but his friend—
another pimp—says he would consider such behaviour dis-
honourable. "On ne lâche pas une femme parce qu'elle a la vérole."
Philippe's development, like that of every strong man, was from
lyricism to objectivity. And objectivity, for him, meant work. The
message which rings out more and more clearly from all his writings
is that work is the only thing in life that strengthens and saves.
Here, he believed, was the way to overcome lyricism and
sentimentality. But lyricism can never be completely banished; the
more honest, the more impassioned our struggle against it, the more
cunningly it will always creep back. In *Charles Blanchard*, his last
novel, he meant to describe the new development, the process of
education culminating in work; it was to have been his *Wilhelm
Meister*. But the odd thing is that no one who has a lyrical talent is
ever granted such fulfilment; they all die before completing the novel
of their lives, and their objectivity remains a question-mark at a
crossroads. Philippe appears in one respect to be a curious exception.
For him the goal was never problematical as it was for the others;
but the steps which should have led to it were never completed.
What remains of his unfinished fragments reveals him as the
exquisite and profound idyllist that he always was. A leap still had
to be made from idyllicism to objectivity, and Charles-Louis Philippe
did not live to make it.

4

Longing is always sentimental—but is there such a thing as a
sentimental form? Form means getting the better of sentimentality;
in form there is no more longing and no more loneliness; to achieve
form is to achieve the greatest possible fufilment. Yet the forms of
poetry are temporal, so that the fulfilment must have a "before" and
an "after"; it is not being but becoming. And becoming presupposes
dissonance. If fulfilment is attainable, it has to be attained—it can
never be there as something natural and stable. In painting there
cannot be dissonance—it would destroy the form of painting, whose

realm lies beyond all categories of the temporal process; in painting, dissonance has to be resolved, as it were, *ante rem*, it has to form an indissoluble unity with its resolution. But a true resolution—one that was truly realized—would be condemned to remain an un-resolved dissonance in all eternity; it would make the work incomplete and thrust it back into vulgar life. Poetry cannot live without dissonance because movement is its very essence, and the movement can only proceed from disharmony to harmony and back again the other way. When Hebbel spoke of a beauty that exists before dissonance, he was uttering only a half-truth; one can try to achieve such beauty, but it can never be achieved. Is there not, then, a sentimental form of poetry? Is not the form-concept of poetry in itself a symbol of longing?

The two opposite poles in poetry are pure lyricism and pure idyll: longing and fulfilment, pure, made form in themselves and out of themselves. Lyricism has to exclude the entire world with all its actions and events in order that feeling may rest within itself, centred on itself, without any tangible object for itself. In the idyll, all long-ing should be reduced to silence; it should be the final, unequivocal and complete cancellation of longing. This is why the idyll is the greatest paradox in poetry, just as tragic painting is the greatest paradox in painting. Longing leads men to actions and events, and no action or event is worthy of becoming the fulfilment of longing. In the idyll, an event in its simple, empirical existence should absorb all longing within itself—longing should be completely dissolved in the event. Yet the event should remain an event, sensual and valuable in itself, and the longing should never lose its strength and bound-lessness. In the idyll, the purely outward aspect of life should be turned into lyricism and music. Lyricism is the wonderful, the magnificent naturalness of poetry; compared to it, all other forms are mere metaphysical compromises. Lyricism is the goal of all poetry of action and events, all poetry of active longing which has some effect upon the world of reality. But it can only be attained by going beyond all externals. At the great moment of tragedy the tragic hero is raised by his destiny high above his own actions. The hero of the pure, great epic races through the adventures of life; like the hero of tragedy, the epic hero rejects all externals, but his rejection, as it were, is horizontal where the tragic hero's is vertical; the dimension and multiplicity of what he leaves behind replaces, in the epic, the intensity of the tragic hero's upward surge. In the idyll there is no question of overcoming externals.

An event described in a matter-of-fact and sensual way is the com-plete expression of a boundless feeling: that is the essential nature of the idyll form. It is an intermediary form between the epic and the lyric, and at the same time their synthesis. Classic aesthetics placed the idyll and the elegy, which are profoundly akin to one another and complete one another, between the epic and the lyric. In that way they became timeless formal concepts and not merely accidental, historical ones. The idyll is the more epic form of the two; since, of necessity, it represents only an event or a destiny—otherwise it would become pure epic—it comes closest in its technique to the short story; yet the form of the short story is, in the last analysis, the furthest removed from the essential nature of the idyll. Today, I think, we should interpret the concept of the idyll more broadly that it was interpreted in classic aesthetics. There have always been imaginative writings which have lacked the epic's aspiration to create an image of a whole world—writings whose action sometimes barely amounts to that of a short story—and yet which go beyond the short story's preoccupation with an isolated, individual case and, out of their strong sense of soul, achieve a different, all-embracing power. In such writings the hero is just one soul and the action only the longing of that soul, and yet hero and action are truly realized. Such writings are usually called lyrical novels; I would rather choose the mediaeval definition of *chante-fable*. But really they are covered by the purest, broadest and deepest concept of the idyll—with a natural inclination towards elegy. (Let me name a few titles chosen at random: *Amor and Psyche*; *Aucassin and Nicolette*; *La Vita Nuova* and *Manon Lescaut*; *Werther, Hyperion*, and Keats' *Isabella*.) That is the form of Charles-Louis Philippe.

We should not call it a minor form. Only its format, its outward contours, are small. Its events appear arbitrary: "merely the accidental passion of subject for subject" as Hegel puts it. Yet it is a form of the strictest necessity; and every necessity is a circle and, as such, complete and world-embracing. Smallness and arbitrariness are the conditions of this form: reality, mirrored in an accidental, small event, becomes transparent; anything can mean anything. It is a paradoxical elevation and deprecation of life; but it is only possible because anything can be soul, because for the ultimate soul-necessity every outward manifestation of the soul is always small and arbitrary. The events are accidental as they are in the short story, but for other reasons. Here, what we call accident does not break through the dull, dead-weight neccesity of the concatenation of outward events; on the contrary, everything external, with all its necessities, is reduced to mere accident by the soul, and everything becomes equally accidental in face of it. Lyric becomes epic, and this signifies the conquest of the outward by the inward. The transcendental in life becomes graphically vivid. The rigour of the form consists in the fact that it remains epic—in the fact that inner and outer are kept together and apart with equal strictness, and the reality of life remains intact and undissolved. To dissolve everything in moods is banal, it can be done at any time; but when the inner-most centre of the soul, pure longing, wanders through corporeal and harshly indifferent reality—even if it wanders there as a stranger, an unknown pilgrim—then this is a sublime truth and a miracle.

The Middle Ages, which had a clearer concept of form than we have today, kept the epic and the lyric in such works strictly apart, perhaps for this very reason. But that is why their mediaeval form could never be anything but an assembly of separate elements, kept together by architectural means; the mysterious separateness-in-unity was then impossible. It became possible with the coming of the modern age and its discovery of atmosphere. What lay behind the appearances of things no longer had to burst through them in order to become visible; it could now be seen in them and between them, in the shimmering of their surfaces and the trembling of their con-tours. The inexpressible could now remain unexpressed. The form of *Werther* is more mystical than that of the *Vita Nuova*.

But the undisciplined pantheism of feeling which is characteristic of our time stopped at the possibility, over-extended it, and dissolved all form into a vague and formless lyricism of longing. The poets became indolent, stopped giving form to either feelings or events, and wrote poems which spilled over chaotically into infinity in a totally unrestrained prose. Atmosphere dissolved everything into mere mood, mere stammering. But this again drove out every element of secrecy, of concealment; by leaving everything unexpressed they finally told everything, loudly and importunately; their depth became triviality, and all their brilliant and richly nuanced flashes add up to a grey and dismal monotony.

They have stopped at the mere possibility; for atmosphere does not release things from the rigidity of their contours simply in order to dissolve them in the immateriality of transient moods, the incorporeality of contourlessness, but in order to give them something new—a gleaming hardness, a soaring gravity. Atmosphere is a prin-ciple of modelling. After the intoxication of Impressionism, Cézanne and his disciples recognized this in painting, and it seems as though in poetry, too, it will be the mission of France to re-create the old form out of the new means of expression available to us. Flaubert still used matter-of-fact realism and sure-fingered, classically pure draughtsmanship as a mask and an irony; but in France today these methods have become the means of expression for a new lyricism in prose. Charles-Louis Philippe was one of the first and perhaps the greatest and most profound of such writers. The stories in his slender books are constructed with rigour and sober matter-of-factness; their lyricism has been so completely absorbed into the clear lines of his drawing that, as things are today, its voice cannot be heard amid the noisy silences of formless novels whose subject is longing. Most people will regard Philippe as a disciple of realism, a poet of poor folk, like many another. And this is right and proper, for it proves that Philippe's longing truly dissolved itself into form.

1910

The Moment and Form

RICHARD BEER-HOFMANN

1

SOMEONE has died. What has happened? Nothing, perhaps, and perhaps everything. Only a few hours' grief, perhaps, or months: and then everything will be calm once more and life will go on as before. Or perhaps something that once looked like an indivisible whole will be torn into a thousand shreds, perhaps a life will suddenly lose all the meaning that was once dreamed into it; or perhaps sterile longings will blossom into new strength. Something is collapsing, perhaps, or perhaps something else is being built; perhaps neither of the two is happening and perhaps both. Who knows? who can tell?

Someone has died. Who was it? It does not matter. Who knows what this person meant to another, to someone else, to the one closest to him, to the complete stranger? Was he ever close to another? Was he ever inside someone else's life? Or was he just a ball thrown this way and that by his own wayward dreams, just a springboard to project himself into the unknown, just a lonely wall with a creeper growing upon it which could never, whatever happened, become one with it? And if he really meant something to someone, what was it? How, through what quality of his, did it happen? Was it the result of his particular character, his own weight and essence, or did it come about through fantasies, unconsciously uttered words, accidental gestures? What can any human being mean to another?

Someone has died. And the survivors are faced with the painful, forever fruitless question of the eternal distance, the unbridgeable void between one human being and another. Nothing remains that they might cling to, for the illusion of understanding another person is fed only by the renewed miracles, the anticipated surprises of constant companionship; these alone are capable of giving something like reality to illusion, which is directionless—like air. The sense of belonging together is kept alive only by continuity, and once this is destroyed, even the past disappears; everything one person may know about another is only expectation, only potentiality, only wish or fear, acquiring reality only as a result of what happens later; and this reality, too, dissolves straightaway into potentialities. Every rupture—unless it is a conscious ending, something which severs all the threads of the past from real life and ties them together in order to give them final and complete form, the static form of a finished work of art—every rupture not only cuts off the future for all eternity, but also destroys the entire past. Two men, two close friends, are talking together for the first time after a year's separation. "But they spoke of almost indifferent things; they knew that a chance word or the darkness of an empty street at night would later loosen their tongues, and they would say something very different to one another. Yet there was no 'later'." There was no more being-together, for one of the two friends died that night and the unexpected, brutal catastrophe illuminates with sudden sharpness what this friend meant to the survivor, what he could have meant to him—this friend whom he had loved, to whom he had always felt close, whom he thought he understood and who, he believed, had always understood him.

The questions pile up, the doubts come down and the lost possibilities whirl around in a mad witches' dance. Everything whirls, everything is possible and nothing is certain, everything flows into everything else—dream and life, wish and reality, fear and truth, the lying denial of pain and the courageous confrontation of sadness. What is left? What is sure in this life of ours? Where is the place, however bleak and bare, however remote from all beauty and richness, where a man may strike solid roots? Where is there anything that does not trickle away like sand between one's fingers just when one would wish to lift that thing out of the formless mass of life and hold it fast, if only for a brief moment? Where is the dividing line between dream and reality, the "I" and the world, deep meaning and fleeting impression?

Someone has died, and a tempestuous force sweeps away the bereaved survivor's questions. Perhaps this death is only a symbol of the survivor's loneliness, of his need to ask all the questions which were always latent in his mind but which the beautiful words and dreams of friendship had always lulled to sleep. This death—the death of the other—perhaps reveals most brutally, with a force which the sweet power of dreams cannot control, the great problem of human beings living together, the problem of what one human being can mean in the life of another. The irrationality of death is perhaps only the greatest accident among the myriad accidents of life; the rupture caused by death, the great estrangement that falls between the dead friend and the living one, is perhaps the same as the thousand estrangements and pitfalls that may occur in any conversation between friends—only in more perceptible, more tangible form. The truth, the finality of death, is dazzlingly clear, clearer than anything else, only, perhaps, because death alone, with the blind force of truth, snatches loneliness from the arms of possible closeness—those arms which are always open for a new embrace.

Someone has died. What is left to the survivor, and what this thing that is left makes of him, is the subject of Beer-Hofmann's few short stories. The world of these stories is that of the Viennese aesthetes: a world in which everything is enjoyed and nothing is held on to, in which reality and dream flow into one another and the dreams forced upon real life come to a violent end; the world of Schnitzler and Hofmannsthal. The heroes of Beer-Hofmann's stories exist in this world, and the richness of their ecstasies and tragedies gives this world its content; souls which are deeply and truly akin to theirs speak a language which sounds like their own. And yet it is not quite their world. Beer-Hofmann is not quite "one of them". His works grow from the same soil as theirs, but other suns and other rains have given different colours and quite different forms to his flowers. He is their brother, and yet they are as profoundly different as only brothers who are very alike can be. These other writers (and not only they) write the tragedy of the aesthete, the great reckoning of lives lived only inwardly, only in the mind, lives consisting only of outward-projected dreams, lives whose solipsism is carried to the point of näivety, whose cruelty to others is hardly cruelty any more, whose kindness is not kindness and whose love is not love; for every other person is so infinitely remote from such a life, so much the mere raw material of the only thing that matters—the life of the soul, the life of dreams—that the aesthete simply cannot be unjust or unkind towards anybody. Whatever he does to another and whatever another may do to him, his dreams will form it and mould it as they will, until it completely corresponds to the mood of his own passing moment. Every event—which after all is only the accidental consequence of a thousand possible causes, among which the real one can never be identified—fits into this, and always in the way that is most beautiful and most harmonious. ". . . In everything he sought nothing but himself and he found nothing but himself in everything. Only his own fate really fulfilled itself, and whatever else happened, happened at a great distance from him; events which he saw played on a stage, although they told the story of others, seemed to concern him alone; everything was only what it could give him: a *frisson*, an emotion, a fleeting smile."

And the reckoning? I have already said it: the brutal ending of dreams forced upon life. When destiny tears apart the finely woven harmonies of dreams so harshly that art is great enough to weave a beautiful, multicoloured carpet out of the frayed threads; when the soul, totally exhausted by a game which is always new and yet forever repeated, longs for truth, concrete, undeformable truth, and begins to recognize that the all-absorbing, all-adjusting nature of its own self is a prison; when every conceivable comedy has already been played on the stage of dreams and the rhythm of the dance begins to become gentler and slower; when one who is at home everywhere and yet nowhere begins to want to settle down at last; when one who understands everything begins to long for a single, powerful, exclusive feeling—that is the reckoning. The lamentation of Hofmannsthal's Claudio, the resignation with which, in Schnitzler's works, some ageing Anatol starts on yet another road that leads to self-created loneliness; tragically ironic meetings, when ironic smiles on sophisticated lips turn bitter and the game is continued only to mask the stifled sobs of a broken soul—or was that, perhaps, its only purpose even before the meetings? In such confrontations life takes its revenge; it is a harsh, ruthless revenge, a concentrated half-hour of humiliation and torment exacted as retribution for the arrogance of a whole lifetime.

Beer-Hofmann's writings grow from the same soil, but his strings are more taut and the sounds he plucks from them are soft and deep where, with any other writer, they would have broken long ago. There is nothing "literary" about his aesthetes; the world which exists inside them is not the product of the isolating ecstasies of their own art or the art of others, but of the turbulent richness of life itself, the golden load of the thousand instants which make up life. Nor is there any resignation or renunciation in them. Their lives are over-sophisticated indeed, but there is also much freshness and naïvety in them, much energy and desire to discover the innermost nature of things, even if it is often mingled with sterile play and self-tormenting scepticism. By such play they hope to embrace life and conquer all its fullness; such play—although they may not know it themselves—is a net which they fling out to catch all the truth that may be learned about life and men. Thus their aestheticism is only a condition, even when it completely fills them, even if they experience it as a whole form of their existence and believe that to feel in this way is the sole content of their lives. Beer-Hofmann's aesthetes are perhaps the most extreme of their kind, and yet they are not tragic—at least not as aesthetes. For what forces them to halt upon their lonely road is not any inherent failure or weakness of theirs, nor does their whole life have to collapse for them to stop and shudder at themselves. No, what happens is that someone dies, and the unexpected, brutal catastrophe which destroys any possibility of true knowledge of the other puts an end to all their play, which never existed for its own sake, and which now loses all its meaning. The spring of the machine which caused the puppets in the puppet theatre to dance is broken, and even if the dance continues for a while longer, it must soon come to an end; even if the fantasies of the soul, no longer inhibited by anything, continue for a while longer to leap wildly and aimlessly from one extreme to the other, in the end they must tire and come to a halt, for the limit which reality imposed on them was their sole reason for existence. And then their life is over.

The aesthete's tragedy in Beer-Hofmann's work is, then, similar to that of Kleist's *Prince of Homburg*, the play of which Hebbel once wrote that in it the shadow of death and the fear of death produce the catharsis which everywhere else is achieved only by death itself. Someone dies and, robbed of their contents, the dreams constructed round that person collapse; and the collapse of these dreams is followed by that of all other dream-constructs. The survivor is now bereft of the entire content of his life, but his will for life engenders a new life all the same—not as beautiful a life as the old one, yet a stronger one; a less harmonious one, less complete in itself, yet one that fits better into the world of other men, into true life; a less sensitive and subtle one, but deeper and more tragic. Perhaps this solitary dreamer is wreathed in a veil of dreams that is more dense and yet more insubstantial than that of any other, yet the veil tears—for this very reason perhaps—before it is too late. Beer-Hofmann's aesthetes are so sensitive that a mere detail, an accidental happening, is enough to change everything within them, yet they are strong enough for the bankruptcy of their life-contents not to cause the collapse of their actual lives. More courageous and more sophisticated, more frivolous and more complex than all others, they connect everything with everything else (the mood of the moment being the sole fixed central point of their world); but when the great experience comes and destroys the connections, it destroys only the contents, leaving the form intact. The experience detaches the form from the content, it relieves his heroes from being the starting-point for all the rest, it gives reality to the outside world and to all those who live in it and puts an end to the delusion that their "I" is something fixed and solid at the centre of the world; it seizes hold of them and throws them into the midst of life, where everything is *really* connected with everything else.

"This is what he learned in that evening hour: his life was not going to fade away like a single solitary note sounded in an empty space. His life existed as part of a great, solemn dance, measured from the beginning of time, permeated by the all-pervasive music of external laws. No harm could befall him; to suffer was not to be an outcast; death did not separate him from the All. Every action was bound up with everything, necessary to everything, indispensable to everything; an action was perhaps a service, suffering perhaps a dignity, and death perhaps a mission.

"And he who sensed this, however dimly, could walk through life as a just man—his eye not turned in upon himself, but surveying the distance. . . . Fear was a stranger to him; whatever surface he might strike, be it harder than rock, righteousness spurted from it like water from a spring, and justice like a never-ending stream."

This, then, is the new world, the way that leads out of aestheticism: a deep, religious sense of everything being connected with everything else. The sense that I can do nothing without striking a thousand resonances everywhere, most of which I do not and cannot know, so that each action of mine—whether I am aware of it or not—is the consequence of many thousands of waves which have met in me and will flow from me to others. That everything truly happens inside me, but that what happens inside me is the All; that unknown forces are my destiny, but that my fleeting moments may likewise be the unknowable destinies of men I shall never know. Thus the accidental becomes necessary; the accidental, the momentary, the never-recurrent is transformed into a universal law, and ceases to be accidental or momentary. It is the metaphysic of Impressionism. From the viewpoint of one in whom the waves meet, everything is accidental—for example, which wave reaches him, and when and where; none of this can have anything to do with his real, inner life-process. Every wave is accidental: the only stable law is that all life is a play of accidental waves. But if everything is accidental, then nothing is accidental, then there is no such thing as accident, for accident has meaning only if it exists simultaneously with the laws of life and supervenes only occasionally, in a few concrete cases.

In such a world, what can a man mean in the life of another? Infinitely much and yet infinitely little. One man can be the other's destiny, his catalyst, his guide, his re-creator and his destroyer, yet all in vain—because he can never reach the other. This is not a tragedy of misunderstanding, of any crude failure of comprehension, nor is it the tragedy of the subtle egoist who creates everything in his own likeness. Here, understanding itself—the deepest and most beautiful, the most tender and loving understanding—is crushed under the wheels of fate. Once again Beer-Hofmann pushes the opposite poles further apart than the others. For them, the tragedy consists in the fact that there exists and can exist no understanding between men; for him, in the fact that understanding can exist, that it is within reach, but that it is useless. Yes, men are capable of understanding everything, of seeing with the deepest love and sympathy everything that happens to another and why, but such understanding is quite irrelevant to what is really happening, and is bound to remain so. From the world of understanding you cannot do more than look across into the world of real life; the gate that separates the two is closed forever and no power of the soul can break it down. Things happen and we do not know why; and even if we did, we should still know nothing. The very most that we can know is what happens within us when fate strikes, and what happens in another who has contributed something to shaping our fate, and in the one whose fate we represent. This we can know, and we can love the other for it, even if our life is destroyed as a result of our meeting. We can exist truly and deeply inside the life of another, yet everyone remains alone with his own innermost fate. Everyone is alone, even in relation to his own self.

Beer-Hofmann's poetry grows out of this vision—a vision in face of whose all-embracing astonishment all our categories lose their meaning: faith and doubt, love and renunciation, understanding and estrangement and all the other words we use. It is a world in which everything is really melted down into one: it contains everything and yet it also negates everything. It is a chorus in which each word we use can only describe the mood of each strophe, but an antistrophe grows out of every strophe and—as in music—they have no existence except together, no meaning nor significance nor reality except as a unity.

2

Every written work, even if it is no more than a consonance of beautiful words, leads us to a great door—through which there is no passage. Every written work leads towards great moments in which we can suddenly glimpse the dark abysses into whose depths we must fall one day; and the desire to fall into them is the hidden content of our lives. Our consciousness allows us to evade them for as long as we can, yet they are always there, gaping at our feet when a view opening unexpectedly before us from a mountain top gives us a touch of vertigo, or when roses whose scent still surrounds us suddenly vanish from our sight in the evening mist. Every written work is constructed round a question and progresses in such a way that it can suddenly stop at the edge of an abyss—suddenly, unexpectedly, yet with compelling force. And even if it leads us past luxuriant palm groves or fields of glowing white lilies, it will always lead to the edge of the great abyss, and can never stop anywhere else before it reaches the edge. This is the most profound meaning of form: to lead to a great moment of silence, to mould the directionless, precipitous, many-coloured stream of life as though all its haste were only for the sake of such moments. Written works differ from each other for no other reason than that the abysses can be reached by many paths, and that our questions always arise out of a new astonishment. Forms are natural necessities for no other reason than that there is only one path leading to the abyss from any one place. A question, with life all round it; a silence, with a rustling, a noise, a music, a universal singing all round it: that is form.

And yet (only today, admittedly), humanity and form are the central problems of all art. If we have any right to enquire into the origin of things which have existed for thousands of years and, after passing through the storms of those millennia, have perhaps become strangers to their own origins—if we have any right to discuss the origins of art, we may say that art becomes possible, and in particular the art of writing came to have a meaning, only because it can give us the great moments we have been speaking about. It is only on account of these moments that art has become a life-value for us, just as woods and mountains and men and our own souls are life-values—but the life-value of art is more complex, deeper, closer and yet more distant than any of these, more coldly objective towards our life and yet fitting more firmly into its external melody. Art can be this, solely because it is human and only to the extent that it is human. And what of form? There have been times when the reply to such a question would have been: why, is there anything else but form? There have been times—at least, we believe there have been—when the thing we call form today, the thing we look for so feverishly, the thing we try to snatch from the continual movement of life in the cold ecstasy of artistic creation, was simply the natural language of revelation—an unstifled scream, the untramelled energy of a convulsive movement. In those times no one asked questions about the nature of form, no one separated form from matter or from life, no one knew that form is something different from either of these; form was just the simplest way, the shortest path to understanding between two similar souls, the poet's and the public's. Today this too has become a problem.

The conflict cannot be grasped theoretically. If we think about form and try to invest the word with meaning, the only meaning which emerges is that form is the simplest way to the strongest, most permanent expression. And then (such analogies, we feel, confirm us a little) we think of the golden rule of mechanics and of that doctrine of national economy which has it that everything strives to achieve the maximum results with the minimum expenditure of force. Yet there is a conflict, and we know it. We know that there are artists for whom form is the immediate reality, and we feel that life has somehow slipped out of these artists' works; they are artists who give us the only goal, leaving us unsatisfied because a goal is satisfying only when it represents an arrival, the long-awaited end of a long, hard road. (From another point of view I might say that these artists give us only the road and not the arrival.) And then there are artists whose souls are so overflowing with riches that form appears to them as an impediment, and having no cup into which to pour their golden wine, they let it evaporate into an empty haze: with sadly lowered heads they renounce all perfection; and works which can never be complete, which can never mature, fall from their weary hands. Hebbel, that great master of form, once put it this way: "My plays have too many intestines, those of other playwrights too much skin."

Alternatively, the question can be posed as a conflict between richness and form. What may, what must be sacrificed for the sake of form? Must anything be sacrificed at all? And why? Perhaps because the existing forms are not the product of our life today, or because our life today is so inartistic, so haphazard, so uncertain and weak, that it is quite incapable of transforming for its own ends whatever aspect of the existing forms could change with time, and must be changed if we are to have a living art. And so today we have either abstract form—the result of thinking about art, of admiring great works of the past and exploring their mysteries—a form which cannot encompass the specific qualities, the beauties and riches of the art of today; or else there is no form at all, and anything that produces an effect does so simply through the power of shared experience, and becomes incomprehensible as soon as the experience is no longer shared. This may or may not be the reason for the conflict, but a conflict there most certainly is; and, just as certainly, there was no such conflict in the really great periods of the past. The Greek tragedies were able to give expression to the most personal lyricism; the great compositions of the Quattrocento remained intact despite the fantastic multicoloured treasures which were packed into them—and, of course, this was still more true of earlier times.

To sum up: there are written works today which produce their effect through their form, and others which do so despite their form. The question for many (it should be the question for all) is whether it is nevertheless possible to achieve harmony: in other words, whether there is or can be such a thing as a style of today. Is it possible to extract an essence from the abstraction of forms, and to do it in such a way that today's life is not wholly drained from it? Is it possible to make the colours, the scent, the flower-dust of our moments—which may be gone tomorrow—endure for ever? Is it possible to grasp the innermost essence of our time, the essence that even we ourselves may not know?

3

Beer-Hofmann and forms: we have to speak of two specific forms, the most rigorous and binding ones, the short story and tragedy. Both these forms handle abstractions; in both, the characters, their relationships and their situation are as abstract as the minimum necessary for illusion permits. The short story is the abstraction of great rationality; in it, several necessities intersect and all possibilities are completely and utterly cancelled out—not only the possibilities thrown up by the story itself, but also those which can be developed intellectually out of the abstract theme. Tragedy is the abstraction of irrationality, a world of disorder, of non-causal factors, dominated by unexpected, destructive, analysis-defying moments. Both (in a manner which absolutely excludes the means used and the effects produced by the other and by all other art forms) utilize only that part of human nature which allows itself to be fitted into their abstract themes.

This is Beer-Hofmann's great stylistic problem (as with all real artists, it is not his problem alone, but in his case we see it at its clearest and sharpest). Chance and necessity are not strictly separated from each other; the one grows out of the other and then again into the other, merges with it, robs it of its specific meaning, renders it unsuitable for the abstract stylization which the form postulates. To put it briefly: the subjects of Beer-Hofmann's stories are irrationalities, matters of chance; but he makes necessities of them, and all the qualities of his style therefore work against the intended effect; and the more so, the more these qualities are strong and authentic. Beer-Hofmann's plays are held together by the power of necessity, but this necessity consists in elevating the accidental to the status of the necessary; and the more subtle and solid the construction he builds out of the interweaving of complementary accidents, the more fragile the whole construction becomes, the more obvious the insecurity of its base. What does this stylistic problem mean for the short stories and the plays? For both it means that their proportions are ruined by the intrusive richness of the momentary And—even if we leave aside the richness of this author's world—the *principium stabilisationis* in both cases is so complicated, encompasses so much and is so flexible and multilinear, that it is almost impossible by means of this *principium stabilisationis* (and yet there is no other means) to simplify men and situations and to keep them at the proper distance from us, in the right relationship to one another and to their background; it is almost impossible to reduce the background to the necessary size, to make it appear only as a background; and then the unrestrained rule of psychology is inevitable.

In the short stories this means that a situation set up in an insoluble way is nevertheless resolved. His short stories achieve surprise just because their form neglects the element of surprise. The resolution can, of course, come only from the inside, through large, richly lyrical analyses of the soul. Beer-Hofmann's short stories are about the development of a human being after an accidental disaster, but the question is precisely this: can the development of a human being be the subject of any art form other than the novel? (In this sense, the novel is not a strict form.) Why is this an important question? Because the development of a soul can never suggest anything other than itself (the less so, the more purely it is of the soul). Why? Perhaps because psychology—we speak here only of art, but this is true outside art as well—is bound to seem arbitrary. The development of a soul cannot be given form by artistic means, by the force of any direct appeal to the senses; the only possible method is to sensualize the beginning and the end of the development, or the partial development, with such energy that even the second stage appears convincing (and this is very rare), so that, looking back from the point of destination, we accept the process of getting there, we accept the actual development as possible—although never as the exclusively possible way, for we can always imagine any number of psychological connections between two points. Furthermore, the smaller the influence of outward factors, the more such a development will concern only the soul, and the more psychological the treatment, the less convincing therefore will be the form-giving; for the possible number and variety of connections between two points increase in proportion with the distance between them. The relative size of their respective worlds is what distinguishes the novel and the short story most obviously from each other. The subject of the short story is the isolated happening, the subject of the novel is the whole of life. The short story selects a few characters and a few outward circumstances from the world, as few as will suffice for its purpose; the novel lets every conceivable element enter into its structure, for nothing is superfluous to its purpose. To summarize the stylistic problem briefly, Beer-Hofmann's short stories, in their schema and intended effect, are like novels, but their starting points and their means of reduction are those of the short story; in this way he loses much of the concentrated power of the short story without gaining anything to make up for it. His short stories fall apart; seen from the perspective of the beginning, the end is weak, while from the viewpoint of the end, the basis appears arbitrary—as does the line of development. Thus whatever is fine in these short stories can only be purely lyrical in character. It is interesting to note that this dissonance appears the more sharply, the more profound, rich and absorbing is Beer-Hofmann's lyricism. Formally speaking, his thinnest short stories are the best.

So far as the plays are concerned, the situation is still more difficult, yet also, perhaps, a little simpler. In the plays Beer-Hofmann deepens the problem still further, so that the two poles no longer exclude one another. (The essential nature of the conflict of style in the short stories is perhaps that Beer-Hofmann wants them to achieve something higher than this particular form can achieve, and therefore he is forced to destroy the limits, the frame, of the form.) The opposite is true of the plays; the thing which is actually shown is stylized upwards until it becomes suitable material for dramatic expression. What does this mean? Drama is always ruled by a world necessity, by an inexorable, always self-fulfilling, all-embracing, cosmic set of laws. The actual content of the play does not matter— i.e., among an unlimited number of possible contents there are always several which are equally suited to serve as the basis for dramatic stylization. From this viewpoint, then, no objection can be made to the fundamental basis of the *Count of Charolais*. What would destroy any other drama—the completely accidental nature of the catastrophes and changes described—here becomes deeply moving and, in some cases, actually dramatic. Here, chance is an *a priori* element of the work, it is present in its very atmosphere; indeed it creates the whole, everything is constructed upon it and out of it, and for this very reason it achieves its dramatic or tragic effect. For the all-determining criterion of whether a moment is dramatic or not is, ultimately, nothing but the degree of its symbolic power—how far that moment encompasses the whole nature and destiny of the characters and how far it symbolizes their lives. Besides this, everything else is merely external, and if this quality is lacking then nothing else will do, neither refinement nor vehemence, neither passion nor vivid pictorial quality. In a few important cases the irrationality remains unprocessed; for the process which cancels out the accidental nature of the accidents, thus making them dramatic, can only—given the means of expression at our disposal today—be a *post facto*, psychological one; it can only be expressed through the souls of those who experience it. Thus any direct sensualization and, with it, full symbolization—the truly dramatic effect—is rendered extraordinarily difficult and almost impossible. Or, to put it better, whether or not the dramatic effect is achieved is not necessarily and organically connected with such sensualization or symbolization; the question is rather whether we have any other means of giving dramatic expression to such a view of the world than that of *post facto* reflection.

This question has not yet been solved in Beer-Hofmann's only play to date. Of the three great turning-points with which it deals, one lies in the play's pre-history, in the past, and is deeply moving and perfectly suggestive. This solution (which we also find in *Oedipus Rex*) was used by Ibsen, and by Hebbel before him, in an attempt to surmount irrationalism. But although this device is effective, it cannot be used in all cases; for—as Paul Ernst has shown from a different viewpoint—it necessarily makes the artist and his art poorer because it allows him too few variations and too little freedom of movement within the play. The other two crucial events in the play (which are not dealt with in this manner) are not convincing enough as happenings, however much we may be gripped by all their consequences. And yet, even from the point of view of the abstract concept of drama, it would be wrong to say that the play is a failure. As always, the path Beer-Hofmann has chosen is the most hazardous, and perhaps for that reason it promises something for the future. None of the scenes is purely psychological; the second, which is the bolder one, is first and foremost *not* psychological. In it, a strange concatenation of chance events causes a woman whose love of her husband and her child is unshakeable and who, in her feeling, remains completely faithful to her husband until death, to be seduced by another man—a man whom she perhaps despises and to whom, in any case, she has always been completely indifferent. A combination of strange accidents brings the two of them together, completely alone, in a darkened room; the young man's melancholy appeals leave the woman completely unmoved, but at the very moment when she feels most secure in her love of her husband, a burning log falls out of the grate and hurts the man whom she has just rejected with such total indifference. And now, although at heart she still remains indifferent to his words, she hears them with a certain human sympathy. It is this unthinking, human sympathy which makes her take the first step (which need not lead to anything further): he asks her to walk back with him for some of the way through the garden.

I want the night
to see the two of us walk through the garden.
Night who is everywhere. I want the night
to be my confidante. Wherever I may find myself

I can then speak to her about you. She
will have seen us. She knows about you and me.
"Night," I shall say to her, "you saw her, did you not? is she
not beautiful?" and I shall complain:
"She does not love me, night, and I love her so much."

Then the garden with its twisting paths, the snowflakes falling in
the moonlight, his strange words still ringing in her ears, lead her to
take the next step and then the next, until it is done, without her
having wanted it, without, perhaps, her realizing what was happening. And when, later, in the great tragic confrontation, when deep
sadness has already replaced the rage and bitterness of the first
moments, and her husband asks the melancholy question:

> What was it then, you proud one,
> that brought you to this pass?

she can only shake her head sorrowfully and answer: "I don't
know," and, groping for words: "He said . . .". It seems to me that
the wonderful and terrible hazards which rule our lives, the terrify-
ing wonders of the strange moments of life, become completely
visible at this point of the play; we can hear them clearly in the
music of the accompanying circumstances; they assume a living
quality which makes us feel directly how inexorable is the rule of
chance over life. Here the accidents, the moments, become symbolic
—symbols of their own sovereign power. This is the first step towards
true dramatic expression. The first step only; for here, too, their suggestive effect is largely a post facto one, and the events serve only as
an explanation and a basis for the feeling that comes afterwards;
they do not give us this feeling with the overpowering force of direct
experience, but only as a faint premonition. At other moments, there
is a sense of immediate experience as well. It is at these moments and
in the path they trace that the first signs of a modern dramatic style
can be detected. What makes the style a modern one are not the
superficial, insignificant features of life today, of little deep-down
interest to anyone (as is the case, for example, with naturalist
drama); it is the fact that our specifically modern way of feeling,
evaluating and thinking, its rhythm, its speed and melody, grows into
the forms, becoming one with them, becoming at last form itself.
Beer-Hofmann's drama is full of an incredible wealth of unsuspected
beauty. The very way in which he poses the question—even if the
day for the answer has not yet arrived—makes it possible for him to
find wonderful new solutions. Since Goethe and Schiller, verse has
been needed to keep dramatic characters at the distance which great
tragedy demands; but Goethe and Schiller gave up the attempt to

invest their characters with full humanity. Schiller wrote to Goethe, with pride or resignation, that individual character really does not belong to drama, and that the "ideal masks" of Greek tragedy were more suitable to drama than the human beings to be found in Shakespeare or in Goethe himself. Beer-Hofmann is the first since Kleist, perhaps, whose verse succeeds in keeping the whole world of the play in tune, so that no character stands out through the excessive realism of his individuation; yet none of the play's flexibility, its fragile subtlety, its momentary quality, is lost as a result.

Beer-Hofmann's technique of depicting human beings, which is deeply bound up with the very nature of the play's construction, is a technique of great moments. (The Browning of *Pippa Passes* and the lyrical scenes of the young Hofmannsthal are a preparation for this development.) Each of his characters comes to life suddenly at a certain point in the play (or, depending on his importance, at several points). And just when his own destiny and character enter into the central axis of the drama, he ceases to be the picturesque background to the fate of the other characters. The force which accumulates in the human intensity of such moments, and this force alone, is what gives life to his characters and sheds a powerful light upon the past and the future. The character is fully worked out, completely nuanced and differentiated, but all this happens only at these moments; all other movements are consequent upon the potential energy released at these moments and, for that reason, it is reduced to a minimum, so that, however intense it may be, it cannot destroy the construction. To sum up: other playwrights of today (e.g., Hofmannsthal) simplify their characters, reducing them to the barest necessities; but Beer-Hofmann stylizes only their forms of expression.

He applies this technique to both the psychological and structural relationships between his characters—to the representation of human relations. Here again a strict choice is made in terms of time; only the most intense moments which are of central significance to the drama are chosen. Beer-Hofmann's characters have no other point of contact; here, he does not experiment with developments. At these moments the contact between characters takes place, as it were, along their entire surface; they have completely entered into the drama because their entire nature is dramatic (and not only a few separate traits); and consequently the author's lyricism—however broad-flowing, however many-voiced it may be—never becomes undramatic. In all the successful moments the breadth of the basis of stylization—that great stylistic hazard which has to be met and overcome—turns into a source of great beauty: nothing outside the strict concern of the drama is included in the relationships between the characters. The work is not threatened by the great danger of modern psychological drama— the danger of the characters becoming broader and more finely nuanced than their dramatic destiny absolutely requires, so that the pure and deep lyricism of their contacts with one another never rises above pure lyricism and so becomes static and, ultimately, uninteresting and flat. Beer-Hofmann also avoids the other major weakness of today's dramatic stylists: the risk that, because a complex and involved inner life is compressed into a few bare outlines, a figure who was perhaps originally intended as normal tends to appear pathological. (Hofmannsthal's Jaffier is perhaps the most striking example of this risk.)

The great isolation in which Beer-Hofmann's characters live, like all the characters in modern drama, does not render their relations with one another joyless, even if the lines of their profiles are drawn a little harshly—in order to make them stand out clearly in the perspective of the play. Beer-Hofmann's characters do not talk past each other, they are not stiff and sharp with one another, their words meet like arms stretched out for an embrace, they intertwine, they seek and find each other, and only behind these encounters do we perceive the eternal loneliness, as vast as ever and all the more shattering for being so affectionate. The precipices which separate his characters from one another are planted with roses; his characters send out rays in all directions, but the roses cannot bridge the precipices, and the rays of light are reflected only in mirrors.

Beer-Hofmann is one of those artists who, without claiming to do so, reject any suggestion of compromise and refuse the superficial heroism of pursuing a narrow programme to its extreme. The old abstractions are too narrow for what he has to say; he wants to create new abstractions so that his whole lyricism may be dissolved into form. This separates him (I mention names only to place him within a context) from Paul Ernst's rigidly stylized, purely artistic architecture as it does from Gerhart Hauptmann's splendid sculptures. Of all today's writers he is the one who is fighting the most heroic battle for form. It seems that a profound intelligence is forcing him to keep the overflowing richness of the moments he describes within strict limits. Forms are still barriers for him, barriers against which he has fought long and hard—not for the sake of what he has to say but, rather, to avoid silence and resignation. In each of his works the edifice he has so beautifully constructed breaks down at several points and sudden perspectives open up before us, sudden glimpses of something—who knows what? Life? His own soul? If posterity, which recognizes only what has been given form and ignores all spontaneous expression, should prove indifferent and uncomprehend-

ing towards him (however justifiable this may be), we still cannot
help loving those moments in which Beer-Hofmann the artist shows
himself to be weaker than Beer-Hofmann the profound and authentic
human being.

1908

Richness, Chaos and Form

A dialogue concerning Lawrence Sterne

THE scene is a simply furnished, middle-class girl's room where new and very old objects are mixed together in a curiously inorganic fashion. The wallpaper is brightly coloured and rather common, the furniture is small, white and uncomfortable in the typical fashion of young middle-class girls' rooms; only the desk is handsome, large and comfortable, and so is the big brass bed in the corner, behind a folding screen. On the walls, the same inorganic mixture: family pictures and Japanese woodcuts, reproductions of modern paintings and of old ones currently in fashion: Whistler, Velasquez, Vermeer. Above the desk, a photograph of a fresco by Giotto.

At the desk sits a strikingly handsome girl. On her lap lies a book: Goethe's aphorisms; she turns the pages and appears to be reading; she is waiting for someone. The bell rings. The girl now becomes immersed in her reading, so that she hears the bell ring only for the second time; she stands up to greet the newcomer. He is a fellow-student from the University, about the same age as she, perhaps very slightly younger: a tall, well-built, fair-haired young man of twenty or twenty-two, his hair parted at the side; he wears pince-nez and a coloured jacket, is studying modern languages, and is in love with the girl. Under his arm he is holding several tattered leather-bound volumes—English authors of the beginning of the nineteenth century. He puts them down on the desk. They shake hands and sit down.

She: When are you going to give your paper at the seminar?

He: I'm not sure yet. I still have to look up a few things. And I must go through a few volumes of the *Spectator* and the *Tatler*.

She: Why take so much trouble—for those people? What you've done is good enough just as it is. Who'll notice if anything's lacking?

He: That may be so. But Joachim. . . .

She (interrupting him): Oh yes, because you always discuss everything with him.

He (smiles): Perhaps not only because of that. And what if it were? I do it for my own sake. I enjoy working, just at the moment. I lik it. It's so nice to deal with little facts. They bring me face to face with many things which otherwise I should have been too lazy to notice. And yet I'm not thinking hard and I don't have to make an effort. I lead a comfortable life—and call it my "scientific conscience". And I like to be called a "serious scholar".

She (delighted with the conversation): Don't be cynical, Vincent. I know very well how important it is for you to round off your material—how deeply serious you are about it all.

Vincent (who is not altogether convinced, but pleased to accept this flattering view): It may be that you're right. Certainly. (Another small pause.) I've brought the Sterne along. As you see, I didn't forget.

She (picks up the volume and strokes the binding): A beautiful edition.

Vincent: Yes, it's the 1808 one. Lovely. Have you seen the Reynolds frontispiece? Splendid, isn't it?

She: And the other engravings, how pretty. Look at this! (For a while they look at the engravings.) What are you going to read me from it?

Vincent: I might start with the *Sentimental Journey*. Then you could read *Tristram Shandy* by yourself later on, if you felt like it. Agreed? (His English accent is very good but rather consciously affected.) Listen now. (He reads the beginning of the journey, the first little sentimental episode with the mendicant friar, the humorous classification of the travellers, the purchase of the chaise, the first sentimental-platonic adventure with the unknown lady. He reads rapidly and nervously, with a pure accent, without any sentimentality, using an ironic tone of voice—so faint as to be almost imperceptible—especially in the sentimental passages. The way in which he is reading suggests that the text is not very important to him: just something, among the many beautiful things that have come his way, that has happened to please him, and even the manner in which it pleases him is a question of mood, of taking pleasure in his own moods. When the two of them are deep in their reading, there is a knock at the door, strong and emphatic, and immediately afterwards Joachim, another fellow-student, enters the room. He is as old as they, perhaps a little older, taller than Vincent, dressed in black, almost shabby. His features are hard and fixed. He too is a student of modern languages and he too is in love with the girl. This is why he is displeased by the atmosphere of quiet harmony which he senses between the pair. He goes up to them and shakes hands. Then he takes the book out of Vincent's hands and says: What are you reading?

Vincent (a little nervously, partly because Joachim's entrance has disturbed them, partly because he senses a disguised challenge in the question): Sterne.

Joachim (accepting the tone, smiling): Don't tell me I'm disturbing you?

Vincent (also smiling): Well, yes, as a matter of fact. Sterne isn't for you. He's beautiful. Amusing. Rich. And perfectly irregular!

She (displeased by the interruption): Are you two going to have another argument?

Joachim: No. At least, not I. And today least of all. (To Vincent.) There's just one thing you've got wrong—don't be afraid, I don't intend to argue—it isn't that Sterne is not for me, although it's true that I don't care for him. It's this one here (he points at the volume of Goethe, which is still lying in the girl's lap) that Sterne doesn't go with. Were you reading that before you started on the Sterne?

She (grateful that somebody has at least noticed her, and for this reason speaking warmly to Joachim, with a touch of concealed irritation against Vincent): Yes, I was reading Goethe. Why do you ask?

Joachim: Because, while you were reading Sterne, you must surely have asked yourself: what would *he* have said to this? Wouldn't he have resented this confusion of heterogeneous bits and pieces? Wouldn't he have despised what you were reading, on account of its raw, disordered state? Wouldn't he have called your Sterne an amateur because he reproduces sentiments just as they are—as raw, unprocessed matter—and makes no effort to unify them, to give them form, however imperfect? Haven't you read what he says about amateurs? Do you remember? "The amateurs' mistake: to want to establish a direct link between imagination and technique." Couldn't this sentence be placed at the head of any critique of Sterne? And, if one had just read such words—if the experience was still fresh in one's mind—wouldn't one find it difficult to become totally absorbed in Sterne's formlessness?

She (a little uncertain, but trying to disguise it by assuming a particularly firm tone of voice): I'm sure there's something in what you say, but Goethe didn't . . . after all, that wasn't quite. . . .

Vincent: I think I know what you want to say; please let me complete your sentence for you. Goethe was never a dogmatist. "Let us be many-sided!" he said. It was this you wanted to refer to, wasn't it?

She (nods a warm and grateful "Yes". Once again, as before the interruption, her silence signifies agreement with Vincent, and both men are aware of it.)

Vincent (continues to speak): "Prussian beets are delicious, especially when served with chestnuts, yet these two noble fruits grow a long

way from one another." I could quote a thousand passages like this.
—No! To speak against such delights in Goethe's name will not do.
Not against any delight, any pleasure. Nothing that enriches us, that
can add something new to our life!

Joachim (a little ironically): You don't say!

Vincent (whose irritation is coming more and more to the surface):
As if I didn't know—and I'm perfectly certain you know it too—
what Sterne meant to Goethe, with what grateful affection he always
spoke about him, as of one of the most important experiences of his
whole life! Don't you remember? Don't you recollect the passage
where he says that the nineteenth century, too, must realize what it
owes to Sterne and learn to see what it could still borrow from him?
Don't you remember? And what about the passage where he says:
"Yorick Sterne's was the most beautiful mind that was ever at work;
whoever reads him must feel fine and free at once"? Don't you
remember?

Joachim (with an appearance of great calm and superiority):
Quotations don't prove anything. You know that as well as I do. I
know that you could go on for another half an hour quoting to the
same effect, and I'm sure you know that I could go on quoting in
support of my point of view without ever leaving Goethe. Each of
us could quote, for our own purposes, Goethe's resigned remark that
it is impossible to convince anyone—because false judgements are
deeply rooted in everyone's life—and that all one can do is to keep
repeating the truth. And each of us could attack the other by quoting
the equally resigned saying that our opponents think they have
defeated us when they simply state their own views over and over
again and pay no attention to ours. No! Quotations support everything and, in reality, are at the basis of nothing. And even if all the
quotations of world literature were against me—still I would know
that in this argument Goethe would be on my side. And even if not
—Goethe could afford to do many things which we can't!—even
then, my first reaction would remain the right one: it is a fault of
style to read Sterne after reading Goethe. I may even be still more
right than I realized at first: it is impossible to love Goethe and
Sterne at the same time. The man to whom Sterne's writings mean
a great deal doesn't love the real Goethe—or doesn't properly understand his own love of Goethe.

Vincent: I think it's you who misunderstood Goethe, not I (looks
at the girl), not we. You love something about Goethe which he himself regarded as secondary. But you're right about one thing: let's
not argue in his name. He can't prove either of us right, he can only
supply us with ammunition; and in any case, it would, I think, be a
matter of considerable indifference to him which one of us was proved

right. Come to think of it, it really doesn't matter a jot which of us
is right.

To be right! To be wrong! What a trivial, unworthy issue! How
little it has to do with the things that really matter! Life! Enrichment! Suppose I concede that you are right (I'm doing nothing of
the sort, mind): suppose I admit that we have been inconsistent,
that the two subjects with which we have occupied ourselves are not
in harmony with one another—what then? If we experience something even a little strongly, the very intensity of the experience
refutes any theory imposed from the outside. It is simply not true
that there can be a strong, decisive contradiction between two powerful experiences. This is inconceivable because the essential lies
precisely where I am putting the emphasis—it lies in the power of
the experience. The possibility that both things can be a powerful
experience in our lives excludes the possibility of contradiction. The
contradiction is somewhere else, outside the two, outside what we
might know about them—in nothingness, in theory.

Joachim (a little ironically): You could say that about anything.
Everything is. . . .

Vincent (interrupts him vehemently): And why not? Where is
unity, where is contradiction? These are not properties of works or
artists, they are just the limits of our own possibilities. There is no
a priori in face of possibilities, and once the possibilities have stopped
being possibilities—once they have been realized—there is no
criticism that can be addressed to them. Unity means being together
and staying together, and the fact of being together is the sole
applicable criterion of truth. There is no higher instance than
this.

Joachim: Don't you see that what you're saying, if one thought it
through to its logical conclusion, would lead to complete anarchy?

Vincent: Not at all. Because there isn't any question here of thinking through or of logical conclusions, but of life. Not of systems, but
of new, never recurring realities. Of realities where each successive
one is not the continuation of the one before but something quite
new, something that can in no way be foreseen or captured by
theories of "thinking through to logical conclusions". The limit and
the contradiction are only inside ourselves, just as the possibility of
unity is inside ourselves. If we feel an insoluble contradiction anywhere, it means that we have arrived at the frontiers of our own self;
if we speak of contradictions we are speaking of ourselves, not of outward things.

Joachim: That's certainly true. But we must never forget that there
are frontiers within us which are not drawn by our own weakness
or cowardice or lack of sensibility—as opposed to our capacity to

receive impressions—but by life itself. And if a warning voice within us forbids us to cross these frontiers, it is the voice of life and not of fear in face of the richness of life. We feel that our life lies only within these frontiers, and whatever is outside them is mere sickness and dissolution. Anarchy is death. That is why I hate it and fight against it. In the name of life. In the name of the richness of life.

Vincent (sarcastically): In the name of life and of the richness of life! That sounds very fine so long as you don't try to apply your theory to anything concrete. As soon as you take it out of the lonely realm of eternal abstraction, it becomes a theory which does violence to the facts. Don't forget that we are talking about Sterne. Is it against Sterne that you are raising your objections—in the name of life and the richness of life?

Joachim: Yes.

Vincent: But don't you realize that that's just where Sterne is practically unassailable? That even if we deny him everything else in the world, we simply have to leave him this one thing—richness, fulness, life? I don't want to speak now of the wealth of small stylistic jewels in his work, nor of that teeming richness which is in every life-manifestation, however small, contained in his writings. I would only ask you to think of the exuberance of certain characters in *Tristram Shandy* and, when you think of these characters, to think also of the marvellous many-coloured variety of their relationships with each other. Heine admired Sterne as a brother of Shakespeare's, and Carlyle loved him as he loved nobody else except Cervantes. Hettner compared the relationship between the brothers Shandy to that between Don Quixote and Sancho Panza—and he thought the relationship in Sterne's book was the deeper one. Don't you see that because it is deeper, it's much richer? The Spanish knight and his fat squire stand side by side, like actor and scenery, and each is no more than a piece of scenery for the other. They complement each other, certainly, but only for us. A mysterious destiny has placed them next to one another and leads them at each other's side throughout their lives. Every life-experience of the one becoms a distorted image of all the life-moments of the other, and this continuous sequence of distorted images is the symbol of life itself—a distorted image of the hopeless inadequacy of the relationship between human beings. Very well, but can't you see that despite all this, Don Quixote and Sancho Panza have no relationship with one another, at least not as human beings? There is no interaction between them except of the kind that usually exists between figures in a picture: a linear and a coloristic one, but not a human one. Daumier was able to express their entire relationship, their entire character, in purely linear terms. It would not be too paradoxical to maintain that everything Cervantes wrote, all the adventures he invented for his heroes, all of it is only a commentary on these pictures, only an emanation of the idea, the aprioristic life —outdoing real life with its vigour and liveliness—which it was possible to express in this linear relationship. Don't you know what it means that this relationship between two destinies could be expressed in such a way? In this fact lies the monumentality and, at the same time, the limit of intensity of Cervantes' idea. It means that his characters have something mask-like about them: the one is tall and the other short, the one thin, the other fat; and the existence of each, being of such a kind, is absolute and excludes its opposite from the start. It means that the relativism, the fluctuation of their relationship is to be found only in life, in adventure, while the two men are as yet completely unbroken. Their gesture vis-à-vis life is unified, their character is mask-like, and there is no communion between them and no possibility of contact.

Sterne, on the other hand, puts relativity into his observation of human character. Both the Shandy brothers are Don Quixote and Sancho Panza at once. Their relationship renews itself at every moment, turns itself inside out and becomes its own self once more. Each of them fights battles with windmills, and each is the uncomprehending, sober spectator of the other's fruitless and aimless battles. To reduce this relationship to any formula whatsoever is impossible. Neither of the Shandy brothers wears the typical mask of a constant attitude vis-à-vis the world. What they do, the way in which they live as the grandsons of the noble knight, all this appears secondary beside the grotesque and sublime inadequacy of their relationship. It has been said, not without justice, that Walter Shandy's inability to cope with objects is the theoretician's eternal impotence face to face with reality. I know that it is possible to say this, and it may be that no one has yet expressed the powerful symbolism of this situation with sufficient precision and depth. Yet what is really profound in this book are the relations between people, not any individual person. The really profound thing is the all-embracing multiplicity and richness of the circle, even if this circle is formed of only two or three persons. How rich—to speak of nothing else—is the relationship between these two brothers! Is it not moving to see how they are conscious of belonging together, how a sense of inner identification—at a depth inaccessible to thought—exists within them, how the great fear that this very thing will separate them, irrevocably and forever, quivers in their innermost souls? It is very moving when each tries, from time to time, to share the other's quixotry, and at other times attempts to cure the other of it—the very content of his life. Yet there is no occasion when their

relationship does not manifest itself in grotesquely comic fashion—
generally with such force that the actual cause of the comedy, the
profound inability of these two souls to meet, is heard only as a
faint accompaniment to the great laughter. I don't know if it has
struck you how the play on words becomes a life-symbol in the
world of *Tristram Shandy*—a symbol of the indicative, mediating
nature of words, a symbol of the fact that words can convey an
experience only if the listener has already experienced the same
thing.

The brothers Shandy speak with one another, not to one another;
each pays attention only to his own thoughts and receives the other's
words, but not his thoughts of feelings. Every word which distantly
relates to the thoughts of one of them sets those thoughts in motion
again, and the other proceeds in the same way. Here the play on
words makes intersecting paths on which the two men, eternally
looking for one another, cross each other unrecognized. Walter
Shandy's relationship with his wife is a similar one, full of the same
tragically grotesque sorrows and melancholy joys. It is full of the
philosopher's sorrow over his wife, who never understands anything
he is talking about, never even becomes aware that she cannot understand him, never addresses any question to him, never becomes angry
or excited over him. The most complex intellectual apparatus cannot
disturb this woman's tranquillity, which makes her accept everything that the philosopher who is her husband may say—and in
consequence of which everything happens just as she wants it to
happen. The philosopher writes a book about how his son should
be brought up out of reach of his mother's influence—and while he
is writing it, the mother, naturally, brings up her son. And think of
his few little satisfactions, sad and humorous at the same time—as
for instance when the wife, wanting to eavesdrop on the love scene
between Uncle Toby and Mrs. Wadman, tells her husband she is
curious and asks him whether she may listen, and the happy
philosopher replies: "Call it, my dear, by its right name and look
through the keyhole as long as you will." And then that other great
inadequacy, Uncle Toby's great, primitive goodness that knows
nothing of life or men, Uncle Toby whose utter helplessness in face
of all reality causes the most painful confusion, the greatest mis-
understanding among quite simple, normal people. Yet in this night
of mutual incomprehension there gleams a faint light of communion
between two men—Uncle Toby and his servant, Corporal Trim, who
once served in the army under him and who is as limited as he, yet
whose passive, kindly nature, the nature of a man born to serve
others, allows him to accept all his former captain's nonsense without
a hint of criticism. In the whole world only these two fools under-

stand one another—and they only because chance has endowed them with the same fixed idea !

This is the world Sterne saw, this is the world whose immense richness he glimpsed, its profound sadness and its absurdity, sadness and absurdity at one and the same time and inseparable from each other. He saw the many-sidedness of this (apparently only two-sided) circle—the tears that turn to laughter, the laughter from which tears spring; the life that becomes true life thanks only to this many-sidedness, and to which I can never do full justice because I cannot observe the centre of the circle from every point on its periphery at the same time. (Pause).

The girl (suddenly): How beautiful! The centre . . . (Vincent looks at her, waiting the applause that is due to come; the girl blushes because she realizes that she has given herself away; in great confusion.) Yes—the theory of the centre—the Romantic theory of the centre. . . .

Joachim (is also embarrassed. But he is embarrassed because he feels that, in view of all his convictions and especially in view of the existing situation, he ought to argue the case of abstract form against Vincent, but he doesn't know how. Many ideas occur to him, but he senses that any argument, in face of such fine and sincere enthusiasm, would be petty, and is afraid of making himself thoroughly disliked by the girl if she, too, feels his arguments to be petty. But on the other hand he knows that for the self-same reason he must, after all, come out with his objections and must not allow a mood conjured up by Vincent to settle upon the three of them. And so he speaks softly and a little uncertainly, with many small pauses.) How beautiful. Yes . . . How beautiful . . . this novel would be . . . if it were like that . . . if it were really like that. What a great novel it might have been.

Vincent (to tell the truth, he is embarrassed too. He senses that there are justified counter-arguments somewhere in the air, and—because he knows Joachim—he can guess roughly from where the counter-attack is going to come. However, he doesn't yet know for certain how the attack will be framed, and still less how he should defend himself. He vaguely senses that he got carried away, but is also aware that he must keep his enthusiasm intact, if only for the girl's sake. For these reasons he begins to talk in a very nervous manner, in short, disconnected sentences whose form suggests that he is throwing them away.): Might have been! Ridiculous! (He tries to keep the conversation off the problem of form for as long as possible.) You know **perfectly** well that I've quoted only a few details out of the infinite richness of the whole. Might have been! I've never heard such a thing!

Joachim (still uncertain and very cautious): Yes, of course . . . there are some things in Sterne's book which you haven't mentioned, and I'm sure you've had to leave out a great deal that might have increased your enthusiasm still further. (The girl, who had been listening to Vincent's speech with enthusiastic approval, now realizes that what he has been saying is, perhaps, a little dubious. She does not want to take sides at this stage, and tosses her head, offended because Joachim seems to be identifying her with Vincent simply because she has expressed support of the latter. Joachim interprets this gesture as agreement with himself and goes on speaking more boldly—yet the girl's irritation is directed at him because of the uncomfortable situation he has put her in.) But please don't forget that there are many other things which you have left unmentioned as well. You've left out many things whose absence—believe me— has done much to advance your argument.

Vincent (like Joachim, he has misinterpreted the girl's gesture. He now speaks more passionately than before, trying to recover his superiority which threatens to slip through his fingers): I think I understand what you are hinting at, but—forgive me—your objection strikes me as extremely petty.

Joachim (interrupting him): I hadn't finished what I was trying to say . . .

Vincent (going on as if Joachim had not spoken): You were saying, more or less; "What a fine novel *Tristram Shandy* would have been if only Sterne had . . . written it". And that I had completely falsified Sterne by leaving out everything that might have damaged. . . .

Joachim: But I. . . .

Vincent: A moment, please. You are thinking, I'm sure, of Sterne's digressions, his episodes which seem to have nothing to do with the subject, his grotesque philosophical passages and much else of the same kind. I know. But how superficial it is to think that everything which at first glance seems out of place—perhaps only from a prejudiced, excessively theoretical point of view—must be disturbing and damaging to the greatness of a work ! Remember that where you can see only confusion and disorder, there may be an intention which, although it may not be clear to you, is nevertheless profound and true. I think Sterne knew very well what he was doing, and he had his own theory of literary balance—admittedly, a rather individual one: "to keep up that just balance betwixt wisdom and folly," he writes in *Tristram Shandy*, "without which a book would not stand together a single year". I think I know the feeling which produced and encouraged this idea of balance. You may remember what I said about Sterne's many-sided view of human beings. Well, his method is the only one or—what does it matter if it is the only one or not?—at any rate an excellent one of bringing such many-sided human beings together and, later, setting them in motion. The shortest way of defining the method would, I suppose, be this: a fact, and all round it a disordered host of associations which this fact evokes. A man steps forward, speaks a word, makes a gesture, or else we merely hear his name, and then he disappears again in a cloud of images, ideas and moods that his appearance on the scene has produced. He disappears in order that all our thoughts may encompass him from every side; and although his reappearance destroys much of the many-sidedness which his earlier appearance had evoked, still the new event creates a similar richness, made even richer by the recollection of what has gone before. That is the novelist's state of mind when he has seen a significant gesture of his character's; the diarist's when he reflects upon his experiences and orders his memories; the state of mind of the true reader, the reader who reads more than the print, when he wants to identify with the characters who are strangers to him. And such, in real life, is the technique whereby any man recognizes another.

Joachim (still speaks a little uncertainly, warming up only slowly as he goes along): There may be something in what you say. Yet I still feel the same as I did before: how fine this novel might have been! Because you're doing the same thing again—you're leaving things out to help Sterne and your own argument. You speak of Sterne as though your words did no more than reveal the immanent rhythm of his apparent chaos, and yet you are extracting from him only what can—with your help—acquire rhythm, and throwing the rest aside—perhaps without realizing it.

Vincent (nervously): That isn't true.

Joachim: To give just one example—an important one (the many dead passages, already unreadable today, would support my point of view anyway): I once read in some English literary historian's work that Sterne uses the word "humour" in the old, Elizabethan sense. And indeed, what else is the eternal theme of blindness and nonsense, the "hobby-horse" of each and every one of his characters, but the "humour" of the characters in Ben Jonson—the abiding quality of a man, so powerfully present in everything he does that it almost ceases to be a quality and it seems as though all his life-manifestations were merely the qualities or properties of this "humour"? Not a quality which a man possesses, but one which possesses the man. I could also say: the "humour" is a mask left over from an ancient, still wholly allegorical culture when life and drama were personified by types: a culture in which the whole nature of a man was compressed into an epigram, an inscription; and for as long as the play continued, he could never, not even for a moment, be anything but true to type. And, by the way, any mask—even one as threadbare and full of holes as the masks worn by Sterne's characters—is still an obstacle to interaction between men: so that, in actual fact, Sterne didn't go beyond Cervantes in this respect.

Vincent (triumphant): Now try to look objectively at what you've just said. I don't mean Sterne's position vis-à-vis Cervantes. The face and the mask are mutually exclusive in concept only; in reality they are simply two poles, and it's quite impossible to tell exactly where the one ends and the other begins.

Joachim (quickly): But here it *is* possible!

Vincent: Well, as I said, that isn't the important thing. But haven't you noticed how everything you said about "humour" fits in with what I said about Sterne's view of humanity? Except that you (a little ironically), *c'est votre métier*, gave formal reasons for what I said, too. What you call "humour" is the centre round which everything is grouped—all the things that Sterne shows from an infinity of aspects in an attempt to do justice to life. I, too, had to presuppose the existence of such a centre, even if I didn't explicitly speak of it, for without one everything would simply have collapsed. And if I define it—as you've already done—then I make the connection even stronger and the substance of this world even richer, its matter still more varied. Because there is unchanging matter in this world, and continually changing matter too; and we can separate the one from the other only in abstraction: just as a face is modelled, for the purpose of our vision, by the air that surrounds it, by light and by shade.

Joachim: I've already said that I don't want to argue (Vincent smiles and Joachim pauses before continuing to speak). Nor am I arguing. (Vincent smiles again, but then his glance falls upon the girl; he sees that she is not smiling with him, and for a moment he feels: how far we are from her just now, both of us, and each as far as the other! He is suddenly afraid, and would like the whole conversation to stop. And so he listens to Joachim impatiently, waiting for an opportunity to express his new mood. But Joachim in the meantime goes on speaking.) There's just one more thing I'd like to say. How wonderful it would be—everything we're talking about—if it were so! If what you call Sterne's method were really his method, if Sterne viewed his characters in the least consistently from the same perspective. Please don't interrupt me just yet! Take the notion of "viewing from the same perspective" as far as you will, but while you do so, think of a particular kind of seeing—unless there is that, there can be no art—and then try to apply it. You'll see how far you can get that way. And incidentally, Sterne himself knew it very well. When he speaks about Uncle Toby's kind-heartedness, he senses

that he can't do it in the same style as when he describes Toby's
nonsense with the building of the fort and all the rest of his innocent
lies and illusions—he senses that it is impossible to use his "hobby-
horsical" method.

Vincent (speaking nervously and very impatiently. He would like
to end the discussion no matter how, but cannot help, even so, wanting to find an argument which, he believes, will clinch the matter.
Yet every word he speaks sweeps him along against his will, so that
he finds it difficult to outline his position in just a few sentences.)
Here you go again, running after Sterne's sovereign extravagances
with your accountant's yardstick! Always the same yardstick!
Sterne could afford to reveal a fault in his own method—especially
a fault which really wasn't one at all. Don't you feel, for all that
you may say, how inexpressibly deep is the connection between
these two traits of Uncle Toby's character? Sterne's sovereignty,
which sees the thousand possibilities and limitations of a method all
at once, is at this point playing with the natural limitations of his
method, of any method. Sterne's sovereignty . . .

Joachim: Or, rather, his impotence . . .

Vincent (would have expected any interjection rather than this. His
resolve to put an end to the debate is becoming weaker and weaker;
he is becoming more and more deeply involved with the subject at
issue, forgetting everything else. Now he says with strong, "objective" indignation): No, really! How can you say such a thing?
Can't you distinguish between play and weakness, between throwing
something away on purpose and letting something fall?

Joachim: Surely, but just because. . . .

Vincent (interrupting): Well, I see the same refinement of naïve
certainty here as in all his compositions. To break up the unity
simply so as to make it felt still more strongly—to make the unity
felt at the same time as the things which are destroying it! To be
able to play: that is the only true sovereignty. We play with things,
but we remain the same and the things stay as they were. But both
have been enhanced during the game and through the game. Sterne
plays, always, all the time, with the gravest notions of man and
destiny. And his characters and their destinies acquire incredible
gravity through the fact that all his playing doesn't really shift them
from the spot where they stand, it just washes against them like the
sea against a cliff, yet the cliff stands firm in the play of the waves,
and the more violently the waves break against them from all sides,
the more we sense the cliff's solidity. And yet he is only playing with
them! It is only his playful will that gives them this gravity; and
although he cannot take away what he has once given, still his playful will is stronger than its children; he could pick them up and play

with them, for all their weight, at any time, whenever he liked. And
this immense force you call. . . .

Joachim: Impotence, yes. The question to ask in such a case is: what
is the writer playing with? And when, and why? Because there is
no need to go any further, or because he can't go any further? Is
the reason for playing really his inability to control his exuberant
strength, or is the whole thing a clever cover-up for weakness?
Because, don't you see, there's nothing in the world that covers up a
disability more successfully than the playful gesture of sovereignty.
I can't help it if I sense something like this in Sterne's gesture—
something that isn't strength. The only *raison d'être* of play—the
only time when play is born out of strength, not incapacity—is
when it only seems to be play. Not until . . . not until *everything
has been said* can we cry out: "Why all this talk?", and break off
and begin playing. And I never have the impression that Sterne has
really said everything—no, not in a single instance. When you turn
my own example against me, you appear to be right—but it's only
an appearance. Because the unity you see in Toby's character doesn't
exist, except perhaps in yourself. Perhaps it exists—I'm inclined to
believe it—in Sterne's vision, too. But I deny that it is present in the
work. In life one can and should continually change the point of
view from which one looks at things. Paintings indicate, in a
sovereign manner, the place from which we must look at them; but
once we have put ourselves in that place, it is all over with the
painting's sovereignty. If we have to look at one part from here and
another part from there, that is no longer a sign of sovereignty but
of impotence. And I feel impotence here, as I do in many other parts
of Sterne's works. And in many other respects as well.

Vincent: Such as?

Joachim: Such as the fact that his works never satisfy us.

Vincent: But that's intentional, of course.

Joachim: Not always. I'd go further and say: not except in a few
cases. Please don't think I'm insensitive to the humour of such
passages as, for instance, the one where Tristram arrives at last, after
long preparations which continually intensify our suspense, at the
grave of the unhappy lovers in order to wallow in tears and
sentimental sensations—only to discover that the famous grave
simply doesn't exist. No, I'm thinking of passages like the one where
—let me just give one small example—he introduces into a story
begun but never concluded, very subtly and at great length, the
episode of Corporal Trim's love story with the Belgian nun—only to
rob everything he has so carefully prepared of all its effect by a
dreadfully weak and banal sentence. I feel the same about a great
deal of Toby's adventures with the widow Wadman—which

Coleridge, for all that he admired and loved much of Sterne's work, called "stupid and disgusting". It's the same everywhere: whenever he comes to the really decisive point, he drops the important thing and turns it into play. Because he can't give it serious literary form, he pretends that he doesn't want to.

Vincent: You forget that both books, as we have them today, are fragments. Who knows where Sterne would have taken the love story between Uncle Toby and the Widow Wadman if he had lived long enough to finish writing it?

Joachim: What I'm saying is that he couldn't have lived that long. His works were planned as fragments—if, that is, they were planned at all. Once he said it as a joke—Kerr quotes the remark in connection with *Godwi*—that he would continue his novel to infinity if only he could get a good contract from his publisher.

Vincent (during the last exchanges he has sensed Joachim's superiority; now he is waiting for his opponent to say something that will lay him open to attack. Therefore he can, as it were, hear only the words): Of course, if you read it like that, then everything is as you say, but then you're reading it quite differently and. . . .

Joachim: You misunderstood me. I'm perfectly aware, believe me, that this was only a joke. But behind such jokes I see Sterne's gesture —the gesture I was speaking about a moment ago. All that Sterne does here—and this, I suppose, was always the technique of his [sarcastically] playful sovereignty—is to reveal his cynicism, but not in the area where he is really cynical. He reveals a weakness in himself and in his works, a weakness which, as you so rightly pointed out, isn't a weakness at all; but he does it only in order to divert our attention from other, real weaknesses that really are there. Not at all in order to make us feel his strength. He is superciliously cynical here because we mustn't see that he would be incapable of composition even if he wanted to compose.

Vincent (feels Joachim's advantage still more strongly, but doesn't want to admit defeat and therefore steers the discussion once more towards the crucial issues): You quoted a passage from *Tristram Shandy* a moment ago; but you forgot to say what Kerr wanted to demontrate by it. . . .

Joachim (has the impression that he has said all there was to be said, and feels—if only fleetingly—a strong distaste for all talk. While Vincent speaks, he looks attentively at the girl, whom he had quite forgotten during the last exchanges, and a mood overcomes him like Vincent's a little while ago; therefore he speaks indifferently): Because I didn't consider it important.

Vincent: But it's very important. The question here is what this

composition that you insist on so much should really have expressed.
Yet one can't argue over the events in the soul which call for
expression; a discussion has meaning only if these events are agreed
upon. Then one can argue over whether the artist succeeded in
expressing them, and how and why. Kerr speaks of Romantic irony
—you surely remember the passage—and quotes Sterne once or twice
in that context. He lists the principal stages in the development of
Romantic irony, from Cervantes by way of Sterne and Jean Paul to
Clemens Brentano—Romantic irony whose central thesis is that "the
artist's arbitrary will suffers no law over itself". Sterne, by the way,
expresses the same thought when he leaves two chapters out of the
sequence—chapters eighteen and nineteen of the ninth volume—
and then inserts them after chapter twenty-five, saying: "All I wish,
that it may be a lesson to the world to let people tell their stories
their own way". You called this arbitrary will "impotence" a
moment ago, and I can understand that—from your point of view—
you're bound to see it like that. But isn't there much that is
doctrinaire in a point of view like yours, and much that does violence
to the facts? It is possible that Sterne didn't want to compose
because, in your sense, he was incapable of composition. But the
question to ask here is whether he *needed* composition. Would it be
important to him if his world-view, the immediate form of his life-
manifestation, his way of feeling and expressing the world, consisted of boundless subjectivity and a Romantic, ironic play with all
things? No writer and no work can do more than give us a
reflexion of the world in a mirror which is worthy of reflecting all
the world's rays.

Joachim (would prefer to say nothing; but he hasn't quite managed
not to listen, and on hearing the word "worthy" he has such a strong
sense of the superiority of his arguments and of Vincent's implicit
admission of that superiority that he is forced to interrupt him):
Yes, a mirror that is worthy. . . .

Vincent: If we go back to the world-view, if we succeed in understanding anything at all as a world-view, then all your allegations of
impotence lose their meaning. Then the only thing that matters is to
feel the intensity of these forces, to enjoy and to love their effect.
Sterne's sovereign play with all things is a world-view, don't you
understand? Not a symptom but the mysterious centre of everything, making all symbols clear, resolving all paradoxes in its
symbolism. All romantic irony is a world-view. And its content is
always the sense of self, intensified into a mystical sense of the All.
Think of the *Athenaeum* fragments, of Tieck, Hoffmann and
Brentano. You must surely know those famous and beautiful lines
from Tieck's *William Lowell*:

All beings are because we've thought them.
The world lies bathed in a dim twilight
And into its shadowy caverns
There falls a gleam that we bring with us.
Why does the world not break into a thousand fragments?
We are the destiny that keeps it whole.

Do you not see how sublimely everything that springs from such a life-sense is elevated to play—or reduced to play? All things are important, certainly, for the all-creating self can make something out of anything; but, for the same reason, because the self can create something out of anything, nothing is really important. All things have died, only their soul-possibilities remain alive, only those moments upon which the self, sole giver of life, has cast its rays. Don't you see that such a sense of life can't find any other adequate expression except for Sterne's or that of his precursors and successors: Romantic irony, sovereign play? Play as religious worship, where every separate thing glows like a sacrifice upon the altar of the holy self; play as life-symbol, as the strongest expression of the only life-relationship that matters, the relationship between self and world? The only sovereign evaluation is this: I alone am really living in the entire world, and I play with all things because I *can* play with all things—because all I can do with the things of this world is to play. Do you not sense the melancholy arrogance inherent in such sovereignty—the resignation that lies concealed in this gesture of mastery over all things? Not even the ultimate sovereignty of the gesture with which Sterne sets the sources of the deepest gaiety flowing by striking the rock of our most ancient sorrow with the wand of his playfulness? Yes, it is true, a work of art can only give us a reflection of the world; but the poets of true subjectivity know it, and through their play they give us a truer image than those others, so earnest and so dignified, who claim to recreate real life among empty shadows.

Joachim: You've used the mirror twice as a symbol of the poet's way of giving form to the world. But the first time you attached an epithet to the word, and by way of epithet I shall try to come back to Sterne, from whom your words have carried you such a long way.

Vincent: I've been talking about Sterne all along—him and nothing else!

Joachim: You wanted to eliminate any criticism of the artist's starting point from our debate, yet quite involuntarily—I can quote your own words—you were compelled to admit the possibility of such criticism. You said the rays are reflected in a mirror which is worthy of reflecting all the rays. Worthy of reflecting—what does that mean? At this point I might ask who is entitled to speak to us; for is it not true that here, too, there are boundaries and here too there is a question of worthy or not worthy?

Vincent: You're exaggerating the importance of the epithet I used.

Joachim: Perhaps you're underestimating its real significance.

Vincent (impatiently, aggressive): You listened to what I was saying much as the brothers Shandy listened to each other. You turn everything into a play on words because you hear only words—and opportunities for making a rejoinder.

Joachim (likewise a little impatiently): That's as it may be. Still, the only important question for me is this: which part of a human self is worthy to serve as a mirror for all the rays of our world?

Vincent: The whole self! Otherwise it has no sense. Otherwise what emerges as "style" or "form" is a falsification, a conscious or cowardly evasion.

Joachim: Yes, of course the whole self. The only question is, whose whole? I shall be very brief—and you may accuse me of being dogmatic. But I want to make myself extremely clear. Kant distinguishes between the "intelligible" and the "empirical" self. To put it in a nutshell: an artist may express his whole self—indeed he must do so —but only the "intelligible" self, not the "empirical" one.

Vincent: That's empty dogmatism.

Joachim: Perhaps not quite as empty as all that. Let us take a closer look at the justification for complete subjectivity—the necessity for it, if you like. Why is it there, and what is the use of it? Perhaps its only right to existence—you hinted at this yourself—is that, without it, we should never be able to discover anything of the truth. In other words, it is the only way to truth. But we must never forget that it is only the way to truth, not the goal to which that way leads; always and only the mirror which reflects the rays.

Vincent: How you do overwork that image!

Joachim: It's a good, meaningful image. With its help, I can perhaps say what I want to say still more clearly and precisely. The self is the mirror that reflects the world's rays for us, and—we did agree it should reflect *all* the rays, didn't we?

Vincent (impatiently): Yes, yes.

Joachim: Then—you see how my simple, almost trivial image illuminates the whole problem—then the question does not even arise which part of the mirror must reflect the rays: the whole, naturally! But the question does arise how the mirror must be constituted in order to reflect all the rays and give a complete image of the world.

Vincent: It may be a distorting mirror.

Joachim: Possibly. But it must not be a clouded one. The highest power of subjectivity is that it alone can communicate real life-contents. But there are subjectivities—and in my opinion Sterne's is one of them—which, instead of performing this essential act with supreme intensity, thrust themselves as an obstacle between me and these life-contents, so that any true and important subjectivity is lost—precisely through them and because of them. Thackeray. . . .

Vincent: Surely you don't mean to quote Thackeray?

Joachim: I can well imagine that you don't care for what he wrote about Sterne; I find much of his petty-bourgeois moralizing displeasing. But I think that's less important than the fact that he and I agree on this particular point. "He fatigues me," writes Thackeray, "with his perpetual disquiet and uneasy appeals to my risible or sentimental faculties. He is always looking in my face, watching the effect." Here you have it, put quite precisely—the thing that so annoys me about Sterne and similar writers. Their lack of tact, their absence of any sense of what is really valuable—even in their own ideas, or rather least of all in their own ideas. They think that because there's something in their soul which is important and interesting because of its life-communicating power, therefore every accidental and uninteresting expression of their accidental and uninteresting nature is equally important and interesting. They push their way in between their own vision and our astonishment; they spoil their greatness with the petty things they add; compromise their depth with shallow confessions; destroy the immediacy of their effect with their effect-anticipating grin.

Vincent (tries to say something).

Joachim (going on quickly): I know what you're thinking. But I'm not speaking now of the few passages where Sterne's pushing himself forward is symbolic—"a symbol of the great play", as you called it. I'm speaking of a thousand other passages where it stands in the way of the effect his symbols ought to produce. Not of individual passages so much as of the whole stylistic and ethical demoralization which results from his attitude. His continual coquetry has eaten into every image, every metaphor; not a single line he wrote is free of the poison. His observations, his experiences, his descriptions: I always have to think of the text Nietzsche proposed as a memento for psychologists: "Beware of cheap psychology! Never observe in order to observe! It creates a false optic, a kind of squint: it leads to falseness and exaggeration. Experience as wanting-to-experience is no good. Don't look at yourself when you are experiencing something. An eye that does that is an evil eye." This cheapness, don't you see, this deep vulgarity is what I sense in all Sterne's writing and especially in Yorick's letters to Elisa. And this isn't just an aversion to Sterne the man—although this, too, I would consider entirely justified—it is the most profound criticism that can be addressed to the artistic quality of his works. They are inorganic, fragmentary. Not because he couldn't complete them but because he couldn't distinguish between value and non-value anywhere, and never chose between the two. He didn't compose his works because he lacked the most elementary prerequisite for composition, the ability to choose and evaluate. Sterne's writings are a muddy flood of unselected matter. They are formless because he could have carried on to infinity, and his death meant only the end of his works but not their completion. Sterne's works are formless because they are extensible to infinity; but infinite forms do not exist.

Vincent (quickly): Oh yes they do!

Joachim: How's that?

Vincent (would really like the argument to end, but he cannot let the last remarks pass unchallenged, and so he tries at least to draw the girl into the conversation): You will, of course, find what I am about to say too paradoxical; but you (turning to the girl) will surely understand me.

The girl (is grateful that somebody is paying some attention to her once more, but is afraid of laying herself open to attack in some way; in order nevertheless to say something, she interjects): You mean the endless melody, don't you?

Vincent (is slightly embarrassed because he finds this remark somewhat meaningless): Yes, that's it, more or less.

Joachim (completely absorbed in the discussion, he finds the girl's remark totally devoid of meaning, and in his "objective" passion he exclaims a little too quickly, at the same time as Vincent): The endless melody?!

The girl (is hurt).

Vincent (naturally notices this at once and promptly turns the situation to his own advantage). Yes—the endless melody as a life-symbol—that was what you meant, wasn't it?

The girl: Of course.

Vincent: As a symbol of reaching out for the infinite, of the boundlessness of life and its immense richness. The endless melody is only a metaphor here, but a profound one, for it hints at things which ten times as many words could not express. Still, I shall try to explain what we mean by it.

Joachim (has realized immediately after his last interjection how clumsy and wounding it was; Vincent's "we" makes him wince, but a glance at the girl's face tells him that to protest would by now be useless, and he says nothing).

Vincent: As I said, if the notion of artistic form has any real meaning, then I have already defined the nature of Sterne's form. Now I should add one more thing: form is the essence of whatever has to be said, condensed to a point where we are conscious only of the condensation and scarcely of what it is a condensation of. Perhaps a still better way of putting it would be this: form gives a rhythm to what has to be said, and the rhythm becomes—later, afterwards— something abstractable, something that can be experienced by itself, so that some people feel it to be—always afterwards—as the eternal *a priori* of all content. Yes, form is the intensification of the ultimate feelings, the strongest feelings, to independent significance. There is no form that cannot be reduced to such ultimate, primitively sublime, simple feelings; no form whose every property—every law, as you would have it—could not be traced back to the specificities of those feelings. But every such feeling—even those aroused by tragedy— is a feeling of our power and of the world's infinite richness, a "tonic" feeling as Nietzsche would say. The only thing that dis- tinguishes different art forms from one another is the fact that the occasions upon which they reveal this power are different. To list and arrange these feelings in some order would be a futile game. For us here it is enough to know that there are works which directly convey this kind of reflection, this metaphysically profound and powerful realization of life, whereas most works of literature can convey it only indirectly. In such works, everything grows quite simply from the feeling that the world is many-coloured and infinitely rich, and that we—to whom it is given to make all its richness our own—are infinitely rich, too. The forms born out of such feeling do not convey the great order, but the great multi- plicity; not the great cohesion of the whole, but the wonderful many- coloured richness of every nook and cranny of the whole. For this reason such works are direct symbols of the infinite: they themselves are infinite. Infiinite variations of endless melodies (he looks at the girl), as you said (the girl returns his glance gratefully). Their form is not the result of inner cohesion, as is the case with all other works, but the blurring of their boundaries in a distant mist, like sea-coasts on the horizon: although the boundaries belong to our vision rather than to the works themselves. For, like the feeling from which they spring, they have no boundaries. And our inability to accept life without any connections is what creates the connections between their various parts—not their airy, playful lightness. They, like the feelings from which they spring, are held together by no firmer link that the fugitive images of our dreams. These are the works of true unbrokenness and freshness, of a richness intoxicated by itself. The writings of the early Middle Ages were of such a kind. Adventures, adventures and more adventures: and when the hero, after a thousand adventures, died at last, his son lived on to multiply the endless adventures. Nothing held this endless series of adventures together except a communion of feeling, a communion of experience, an infinitely powerful experiencing of the world's many-coloured richness expressed in a varied series of endless adventures.

Sterne's works, too, were born from such feelings. Yet he did not inherit the blissful sense of richness of a naïvely poetic world; what he created was done in the very teeth of his unpoetic, poverty-stricken epoch. That's why everything in him is so conscious and so ironic: because the possibilty of a naïve feeling, spontaneously making life and play equivalent to each other, was no longer there. Friedrich Schlegel used a beautiful expression to describe this form: he called it "arabesque". And when he said that the humour of Sterne and Swift was "the nature poetry of the upper classes in our era of history", he showed that he had recognized the roots of this kind of poetry and its position in the life of today.

Joachim: There's certainly much truth in what you're saying; but think of what Friedrich Schlegel says directly after the sentence you've just quoted. Quite apart from the fact that he hadn't a particularly high opinion of the arabesque form.

Vincent: Well, in some respects he was still a dogmatist in defence of the old forms.

Joachim: Not any longer when he wrote this. The more important thing, however, is that he rates Jean Paul higher as an exponent of this form, whatever he may have thought of it—"because his imagination is much more morbid and therefore more bizarre and fanciful". Perhaps I'm interpreting this judgement correctly if I say that Sterne's form resembles Jean Paul's, but in Jean Paul the form is more organic to the material, to the innermost nature of his view of the world and of human relationships; that is why his lines can meander more boldly, more richly, more lightly than in Sterne, and yet the picture as a whole is more harmonious. You yourself said that Sterne's world is made up of a variety of materials, and this multi-material character is perhaps the real reason for the disturbing, annoying quality of his writing. Every "now" in Sterne refutes both the past and the future, every gesture of his compromises his words, and his words spoil the beauty of the gestures. I am thinking of the violent dissonances of material—of course I can only point to them very briefly. Every character, every relationship in *Tristram Shandy* is so top-heavy, made of such heavy stuff, so lacking in grace, that the contours, which are stylized into lightness, continually contradict what is inside them by their arabesque quality. It's true you said that the illusion of heaviness is intensified by the author's playfulness. That might be significant if heaviness were a goal and if this contrast increased the grotesque quality of the work. But we know that this

is not so. We feel at every step that the one compromises and
weakens the other—the heaviness weakens the arabesque, the grace-
fulness interferes with the natural *gravitas* of the work. This disharmony is perhaps still more apparent in the *Sentimental Journey*,
although the reasons for it are much subtler there. There, the
contradictions within each single sentence spring from the
dissonance in the sentiment which underlies the whole book. In a
word, the content of the *Sentimental Journey* is the playful enjoyment of sentiment, an amateur approach to sentiment if you will. But
such an approach is a *contradictio in adiecto*: one can conceive of
an amateur approach to sensation, perhaps, but not to sentiment. By
"amateur approach to sentiment" I mean that all one's inner
reactions to things are so distanced that the fitting of these things
into bizarre arabesques becomes the natural form of expression, or
that one's moods are so morbidly over-refined that they can bend
over from left to right and back again of their own accord. Yet
Sterne's sentiments are simple and often quite ordinary, even vulgar.
They are healthy, there's nothing over-refined or morbid about them.
But that is how he sees them, and he fits them into his life as though
they were like that; and so he robs them of their fine, healthy
strength without being able to endow them with the subtle flexibility
of morbid sensations. However, the dissonance in the *Sentimental
Journey* is less marked, and I can understand the French who prefer
it to *Tristram Shandy*, for all the superb ideas contained in the latter.
Vincent: Yes, but Jean Paul thought highly of *Tristram Shandy*,
and he was right. Of course the *Sentimental Journey* is the gate
through which we arrive at a deep understanding of Sterne—and
through which, heavily laden with the treasures of his kingdom, we
return into real life. For whatever we may say about the purely
artistic value or lack of value of these works—and I don't suppose we
shall ever convince one another on this issue—the reason why they
really matter to us is, after all, that they show us a way into life, a
new way towards the enrichment of our life. Sterne said himself
where this way leads to; in a letter in which he discussed A
Sentimental Journey he wrote: "My design in it was to teach us to
love the world and our fellow creatures better than we do." If we
don't read this as a purely programmatic statement but consider it in
terms of the actual result—the overwhelmingly powerful effect of
his writings—then Sterne as an educator becomes far more important
to us than the "aesthetic value" or the "significance in terms of
literary history" of his works. Richness as an ethic, knowing how to
live, knowing how to draw life from everything that comes to hand,
that is what these writings teach us. "I pity the man," he wrote,
"who can travel from Dan to Beersheba and cry: ' 'Tis all barren';

and so it is; and so is all the world to him who will not cultivate the fruits it offers." All Sterne's works proclaim this, with a preacher's enthusiasm and conviction, with the ever-recurrent gesture of opening up the world; everything he wrote proclaims such a worship of life. Here, the difference between great and small, heavy and weightless, amusing and dull, ceases to have any meaning; distinctions between materials or qualities—like those you spoke of a moment ago —become meaningless because everything meets and merges in the unity of great, intense experience; but without such experience—as mere possibility, that is to say—there is nothing, and everything is irrelevant to the same degree. Life is made up of moments; every moment is so filled with the energy of life that, beside its living reality, things of which we know only that they once were and may one day be again, are lost in empty nothingness—things that merely bind and oblige us, but do not fecundate our lives. Sterne's is the most powerful affirmation of life, despite and against everything. There isn't a "No" anywhere in the world that could begin to measure itself against this "Yes". Sterne's "Yes" is always addressed only to moments, and there is no moment which could not give him —everything. "Were I in a desert," he says, "I would find out wherewith in it to call forth my affections." Remember when he arrives in Paris and realizes that he hasn't got a passport? He knows that unless he can get hold of one within a few hours he may be put in the Bastille for months. Remember how he goes out in search of a passport? And all the things that happen to him in the process of looking for it? How much he experiences, and how every experience matters more to him than what he is searching for? In the end, it falls quite accidentally into his lap and is of no more importance to him than all the rest has been. Do you not sense here that all the digressions and excursions that we find in his writings are for him a philosophy of life? Life is only a way: we do not know whither it leads: and what do we know of its Wherefore? The way itself is value and happiness, the way is beautiful and good and enriching. We should accept every digression with joy, no matter what has occasioned it or why. If I consider the characters in *Tristram Shandy* and their destinies from this point of view, they seem to acquire a depth which is quite new: because everything that separates them from each other, everything that hurls them blindly, tragi-comically, against reality makes their lives infinitely richer than reality could ever do. Their imaginings, their castles in the air, their fantasies, their play—these are life, and everything else, compared with which we normally call their life "unreal", appears empty and schematic. That deep alienation that exists between men is turned into jubilant joy, because what separates men gives them life— because any other communicable life would be empty, schematic, devoid of content.

Joachim: You're wrong! Wrong! I deny that there can be an ethic of moments, and I deny that the life-form you have just described can be really rich. (A little more calmly.) I'm thinking of Sterne—whom you've once again forgotten—and I deny that he has real richness or that the chaotic disorder of his experience is enriching to us. No! Chaos in itself is never richness. That which creates order springs from roots in the soul just as deep as chaos, and therefore only a soul in which both—chaos and order, life and abstraction, man and destiny, mood and ethic—are present in equally powerful degrees can be complete and for that reason rich. Only when they are present together, when they grow together organically into an inseparable, living unity at every single moment, only then is a man really a man and his work a real totality, a symbol of the world. And only in the works of such men is chaos really chaos—where every deep, fundamental conflict grows organically together into meaningful unity because everything in the prisons of schematic ideas is really alive and vital, because, under the ice of the abstractions, everything is glowing and seething with life. If chaos alone is present in a work, then the chaos itself becomes weak and powerless because it is present only in a raw state, empirical, static, unchanging, without movement. Only contrast brings things really to life; only constraint brings forth real spontaneity, only in something that is formed do we feel the metaphysic of formlessness; only then do we feel that chaos is a world principle.

Ethics! The order that comes from the outside! The law imposed upon us, the law we cannot transcend! You speak about it as though it did nothing but shrivel up the soul. You do so in Sterne's name, it's true, and there you are right—he felt it to be so, but only out of an instinct of self-preservation, the self-defence of a weak man who is wary of making any value-judgement because he is afraid that, were he even a little honest, all his feelings and experiences would seem too light—even to himself. Such men evade all constraint because any constraint would stifle them once and for all; they run away from all battles because they know they will be defeated. In the lives of such men everything is of equal importance because they are not capable of choosing the really important things, of experiencing them through to the end. Sterne's whole life is an episodism of the soul. It's true that many things have a more powerful effect in his works than in most others, but all really great things are reduced to a thousandth of their size. Remember—to quote only the most obvious example—that in the diaries of his journey through France there is everything . . . except Paris. This is not an attempt to stand accepted values on their head, not a pre-figuring of *Trésor des Humbles*; the great things are not small because the small ones are great; no, this is anarchy, the anarchy of sheer incapacity. The contours of the great things are dimly visible through Sterne's episodes, as through a dirty window—but they remain dim, they are neither grasped nor rejected. Things are the same to him as they are to those who do make value-judgements—it's only that some things are too strong, too big for him. Yet real richness lies in the ability to evaluate, just as true strength lies in the strength to choose—in that part of the soul which is free from episodic moods, the ethical part. It lies in determining certain fixed points for life. This strength, with sovereign power, creates distinctions between things, creates a hierarchy of things; this strength, which projects a goal for the soul out of the soul itself and thus gives solid form to the soul's contents. Ethics or—since we're speaking of art—form, unlike the moment and the mood, is an ideal outside the self.

Vincent (a little superior and sarcastic): That's the view of Gregers Werle.

Joachim: I wouldn't deny it for a moment.

Vincent: You should never forget that there's something—forgive me—foolish and ridiculous about Gregers.

Joachim (vehemently): But only because he tries to make his ideal demands prevail against a nonentity, a Hjalmar! And even so, how much richness and strength there is in him, for all the outward absurdity! And how terrible the inner poverty of the richness you have described! I suppose you take it for irony when Sterne says somewhere, speaking of himself, how wretched his conflicts make him—conflicts into which he would never been flung by worthier sentiments. But try and remember the letter in which he confesses so frankly and sorrowfully to the great inner bankruptcy of his anarchic sentiments: "I have torn my whole frame into pieces by my feelings". He tore his work to pieces, not only by his feelings, but also by his ideas, his moods, his jokes. He diminished his own greatness and made his life pitiful and worthless. You know very well what his life was made up of—an endless series of love affairs begun in play, abandoned in play, never enjoyed and never suffered through to the end; nothing but platonic flirtations, tender and feeble, delicate and frivolous, sensitive and sentimental. Such was the content of his life: beginnings that could never have a continuation, that came and vanished without trace, never advancing him even by an inch. Episodes that always remained the same, always finding and leaving the same man, weak, witty and lachrymose, capable neither of really living nor of really giving form to life. Only the ability to apportion value gives a man strength to grow and to develop—only the ability to create order, to make a beginning and an end; for only an end can be the beginning of something new, and only by constant beginnings can we grow to greatness. In episodes, however, there is neither beginning nor end, and a mass of disordered episodes is not richness but a lumber-room. And the impressionism which produces them is not a strength but an incapacity. (A long and rather awkward silence. The girl has hardly listened to the objective contents of what has been said throughout, but precisely for this reason she has sensed very strongly the personal element in it—the element of courtship. Yet just because she senses only this half-unconscious content, she misunderstands both men and puts more into their words than is there. This personal interpretation of the whole argument expresses itself particularly in her irritation with Joachim, whom she finds exceptionally tactless and, at the end, offensive. Vincent, too, has been conscious of the personal aspect of what has been said towards the end, although quite differently; he feels it is an expression of Joachim's view of the world, and in it he senses a strength greater than his own. It seems almost impossible to him that the girl should not have noticed this. Both men have thrown themselves into the debate so wholeheartedly that Vincent feels his defeat—and at this moment he feels very much defeated—to be a defeat all along the line, and he does not dare to speak again until he knows how the land lies. For a moment he feels so badly beaten that best of all he would like to go away and give up the struggle. Joachim interprets the silence still more incorrectly. He expected a very strong reply from Vincent, whom he has attacked personally and perhaps unjustly. The fact that no reply is forthcoming makes him think that he is wasting his time, since nobody is listening to him anyway. The feeling becomes so strong, especially as he feels the girl to be very hostile towards him, that he decides to go. And that, having offered some perfunctory and transparent excuses, is what he does. After the strained friendliness of the farewells, another silence falls between the two young people who remain behind, and once more each of them misunderstands the other's silence. Vincent now sees the absent Joachim still more as the winner of the argument, and is afraid that the girl is thinking the same. At the same time he feels that something must happen, and promptly. His glance falls suddenly upon the book, and he picks it up with nervous indecision.) This discussion has quite spoilt our pleasant reading. How sterile any discussion must seem compared with the living beauty of life! (The girl looks at him; he does not notice.) Listen to this! (He begins to read, in a voice which, now, is very warm and a shade too sentimental. He would like to use Sterne to recapture the mood of the first half-hour, which the discussion has destroyed. The girl is at first unable to suppress her disappointment that literature is once more about to occupy the centre of the stage. But she manages to adjust herself, and tries to disguise her nervousness by extreme attention. Vincent is very nervous too, and so, when he reaches a passage which is really quite without style, he mistakes the girl's badly disguised restlessness for agreement with the absent Joachim. He bangs the book shut.) That really is an unsatisfactory passage. (He starts turning the pages more and more nervously, and finally starts reading again, with a certain defiance, at the most sentimental place of all—the meeting with Maria of Moulins. The same play of disappointment and mis-understanding. He watches the effect of every word he reads with anxious attention, senses the falseness and weakness of Sterne's sentimentality more and more strongly, and finally puts the book down in irritation, stands up and starts walking nervously up and down the room.) It's no good. This discussion has completely spoilt our reading. I can't read any more today.

She (very sentimentally): What a pity. It was so lovely—wasn't it? He (suddenly understanding the situation, very sentimental): Oh yes, it was. (In a soft voice.) We'll go on another time—all right? *She*: All right. . . .

He (standing very close behind her; softly): Another time . . . (Suddenly bends down and kisses her.)

She (her transfigured face shows her relief that the thing for which the whole argument was only a highly unnecessary preparation has happened at last; and she returns his kiss).

1909

The Metaphysics of Tragedy

PAUL ERNST

Nature makes a man from a child, and a chicken from an egg;
God makes the man before the child and the chicken before the egg.
Meister Eckehart: *The Sermon of the Noble Soul*

1

A DRAMA is a play about man and his fate—a play in which God is the spectator. He is a spectator and no more; his words and gestures never mingle with the words and gestures of the players. His eyes rest upon them: that is all. "Whoever sees God, dies," Ibsen wrote once; "but can he who has been seen by God continue to live?"

Intelligent men who love life are aware of this incompatibility, and they have some unkind things to say about drama. Their clear hostility does greater justice to the nature of drama than the apologies of its timorous defenders. The enemies of drama say that it is a falsification of reality; it makes reality cruder than it is. Not only does it—even in Shakespeare—take away the richness and fulness of reality, not only do the brutal events of drama always just choose between life and death, cheating reality of its exquisite psychological subtleties: the principal reproach is that drama creates a vacuum between human beings. In drama, there is only one person who speaks (his technique being a perfect reflection of his innermost nature) while the other merely answers. But the one begins and the other ends, and the quiet, imperceptible flux of their relationship with one another, which real life alone can really bring to life, become lifeless and rigid in the harsh process of the dramatic description. What these critics say is full of the most profound truth. But rash defenders of drama come forward and invoke Shakespeare's richness, the restless shimmering of naturalistic dialogue, the blurring of all the contours of fate in Maeterlinck's destiny plays. They are rash defenders indeed, for what they have to propose in defence of the drama is only a compromise—a compromise between life and dramatic form.

Life is an anarchy of light and dark: nothing is ever completely

152

fulfilled in life, nothing ever quite ends; new, confusing voices always mingle with the chorus of those that have been heard before. Everything flows, everything merges into another thing, and the mixture is uncontrolled and impure; everything is destroyed, everything is smashed, nothing ever flowers into real life. To live is to live something through to the end: but *life* means that nothing is ever fully and completely lived through to the end. Life is the most unreal and unliving of all conceivable existences; one can describe it only negatively—by saying that something always happens to disturb and interrupt the flow. Schelling wrote: "We say a thing 'lasts' because its existence is not in conformity with its nature."

Real life is always unreal, always impossible, in the midst of empirical life. Suddenly there is a gleam, a lightning that illumines the banal paths of empirical life: something disturbing and seductive, dangerous and surprising; the accident, the great moment, the miracle; an enrichment and a confusion. It cannot last, no one would be able to bear it, no one could live at such heights—at the height of their own life and their own ultimate possibilities. One has to fall back into numbness. One has to deny life in order to live.

What men love about life is its atmospheric quality, its uncertainty, forever swinging this way and that, like a pendulum—but one that never swings out as far as it can go. They love the great uncertainty of life which is like a monotonous, reassuring lullaby. But the miracle is what determines and is determined: it bursts incalculably into life, accidentally and out of context, and ruthlessly turns life into a clear, an unambiguous equation—which it then resolves. Men hate and fear the unambiguous. Their weakness and cowardice make them welcome any obstacle that is imposed from the outside, any barrier that is put in their way. Unimaginable, eternally unreachable Gardens of Eden for idle dreams bloom for them behind every rock face whose sheerness they can never conquer. Life for them is longing and hoping, and what fate puts out of their reach is turned cheaply and easily into inner riches of the soul. Men never know life at the point where all the streams of life converge. Where nothing is fulfilled, everything is possible. But the miracle is fulfilment. It snatches from life all its deceptive veils, woven of gleaming moments and infinitely varied moods. Drawn in hard and ruthless outline, the soul stands naked before the face of life.

Only the miracle, however, has reality before the face of God. For God there is no relativity, no transition, no nuance. His glance robs every event of all that is temporal and local about it. Before God, there is no difference between seeming and substance, appearance and idea, event and destiny. The question of value and reality loses all its meaning: before the face of God, value creates reality and does not have to be dreamed or imagined as reality. This is why every true tragedy is a mystery play. Its real, central meaning is a revelation of God before the face of God. The god of nature and destiny, who is always speechless and always unredeemed, brings forth the voice of the god who slumbers inside man, the voice which, in life, has fallen silent; the immanent god awakens the transcendental god into life. "Because, without a creature, God cannot desire to have effect or movement, he desires to have effect and movement in and with the creature," says the little book of the perfect life; and Hebbel speaks of "God's inability to conduct a monologue".

By contrast, the gods of reality, of history, are obstinate and rash. The power and beauty of pure revelation do not satisfy their ambition. They want not only to be the spectators of the fulfilment of revelation, but also to direct and accomplish that fulfilment. Their hands tug wilfully at the enigmatic yet obvious tangle of the threads of fate and, by entangling them still more, achieve a perfect yet meaningless orderliness. They walk on to the stage and their appearance reduces man to a puppet, destiny to providence; that which, in tragedy, is a grave event becomes, in life, a gratuitous gift of redemption. God must leave the stage, but must yet remain a spectator; that is the historical possibility of tragic epochs. And because nature and fate have never been so terrifyingly soulless as they are today, because men's souls have never walked in such utter loneliness upon deserted paths, because of all this we may again hope for the coming of tragedy—once all the dancing shadows of a friendly order, which our cowardly dreams have cast upon nature to allow us a false sense of security, have entirely disappeared. "Only when we have become completely godless," says Paul Ernst, "shall we have tragedy once more." Think of Shakespeare's Macbeth, whose soul could not bear the gravity of the necessary way to the necessary goal. Witches still dance and sing round him at the crossroads of fate, and awaited miracles proclaim to him that the day of the ultimate fulfilment has come. The wild chaos which surrounds him, which is re-created by all his actions, which entangles his will, is truly chaotic only to the blind eyes of his longing, and only as chaotic as his own frenzy must be to his own soul. In reality both are a judgement of god: the same hands of the same providence guide both. Deceptively, they raise him to the heights, deluding his longing with fulfilments; deceptively they place every victory in his hands; everything he does succeeds, until everything has been fulfilled—and then everything is snatched from him all at once. Outside and inside are still one in Macbeth: the same hand guides the destiny and the soul. Drama, here, is still a judgement of God, and every stroke of the sword is still part of the divine plan of providence. Or take Ibsen's Jarl, who in his dreams was always a king and who could not be a king except in his dreams. What he hopes to obtain from the struggle of different forces is a judgement of God, a verdict upon the ultimate truth. But the world round him goes on its way, untouched by such questions or answers. All things have become dumb, and laurels or defeats are awarded indifferently at the end of the struggle. Never again will God's judgement be clearly heard in the workings of destiny. It was God's voice that gave life to the whole; but then that life had to go on by itself, alone, and the judging voice fell silent forever. This is why Jarl can be victorious where Macbeth was defeated; he is the victim doomed to perish, and as victor he is even more defeated than he would be as loser. The tones of tragic truth ring out pure and clear : the miracle of life, the destiny of tragedy is merely what reveals souls. Too alien from one another to be enemies, the two face one another—that which reveals and that which is revealed, the revelation and its object. What is revealed is alien to that which has occasioned its revelation—higher, and coming from a different world. The soul, having become Self, measures its whole previous existence with a stranger's eye. It finds that previous existence incomprehensible, inessential and lifeless; it can only dream that once it was different, for this new way of being is being. It was but idle accident that dictated the dreams, and but the accidental ringing of a distant bell that brought awakening in the morning.

Naked souls conduct a dialogue here with naked destinies. Both have been stripped of everything that is not of their innermost essense; all the relationships of life have been suppressed so that the relationship with destiny may be created; everything atmospheric between men and objects has vanished, in order that nothing should exist between them but the clear, harsh mountain air of ultimate questions and ultimate answers. There, at the point to which the miracle of accident has raised a man and his life, tragedy begins : and this is why he is forever banished from the world of tragedy. For he can no longer put into that life the hazardous and enriching things he puts into ordinary life. Tragedy can extend in only one direction : upwards. It begins at the moment when enigmatic forces have distilled the essence from a man, have forced him to become essential; and the progress of tragedy consists in his essential, true nature becoming more and more manifest. A life that excludes accident is flat and sterile, an endless plain without any elevations; the logic of such a life is the logic of cheap security, of passive refusal before everything new, of dull repose in the lap of dry common sense. But tragedy needs no further accident; it has incorporated accident into its world forever, so that it is always and everywhere present in it.

The question of the possibility of tragedy is the question of meaning and essence. It is the question whether everything that is there, is—just because, simply because, it is there. Are there not degrees and gradations of being? Is "being" a property of all things, or is it a value-judgement passed upon things, a distinction and differentiation between them?

This, then, is the paradox of drama and tragedy: how can essence come alive? How can it become the sensual, immediate, the only real, the truly "being" thing? Drama alone creates—"gives form to"— real human beings, but just because of this it must, of necessity, deprive them of living existence. Their life is made up of words and gestures, but every word they speak and every gesture they make is more than gesture or word; all the manifestations of their life are mere cyphers for their ultimate relationships, their life merely a pale allegory of their own platonic ideas. Their existence can have no reality except the reality of the soul, the reality of lived experience and faith. "Lived experience" is latent in every event of life as a threatening abyss, the door to the judgement chamber: its connection with the Idea—of which it is merely the outward manifestation —is no more than the conceivable possibility of such a connection in the midst of the chaotic coincidences of real life. And faith affirms this connection and transforms its eternally unprovable possibility into the *a priori* basis for the whole of existence.

Such existence knows no space or time; all its events are outside the scope of logical explanation, just as the souls of its men are outside the scope of psychology. Let me be more precise: the time and space of tragedy have no perspective that might modify or mitigate them, and neither the outward nor the inner reasons for action and suffering in tragedy ever affect their essence. Everything counts in tragedy, and everything has equal force and weight. There is in tragedy a threshold of life-possibility, of the ability to be aroused into life; everything that is on the right side of this threshold, everything that can live, is always present, and everything is present in equal measure. For a character in tragedy, to be there at all—to exist—is to be perfect. Medieval philosophy had a clear and unambiguous way of expressing this. It said that *ens perfectissimum* was also *ens realissimum*; the more perfect a thing is, the more it *is*; the more a thing corresponds to its idea, the greater is its being. But how does one experience one's idea, and one's identification with that same idea, in real life? (For tragedy is the most real life that is.) In lived life, this is not a question of epistemology (as it is in philosophy), but the painfully and immediately experienced reality of the great moments.

The essence of these great moments is the pure experience of self.

In ordinary life we experience ourselves only peripherally—that is, we experience our motives and our relationships. Our life ordinarily has no real necessity, but only the necessity of being empirically present, of being entangled by a thousand threads in a thousand accidental bonds and relationships. But the basis of the whole network of necessities is accidental and meaningless; everything that is, could just as well be otherwise, and the only thing that seems really necessary is the past, simply because nothing more can be done to change it. But is even the past really necessary? Can the accidental flow of time, the arbitrary displacement of one's arbitrary point of view vis-à-vis one's lived experience, change the essential nature of that experience? Can it make something necessary and essential out of the accidental? Can it transform the periphery into the centre? It often seems that it can, but that is only an illusion. Only our momentary and accidental knowledge makes something rounded and changeless of the past. The smallest modification of that knowledge, such as any accident may occasion, sheds new light upon the "unchangeable" past, and suddenly, in that new light, everything acquires a different meaning and actually becomes different. Ibsen only *seems* to be a disciple of the Greeks, continuing in the tradition of the drama of Oedipus. The real meaning of his analytical dramas is that there is nothing unchangeable about the past—that the past, too, is flowing, shimmering and changeable, constantly transformed into something different by new insights.

The great moments of life, too, bring new insights, but these only seem to belong to the series of continual, eternal re-evaluations. In reality they are an end and a beginning, giving men a new memory, a new ethic and a new justice. Many things disappear which before appeared to be the very cornerstones of life, while small, barely perceptible things become the new supports of life. A man can no longer walk along the paths where he used to walk, nor can his eyes find any direction in them; yet now he easily climbs pathless mountain peaks and strides confidently over bottomless marshes. A deep forgetfulness and a clairvoyance of the memory overpower the soul; the blinding light of the new insight illuminates its centre, and everything that belongs to the centre blossoms into life. This sense of necessity is not the result of the inescapable workings of causality; it is without cause, it leaps across all the causes of empirical life. Being-necessary now means being intimately bound up with the essence; it needs no other reason, and the memory retains only this one necessary thing and simply forgets the rest. This alone, then, is the defendant before the judgement and the self-judgement of the soul. Everything else is forgotten, all the whys and wherefores; this alone is weighed upon the scales. The judgement is a cruelly harsh one, without mercy or reprieve; sentence is passed ruthlessly upon even the smallest fault, the faintest suggestion of a betrayal of the essence. Anyone whose sketchiest, long-forgotten gesture implies that he may once have fallen short of his own essence is excluded from the circle of real men. No richness or grandeur of the soul's gifts can alter this judgement, and a whole life filled with glorious deeds counts as nothing before it. But it forgets, with radiant clemency, any sin of ordinary life which has not encroached upon the centre; even to speak of forgiveness is to exaggerate, for the judge's eye simply passes over such sins without noticing them.

Such a moment is a beginning and an end. Nothing can succeed it or follow upon it, nothing can connect it with ordinary life. It is a moment; it does not signify life, it *is* life—a different life opposed to and exclusive of ordinary life. This is the metaphysical reason for the concentration of drama in time, of the condition of unity of time. It is born of the desire to come as close as possible to the timelessness of this moment which yet is the whole of life. (Unity of place is the natural symbol of such sudden standing still in the midst of the continual change of ordinary life, and is therefore a technically necessary condition of dramatic form-giving.) Tragedy is only a moment: that is the meaning of the unity of time; and the technical paradox contained in trying to give temporal duration to a moment which, by its very nature, is without such duration, springs from the inadequacy of expressing a mystical experience in terms of human language. "How can one give form to what is without image, or prove what is without evidence?" asks Suso. Tragic drama has to express the becoming-timeless of time. To fulfil all the conditions of unity is actually to unite the past, the present and the future. Not only is their empirically real sequence disturbed and destroyed by turning the present into something secondary and unreal, the past into a threat, the future into a familiar experience (although perhaps an unconscious one); even the way in which these moments follow one upon the other is no longer a sequence in time. In terms of time, such drama is completely and rigidly static. Its moments exist in parallel rather than in series; it no longer lies within the plane of temporal experience. Unity of time is a paradoxical notion in any case; any attempt to limit time or to make it circular—and this is the only way to achieve unity of time—contradicts the very nature of time. (One need only think of the inner rigidity of the circular movement in Nietzsche's theory of recurrence.) But drama interrupts the eternal flow of time not only at its beginning and its end, bending the two poles towards each other and melting them together; it carries out this same stylization at every instant of the drama; every moment is a symbol, a reduced-scale image of the whole, distinguishable from it only by its size. To fit these moments together must therefore be a matter of fitting them *into* one another, not *after* one another. The French classicists looked for rational reasons to explain their true insight in this matter, and by formulating the mystical unity in a rationalistic way, they reduced the profound paradox to something trivial and arbitrary. They made of this supra- and extra-temporal unity a unity *within* time, of the mystical unity a mechanical one. Lessing—although there is much one could disagree with him about, precisely on this issue—was right to feel that Shakespeare came essentially closer to the Greeks than their apparent successors; but he, like the French, offered explanations which were superficial, rationalistic, and therefore false.

The tragic experience, then, is a beginning and an end at the same time. Everyone at such a moment is newly born, yet has been dead for a long time; and everyone's life stands before the Last Judgement. Any "development" of a character in drama is merely apparent; it consists of the experiencing of such a moment, of the character being raised into the world of tragedy inside whose periphery, until then, only his shadow could enter. It is this character's becoming-man, his awakening from a confused dream. It always happens suddenly and all at once; the preparatory part is there only for the spectator's sake, it prepares the spectator's soul for the leap of the great trans-formation. The tragic character's soul ignores everything pre-paratory, and everything changes in a flash, everything suddenly becomes essential when the fateful word is spoken at last. Likewise, the tragic character's composure (or serenity or rapture) in the face of death is heroic only in appearance, only in the ordinary language of psychology. The dying heroes of tragedy—as a young dramatist once put it—are dead a long time before they actually die.

The reality of such a world can have nothing in common with that of temporal existence. Realism is bound to destroy all the form-creating and life-maintaining values of tragic drama. We have already listed all the reasons for it. Drama is bound to become trivial if its lifelikeness conceals that which is dramatically real. And life-likeness fitted into a genuinely dramatic structure becomes superfluous and is ignored by the senses. The inner style of drama is realistic within the mediaeval, scholastic meaning of the word, but this excludes all modern realism.

Dramatic tragedy is the form of the high points of existence, its ultimate goals and ultimate limits. Here the mystical-tragical experience of essentiality becomes separate from the essential experience of mysticism. The peak of existence, experienced in mystical ecstasy, disappears in the cloudy sky of the Unity of the All; the intensification of life which results from such ecstasy makes the person who experiences it merge into all things, and all things into each other. The real existence of the mystic begins only when all differentiation has vanished forever; the miracle which his world has created must destroy all forms, for his reality—the essence—exists only behind the forms, disguised and concealed by them. The miracle of tragedy is a form-creating one; its essence is selfhood, just as exclusively as, in mysticism, the essence is self-oblivion. The mystical experience is to suffer the All, the tragic one is to create the All. In mysticism, it is beyond all explanation how a self can absorb everything into itself, how, in a state of melting flux, it can destroy everything distinctive about itself and the whole world and yet retain a self to experience this cancellation of the self. In tragedy, the opposite is just as inexplicable. The self stresses its selfhood with an all-exclusive, all-destroying force, but this extreme affirmation imparts a steely hardness and autonomous life to everything it encounters and—arriving at the ultimate peak of pure selfhood— finally cancels itself out. The final tension of selfhood overleaps everything that is merely individual. Its force elevates all things to the status of destiny, but its great struggle with the self-created destiny makes of it something supra-personal, a symbol of some ultimate fate-relationship. In this way the mystical and the tragic modes of experiencing life touch and supplement one another and mutually exclude one another. Both mysteriously combine life and death, autonomous selfhood and the total dissolving of the self in a higher being. Surrender is the mystic's way, struggle the tragic man's; the one, at the end of his road, is absorbed into the All, the other shattered against the All. From being at one with all things, the former leaps across into the deeply personal world of his ecstasies; the latter loses his selfhood at the moment of its truest exaltation. Who can tell where is the throne of life, where that of death? They are the poles which ordinary life melts together and mutually weakens, for only thus—bereft of strength and scarcely recognizable—can ordinary life bear either life or death. Each, separately, means death —the ultimate frontier. But their relationship to one another is that of fraternal enemies: each represents the sole real victory over the other.

The wisdom of the tragic miracle is the wisdom of frontiers. A miracle is always unambiguous, but everything unambiguous divides and points in two directions. Every ending is always an arrival and a cessation, an affirmation and a denial all at once; every climax is a peak and frontier, the point of intersection between life and death. The tragic life is, of all possible lives, the one most exclusively of this world. That is why its frontier always merges into death. Real, ordinary life never reaches the frontier; it knows death only as something frightening, threatening, meaningless, something that suddenly arrests the flow of life. Mysticism overleaps the frontier and thus robs death of any value as reality. But for tragedy, death—the frontier as such—is an always immanent reality, inseparably connected with every tragic event. The reason for this is not only that the ethic of tragedy must have as its categorical imperative the continuance unto death of everything that has begun; nor is it only that the psychology of tragedy is a science of death-moments, of conscious last moments when the soul has already given up the broad richness of existence and clings only to what is most deeply and intimately its own. Quite apart from these and many other negative reasons, death is also—in a purely positive and life-affirming sense—the immanent reality of tragedy. The experiencing of the frontier between life and death is the awakening of the soul to consciousness or self-consciousness—the soul becomes conscious of itself because it is thus limited, and only because and in so far as it is limited. This is the question posed at the end of one of Paul Ernst's tragedies:

> Can I still want when there is nothing that I cannot do
> And others are no more than puppets on my strings?
> . . . Can a god win glory for himself?

and the answer to the question is this:

> There must be limits to what we can achieve
> Or else the world we live in is a lifeless desert.
> We only live by what is not attainable.

"Can a god win glory for himself?" Put more generally still, the question might run: Can a god live? Does not perfection cancel out being? Is not pantheism, as Schopenhauer said, just a polite form of atheism? Could it be said that the various forms of God's becoming man, God's dependence on the ways and means of the human form, are a symbolic expression of this feeling—the feeling that, in order to come alive, even God must forsake his formless perfection?

The double meaning of the frontier is that it is simultaneously a fulfilment and a failure. In a confused way this is the metaphysical background to ordinary life, the simple recognition that a possibility can become a reality only when all other possibilities have been eliminated. Here, however, the primal possibility of a soul becomes the only reality; the contrast between it and other souls is not only that between something realized and something merely possible, but that between the real and the unreal, between the necessarily thought and the unthinkable and absurd. This is why tragedy is the awakening of the soul. The recognition of the frontier extracts the soul's essential nature, lets everything else fall away, but gives to this essential nature the existence of an inner and only necessity. The frontier is only outwardly a limiting and possibility-destroying principle. For the awakened soul it is the recognition of that which is truly its own. Everything human is possible, but only if one has an abstractly absolute idea of man. Tragedy is the becoming-real of the concrete, essential nature of man. Tragedy gives a firm and sure answer to the most delicate question of platonism: the question whether individual things can have idea or essence. Tragedy's answer puts the question the other way round: only that which is individual, only something whose individuality is carried to the uttermost limit, is adequate to its idea—i.e. is really existent. That which is general, that which encompasses all things yet has not colour or form of its own, is too weak in its universality, too empty in its unity, ever to become real. It is too existent to have real being; its identity is a tautology; the idea is adequate only to itself. Thus tragedy's answer to Plato's verdict is to transcend platonism.

The deepest longing of human existence is the metaphysical root of tragedy: the longing of man for selfhood, the longing to transform the narrow peak of his existence into a wide plain with the path of his life winding across it, and his meaning into a daily reality. The tragic experience, dramatic tragedy, is the most perfect, the only perfect fulfilment of this longing. But every longing fulfilled is a longing destroyed. Tragedy sprang from longing, and therefore its form must exclude any expression of longing. Before tragedy entered life, it became a fulfilment and therefore abandoned the state of longing. That is the reason for the failure of modern tragedy. It wanted to introduce the *a priori* of tragedy into tragedy itself, it wanted to turn a cause into an active principle; but it succeeded only in intensifying its lyricism until it became a kind of soft-centred brutality. It never crossed the threshold of dramatic tragedy. Its atmospheric, yearning, indefinite, tremulous dialogues possess lyrical value but are entirely outside dramatic tragedy. Its poetry is the becoming-poetic of ordinary life, that is to say only the intensification of ordinary life and not its transformation into dramatic life. Such stylization is opposed to dramatic stylization, not only by its method but also in its aim. Its psychology emphasizes that which is momentary and transient in human souls; its ethic is one of understanding all and forgiving all. It tones down, softens and prettifies people in a poetic manner. That is why the public today are always complaining about the harshness and coldness of the dialogue of any tragic playwright; yet this harshness and coldness is only an expression of the playwright's contempt for the puny transports with which everything tragic has to be surrounded nowadays because those who deny the tragic ethic are too cowardly to deny tragedy itself, and those who affirm it are too weak to bear it in its undisguised majesty. Nor does the intellectualization of the dialogue, confined to a clearly conscious mirroring of the sense of destiny, mean coldness: it means human authenticity and inner truth in this particular sphere of life. In tragic drama, to simplify the characters and events is not a form of poverty but a form of richness given by the very nature of the genre. People occur in such drama only when the encounters between them have acquired the status of destiny, and moments of destiny are the only ones depicted. The inner truth of such moments thus becomes an intelligible outward truth, and the concentrated, formula-like expression of this truth in the dialogue reflects not cold intellectualization but the lyrical maturity of the character's own sense of destiny. Here, and only here, the dramatic and the lyrical cease to be mutually opposing principles; here lyricism is the true drama carried to its highest peak.

2

Brunhild is the first success granted to Paul Ernst as a writer of tragedies. As a theoretician, he foresaw it long ago; he felt obliged, as a matter of deepest principle, to reject even the finest works created today or in the recent past, and he tried to explain this in terms of the very essence of drama. And so, in one or two of his theoretical studies, he worked right through to that essence—to absolute drama, if we are to use his own terminology. But his theories were for him simply means to an end, to be justified retrospectively by the attainment of that end in practice. *Brunhild* is his first real action, the first steel cast without any dross, a work that has faults but no flaws.

It is Ernst's first "Greek" drama—the first resolute departure from the path along which great German drama has travelled since the days of Schiller and Kleist: the path whose goal was to marry Sophocles with Shakespeare. The German dramatists' titanic struggle for a modern-classical dramatic style sprang from their reluctance to make the sacrifice which Greek drama demands. They sought—and Ernst's early tragedies are attempts in the same direction—a simple monumentality equivalent to that of the Greeks, but without forfeiting the Shakespearean multiplicity of colours and events. Such attempts were bound to fail, because they had to accommodate two ways of giving form to relationships, the way of drama and the way of life—two ways which are mutually exclusive because the one must inevitably inhibit or even destroy the working of the other.

Ernst has found the strength to make the great sacrifice—the sacrifice of all outward richness of life for the sake of achieving an inner richness, the sacrifice of all sensual beauty for the sake of thrusting through to the deeper, non-sensual beauty of the ultimate sense of life, the sacrifice of all material content so that the pure soul-content of pure form may be revealed. His is the *tragédie classique* reborn: he deepens and interiorizes the aims of Corneille, Racine and Alfieri. It is a genuine return to the eternally great model for all drama that seeks the soul of form—the *Oedipus* of Sophocles.

Everything here, as in the *Oedipus*, is reduced to the maximum economy and intensity. A courtyard between castle and church is the only setting; only the two pairs of lovers and Hagen are allowed upon the stage, and the time allotted for the unfolding of destiny is the span of one brief day.

The play begins at dawn after the wedding night, and the sun has not yet set when Siegfried is carried home dead from the hunt and, when Brunhild has committed suicide, they are burned together upon the funeral pile, separated from each other only by Siegfried's sword. This concentration of events is not merely outward. In the inner relationships of the play, in the intimate contacts between the characters, their loves and hates, their ascents and falls, in their words which mirror their inner lives, there is not a trace of superfluity or ornamentation for its own sake—but only destiny and necessity. The gestures and words of the characters are, by their deepest nature, Greek—indeed, being more consciously stylized, perhaps more Greek than those in many ancient tragedies. The consciousness of the dialectic of their destiny is perhaps still clearer and more penetrating than in Hebbel, and their expression—as in Hebbel and in the Greeks —is an epigrammatically pointed and concise fitting together of the essentials. But just as in Hebbel and in the Greeks—just as in any genuine tragedy—this rationalizing, which we might call mystical rationalism, never banalizes the inexpressible quality of destiny. For it is not will, and still less reason, that is responsible for the tragic entanglement of men and deeds. The fact that these are noble men and women of great and penetrating intellect, men and women who recognize their destiny and salute it in respectful silence, cannot make any difference to the workings of destiny but only deepens its mysterious and inexplicable quality.

This tragedy is a mystery play about sacred and profane love. The one kind of love is limpidly clear, it points forward and upward, it is necessity itself; the other is confusion and eternal darkness, aimless, planless and pathless. *Brunhild* is a mystery play about love among superior and inferior human beings, about love equal and unequal, about love which elevates and love which debases. Gunther as king and hero has been spoilt for tragedy, and Ernst does not attempt to rescue him; indeed, he sacrifices Kriemhild as well. They are the inferior pair of lovers, beings with lower instincts, who do not seek equality in love, beings who must never hope to create anything in their own likeness but must always fear it, beings for whom the mere existence of others striding more freely towards goals invisible to them is a dread and a reproach; beings who want to be happy but who practise vengeance and fear it. Siegfried and Brunhild are the other kind.

It is a mystery play about greatness, happiness . . . and about the frontiers. About that greatness which seeks itself and finds happiness and, in the warm darkness of happiness, longs once more for itself, and eventually reaches the frontiers and finds tragedy and death. About happiness which longs for greatness, yet can only pull greatness down to its own level; which can make the path of greatness longer and harder, yet can never stop greatness in its tracks, and has to stay behind, empty and alone. Greatness wants perfection—it is bound to want it—and perfection is tragedy, the final end, the falling silent of every note. Tragedy as the privilege of greatness: Brunhild and Siegfried are burned upon the same funeral pile, but Gunther and Kriemhild remain alive. Tragedy as universal law, as the final goal which yet is but a beginning in the eternal circle of all things.

> For we are like the green earth that waits for snow
> And like snow that waits for the thaw.

But man is conscious of his fate, and so his fate means more to him than the crest of a wave that is bound to sink into the trough and, later to become a crest once more, a game repeated over and over again for all eternity. Man is conscious of his fate, and calls this consciousness "guilt". And by feeling that everything that had to happen to him is of his own making, he draws firm contours round everything inside himself which accidentally happens to enter the flowing circumference of his accidental life-complex. He makes a necessity of it; he creates frontiers round himself; he creates himself. Seen from the outside, there is no guilt, there can be no guilt; every man sees every other's guilt as an accident of fate, as something which the slightest, faintest breath of wind might have caused to be otherwise. Through guilt, a man says "Yes" to everything that has happened to him; by feeling it to be his own action and his own guilt, he conquers it and forms his life, setting his tragedy—which has sprung from his guilt—as the frontier between his life and the All. Greater men draw such frontiers round larger parts of their lives than lesser men do; they leave nothing outside that once belonged to their lives. And that is why tragedy is their privilege. For the lesser kind there is happiness and unhappiness and revenge, because they always feel it is the others who are guilty. For them, everything comes only from the outside, their life can merge nothing into itself: they are untragic and their life is without form. But for one of the higher kind, the guilt of another—even if it destroys him—is always only fate. Herein is the deep mystery of guilt and entanglement and fate.

All this is built into the sheer architecture of a rigid, transitionless dichotomy. A thousand threads of fate connect the two greater human beings with the two lesser ones, yet not one of these threads constitutes a real link. So ruthlessly sharp is this inner division within the couples that the play might perhaps have disintegrated had Ernst not bridged the gap by a wide arch which connects the opposite sides, even if it emphasizes still more strongly the breadth of the abyss which lies between them. This connecting arch is Hagen. He represents the higher being as servant, with his servanthood as his greatness and his frontier; the man who has all the greatness and all the guilty awareness of fate inside him, yet around whom frontiers have been drawn by something outside and far beyond his own self. This man is not yet tragic—however harsh the blows which fate may deal him—because his "must", for all its interiority, still comes from the outside; yet he is capable of experiencing events as his own—in other words, as fate. His frontiers are drawn both on the outside and on the inside; and so the firmly delimited, formed quality of his life places him above the two lesser beings, and yet he stands below the two higher ones because he is, after all, their vassal—their highest vassal, the nearest to their throne—but no more than that, because his frontiers limit him, too, because his possibilities of conquering life are predetermined for him and not by him.

The crystalline transparency of the words conveys most strikingly the mysterious, unfathomable quality of the work. Just as their clarity cannot reveal the workings of fate, so the lucid consciousness with which they say everything that is essential about each character cannot, after all, bring the characters closer to one another or make them understand one another. Each word is a Janus' head; the one who says it sees always only one side, the one who hears it sees the other, and there is no possibility of the two coming closer together; each word that could serve as a bridge needs a bridge in turn. And, in the same way, the actions of the characters are not a sure sign of anything: the good man commits the evil deed, and, often, the other way about; longing conceals the true path, duty destroys the strongest bond of love. And so, at the end, each stands alone, for there is no communion in the face of fate.

3

Such a simplifying of dramatic conditions, however, entails grave sacrifices. The historical element of the play (by which we mean everything that is colourful and unrepeatable about it) is, after all, much more than just an impediment to strict stylization. The playwright's sensual, artistic pleasure in imagining the rich world outside is not his only motive for introducing this "historical" element. The relationship between history and tragedy is one of the deepest paradoxes of dramatic form. Aristotle was the first to express it by saying that drama is more philosophical than history. But does not drama, by thus becoming "more philosophical", lose its own very special essentiality? Surely its deepest meaning, the pure immanence of its laws, the perfect concealment of ideas within facts, the perfect disappearance of ideas behind facts—surely all these are put at risk by its becoming "more philosophical than history"? The point at issue is not the unity of idea and reality, but an involved, confused, indistinguishable convolution of the two. When we feel that something is "historical", then hazard and necessity, accidental happenings and timeless laws, causes and effects lose their absoluteness and become no more than possible points of view vis-à-vis facts which may modify such notions but can never completely absorb them. Being-history is a completely pure form of being; one might say it is Being as such. Something is because it is, and as it is. It is strong and great and beautiful simply because it is incomparable and incompatible with any *a priori* imposed by an order-creating rationality.

Yet there *is* an order concealed in the world of history, a composition in the confusion of its irregular lines. It is the undefinable order of a carpet or a dance; to interpret its meaning seems impossible, but it is still less possible to give up trying to interpret it. It is as though the whole fabric of fanciful lines were waiting for a single word that is always at the tip of our tongues, yet one which has never yet been spoken by anyone. History appears as a profound symbol of fate—of the regular accidentality of fate, its arbitrariness and tyranny which, in the last analysis, is always just. Tragedy's fight for history is a great war of conquest against life, an attempt to find the meaning of history (which is immeasurably far from ordinary life) in life, to extract the meaning of history from life as the true, concealed sense of life. A sense of history is always the most living necessity; the form in which it occurs is the force of gravity of mere happening, the irresistible force within the flow of things. It is the necessity of everything being connected with everything else, the value-denying necessity; there is no difference between small and great, meaningful and meaningless, primary and secondary. What is, had to be. Each moment follows the one before, unaffected by aim or purpose.

The paradox of historical drama is the combining of both these necessities: the one which flows without cause from the inside, and the other which flows meaninglessly outside; its goal is the becoming-form, the mutual intensification of two principles which appear to be fundamentally exclusive of one another. The further the two are from each other, the more profound tragedy seems to become. For they touch one another only when carried to an extreme; they delimit and strengthen each other by their categorical opposition to one another. This is why a playwright is attracted precisely by the historical element of a story, not by the general meaning which can be read into it. Here, he thinks, he can find the ultimate symbol of human limitation, pure constraint upon pure will, the clear, un-ambiguous resistance of matter to creative, form-imposing will. The unselective power of that which exists just because it exists ruthlessly separates the action from the intention, and drives the man who intends an action to execute it with a purity which defiles the inner purity of the intention and separates the action from its aim. The idea which lay hidden in the action or life-situation is revealed, destroying the real idea that lay timeless and uncreated within it, the one which alone could have elevated it to essential being. The power of what merely "is" destroys what it "should be". The young Hebbel wrote in his diary: "A good Pope is always a bad Christian."

This is the meaning of Paul Ernst's historical tragedies—the experience of his heroes, Demetrius and Nabis, Hildebrand and the Emperor Henry. Before these men meet one another, everything that is lofty and noble in them lies unseparated within their souls, just as all the possibilities for good and evil lies unseparated in every action which expresses them. But their meeting separates everything within a single instant. These men experience the only real dis-appointment there is: the disappointment of complete fulfilment. I do not mean the fear that reality will destroy their illusions, that fear which makes Romantics flee from life and its actions; the men in such plays live in the world of tragedy, not of ordinary life. I am speaking of the disillusionment of fulfilment: the disillusionment which follows action, which was inherent in past actions and will follow again upon new ones. Such men do not wearily abandon the struggle. The inner innocence which makes them reach out of every-thing—greatness and goodness, power and freedom, the way and the goal—reveals a disproportion between longing and fulfilment which is not the disproportion between idea and reality, but between dif-ferent ideas. The noble man is always chosen for kingship. Every-thing in him strives towards that end. But kingship and the idea of kingship do not allow of nobility; the highest goals, the innermost essence of kingship demands something different—harshness and wickedness, ingratitude and compromise. The royal soul wants to fulfil the ultimate value of its personality in a royal life, for everywhere else it is confined and constrained; yet the throne makes the same demands upon all, and just because the royal soul is nobly conscious of duty, it is forced to do things which are alien and repulsive to it. Thus it is that Demetrius and Nabis stand face to face, the victorious rebel who is a king's son and the mortally wounded usurper. The young king strides impetuously into the hall where his own father's defeated murderer awaits him; but the dying man has only to utter a few words full of harsh wisdom, and a different Demetrius steps over his dead body to ascend the throne. Nabis has not spoken to the man who has defeated him, but to the heir who is to inherit his kingdom; he has spoken the words of a man disappointed in the deepest recesses of his soul, a man who wanted to do good, "the good that is not hard to understand", yet oceans of blood had to flow and his soul had to wither inside him in order that he might become a king such as his sense of duty and the age in which he lived required. And Nabis' corpse has scarcely grown cold before a new Nabis is seated upon his throne, broken, forsaken by joy, forced to be cruel, alone and friendless: Demetrius, the young king with the pure and hopeful soul, surrounded by a host of devoted friends, Demetrius who heard Nabis speak those words.

In the snow-filled castle courtyard at Canossa, where Gregory and Henry meet for the first and last time, victory and defeat are still more difficult to disentangle. The Pope and the Emperor, who already in the first four acts of their lives had been each other's destiny, now meet at last. God has given the Pope a gentle soul and a happiness-desiring, happiness-bestowing one to the Emperor, but the great struggle between them has crushed everything human, everything specific to themselves, in them both. Hildebrand has had to become harsh and cruel; he has not only had to discard all ordinary happiness, but also to sacrifice and betray the poor whom he once saw it as his mission to help. He has had to do this in order to receive into his hands the power of creating God's kingdom. He has had to become a sinner and to appear a saint, and the path of redeeming, alleviating repentance, open to all other men, is closed to him; his soul will go down into hell to eternal damnation. All his sacrifices are in vain. The adulterer whom he has excommunicated, the Emperor who stands in the way of his plans, now kneels before him feigning contrition like the clever statesman that he is, and he, the unredeemed, must break his only weapon with his own hands by withdrawing the excommunication. The emperor has won, but the radiant man who

reached out for happiness with gleaming hands, who effortlessly gave
and received happiness, Henry the man, is dead. Gregory leaves
Canossa bowed and beaten; Henry will enter Rome as the victor.

> I rose a different man from when I knelt.
> He must curse God because he wanted what was right;
> I have done wrong, yet I bless God.
> He goes to die, I am already dead:
> His death is death, but mine is life.

Henry has won, Gregory is beaten. But did the Emperor win?
And was the Pope defeated? The march on Rome has become
possible, Gregory will be deposed, but did not the king of the world,
the lord of all the world's glories, kneel as a penitent before a priest?
Did not the Emperor bow before the Pope? And will not the priests,
whom Gregory has deprived forever of all human semblance and
capacity for happiness, always stand henceforth as judges over every
mortal? Did not Henry forget the Emperor when he won, and
Gregory forget the Pope when, lamenting, he broke his sword?

This necessity—perhaps the truest and certainly the most real of
all—nevertheless has something humiliating about it. The heroes
who await death here as their redemption from life are not only
broken but defiled and estranged from their own selves. The heroes
of tragedy always die happy, already alive in their death; but here
death is not the absolute exaltation of life, the direct extension of a
life lived in the right direction, but only an escape from oppression,
from the impurity of the real world—a return of the soul from an
alien life itself. The hero, it is true, does not feel any remorse on
account of his deeds or of their vanity, and he does not return to the
naïvely beautiful dreams he used to dream before he came into contact with reality. He knows that all the struggles, all the
humiliations, are necessary for his life, for his becoming-manifest,
for his only possible redemption. And yet this only possible redemption is not the true one, and that is the deepest disappointment of
his soul. The frontiers which historical happenings draw round his
soul, the frontiers to which history drives his soul, are not its true,
specific frontiers—they are common to all men to whom these things
might happen, to all those who might breathe the same air. The
development which is granted or thrust upon the heroes of these
tragedies always has about its nature something deeply alien to them.
They become essential indeed, and their souls, relieved of the
oppression of ordinary reality, breathe deeply and happily; but an
alien being becomes real within them when the final forces are
released. Death is the return, the first and only attainment of their
own essence. The great struggle is only a roundabout way of getting

there. History, through its irrational reality, forces pure universality upon men; it does not allow a man to express his own idea, which at other levels is just as irrational: the contact between them produces something alien to both—to wit, universality.

Historical necessity is, after all, the nearest to life of all necessities. But also the furthest from life. The realization of the idea which is possible here is only a roundabout way of achieving its essential realization. (The said triviality of real life is here reproduced at the highest possible level.) But the whole life of the whole man is also a roundabout way of reaching other, higher goals; his deepest personal longing and his struggle to attain what he longs for are merely the blind tools of a dumb and alien taskmaster. Only very few become conscious of this; Pope Gregory knows it at a few ecstatic moments of his life:

My body is a stone
which a boy's hand threw into the lake
My "I" is the force which draws circle upon circle on the water
when the stone has long lain slumbering at the bottom.

Neither side of historical necessity lends itself to dramatic form-giving; the one is too high for it, the other too low, and yet their indissoluble and inseparable unity is the only true nature of history. It is at this point that the technical paradoxes of historical tragedy spring from the metaphysical paradox of the relationship between tragic man and historical existence: the paradox of inner distance between the spectator and the characters, the paradox between the characters' different degrees of life and life-intensity, the clash beween the symbolic and the lifelike in the characters and events of historical drama. The historical view of life does not allow of any abstraction of place or time or the other principles of individuation: the essential part of men and events is inseparably bound up with the apparently secondary and accidental; the characters of historical drama must "live" and the events portrayed must show all the colourful variegation of real life. This is why Shakespeare's plays, although anti-historical at the core, could—on account of their immense richness and life-likeness—be seen as the greatest examples of historical drama, and indeed had to be seen as such. Shakespeare unconsciously represents the empirical element in history, and he does it with unequalled power and unparalleled richness. But the ultimate meaning of history, wherein it goes beyond everything personal, is so abstract that in order to represent it we would have to out-Hellenize everything we know of Greek drama. The paradoxical dream of synthesizing Sophocles with Shakespeare sprang from the wish to create a historical drama.

Any attempt at such a synthesis must, however, introduce a certain duality into the characters of the drama. Where the heroes are concerned, a solution of the problem is conceivable—the dualism we speak of could simply become their central experience; the flaw could be placed at the centre of the work and in that way, perhaps, be transcended after all. No one has yet succeeded in doing this, yet that does not prove that the problem is insoluble. But the impossibility of artistically creating a historical-dramatic destiny (i.e. one in which the historical element is really important and not just an accidental expression of a purely and timelessly human conflict) is crucial as a matter of principle, too. The human beings in whom destiny becomes form are split into two fundamentally different parts: the ordinary human being standing in the midst of real life is turned suddenly, in a single instant, into a symbol, the vector of a supra-personal, historical necessity. And since this becoming-symbol does not grow from the innermost recesses of the soul but is carried by alien forces to other alien forces, and the human personality is only an accidental connecting link, only a bridge for the progress of a destiny which is a stranger to it, it must irreparably destroy the unity of the character. The motives at work in the characters are alien from them and raise them into a sphere where they are bound to lose all their humanity. But if this impersonal element has been given form in drama, then the character must, during the not-yet or no-longer symbolical part of his life, float incorporeally among the living; he should be seen differently from everything round him, and yet should form a single, indivisible world with his environment. Gerhart Hauptmann always chooses to create individual human beings, and must therefore renounce the higher necessity of the historical—that which should be the true meaning of his plays. Paul Ernst's goal is the precise opposite. But when his Kallirhoë, the bride of Demetrius, is suddenly transformed by her own recognition of an historical necessity from a living and loving creature into the mere executor of that necessity, such concretization of something purely abstract has an almost grotesque effect; the purely symbolic figures in *Canossa* (the old peasant most particularly) are unsatisfactory, and in the *Gold* tragedy this tendency is carried to baroque proportions.

Form is the highest judge of life: the tragedy which finds expression in history is not completely pure tragedy, and no dramatic technique can wholly disguise this metaphysical dissonance; insoluble technical problems are bound to spring up at every point of the drama. Form is the only pure revelation of purest experience, but just for that reason it will always stubbornly refuse to be imposed on anything that is oppressive or unclear.

4

Form is the highest judge of life. Form-giving is a judging force, an ethic; there is a value-judgement in everything that has been given form. Every kind of form-giving, every literary form, is a step in the hierarchy of life-possibilities: the all-decisive word has been spoken about a man and his fate when the decision is taken as to the form which his life-manifestations can assume and which the highest moments of his life demand.

The most profound verdict which tragedy pronounces, then, is an inscription over its gate. Just as the inscription over Dante's gates of hell tells all who enter to abandon hope, so this inscription eternally refuses entrance to all who are too weak or too lowly to dwell in the kingdom of tragedy. In vain has our democratic age claimed an equal right for all to be tragic; all attempts to open this kingdom of heaven to the poor in spirit has proved fruitless. And those democrats who are consistent about their demand for equal rights for all men have always disputed tragedy's right to existence.

In *Brunhild* Paul Ernst wrote his mystery play about tragic men and women. *Ninon de l'Enclos* is its counterpart—a play about un-tragic people. In the former he gave form to human beings as he most fervently desired them to be; in the latter he gave life to figures essentially most alien to him. But the man who wrote the latter play, too, is a writer of tragedy and therefore he had to carry it to an extreme—to the point of tragedy; only, at the moment of the ultimate decision, his heroine slips out of the tentacles of tragedy, consciously refuses everything noble and fatal that had previously hung like a halo about her head, and rushes back into ordinary life, which has been waiting eagerly to receive her. Her motto is carved upon this final moment: it defines her value and at the same time her limitation. As a result of the struggle for freedom which she has fought against herself, she has become strong enough to be able to breathe the air of tragedy, to live within the periphery of tragedy. But, like all human beings of her particular kind, she lacks the final consecration of life. She is the highest of an inferior species: this is the verdict which the dramatic form passes upon the value of her life. She wanted to attain the highest for herself, and has attained it—the highest, which is freedom; but her freedom is simply liberation from all bonds, not, in the last analysis, a freedom organically born out of her innermost self, identical with the highest necessity—not the completion of her life. Her freedom is the freedom of harlots. She has freed herself from every strong interior bond —from man and child, fidelity and great love. She has made heavy sacrifices for this liberation, accepting many smaller, humiliating bonds, such as love that is sold or given away for the sake of a passing whim may create in a woman's life. She has suffered greatly from her loss and has borne with pride the trials imposed upon her by her self-appointed fate—but still it has only been an easing of her life, an escape from its heaviest necessities. Such self-liberation of a woman is not the fulfilment of her essential necessity as is the real self-liberation of a tragic man, and the conclusion of the play raises a question which Ernst the theoretician had foreseen long before: can a woman be tragic in herself and not in relation to the man of her life? Can freedom become a real value in a woman's life?

The core of Paul Ernst's life's work is the ethic of poetic literature, just as that of Friedrich Hebbel's was the psychology of poetic literature. Because, for both, form has become the goal of life, a categorical imperative of greatness and self-perfection, Ernst is always thought of as a cold formalist and Hebbel as a metaphysician of pathology. But whereas the fate of Hebbel's heroes is the tragically impotent struggle of real men for the perfect humanity of men who live in formal works of art—in other words, the profoundly problematic, psychologically experienced high moments of empirical living—Ernst places this perfect and rounded higher world as a warning, a call to action, a light and a goal upon the path of men, but is not concerned with their actual becoming-real. The validity and strength of an ethic does not depend on whether or not the ethic is applied. Therefore only a form which has been purified until it has become ethical can, without becoming blind and poverty-stricken as a result of it, forget the existence of everything problematic and banish it forever from its realm.

1910

SOURCES AND REFERENCES

Original Hungarian edition: A lékék és a formák (Kisérletek), Franklin Társulat Nyomda, Budapest 1910, including:
Levél a "Kisértröl": first publication.
Rudolf Kassner: first published in Nyugat, Vol. 1, 1908, pp. 733 ff.
Theodor Storm: first publication.
Novalis: first published in Nyugat, Vol. 1, 1908, pp. 313 ff.
Richard Beer-Hofmann: first published in Nyugat, Vol. 1, 1909, pp. 151 ff.
Sören Kierkegaard és Regine Olsen: first published in Nyugat, Vol. 2, 1910, pp. 378 ff.
Stefan George: first published in Nyugat, Vol. 2, 1908, pp. 202 ff.
Beszélgetés Laurence Sternéröl: first publication.

The essay on Charles-Louis Philippe included in the German edition was first published in Die neue Rundschau, XXII, 1911, pp. 192 ff., under the title Über Sehnsucht und Form (On Longing and Form). The essay on Paul Ernst appeared at the same time under the title A tragédia metafizikája in Szellem, 1911, pp. 109 ff., and in German in Logos, Vol. 2, 1911, pp. 79 ff.

Italian translation: L'anima e le forme, introduction by Franco Fortini, translation by S. Bologna, Sugar Editore, Milano 1963

Lukács often drew attention to the "unity of continuity and discontinuity" in the relationship between his early writings and those of his "mature Marxist period" (cf. Preface to Deutsche Literatur in zwei Jahrhunderten (German Literature in Two Centuries), Works, Vol. 7, Neuwied 1964, p. 7). It is therefore important to trace the development of the subjects broached in this volume throughout the author's subsequent work.

For the Letter to Leo Popper, cf. especially Aesthetics, Works, Vol. 11, Neuwied 1963, Chapter 10. pp. 778 ff.
For the essay on Kierkegaard, cf. Die Zerstörung der Vernunft (The Destruction of Reason), Works, Vol. 9, Chapter 2, Section V.

For the essay on Novalis, of which Lukács said in 1963 that it was the first of his essays "to be taken seriously", cf. *Skizze einer Geschichte der neueren deutschen Literatur* (Sketch for a History of Modern German Literature), Neuwied 1963, pp. 76 ff.

For the essay on Storm, cf. ibid, p. 128, and especially the Preface to *Deutsche Realisten des 19. Jahrhunderts* (German Realists of the Nineteenth Century) in *Deutsche Literatur in zwei Jahrhunderten*, Works, Vol. 7, pp. 187 ff., also the essay on Keller, ibid., pp. 334 ff.

For Stefan George, cf. *Repräsentative Lyrik der Wilhelminischen Zeit* (Representative poetry of the Wilhelmine Period) in: *Skizze einer Geschichte der neueren deutschen Literatur*, op. cit., pp. 170 ff.